PRAISE FOR MATTHEW P. MAYO'S WORK:

"... I can't recommend it highly enough. The man knows the West and, better still, knows how to tell a story."

—Andrew Vietze, award-winning author of
Becoming Teddy Roosevelt

"An excellent variety of great stories, told in superb narrative style."

—John D. Nesbitt, Spur Award–winning Western
author of Trouble at the Redstone

"Mayo brings the West alive. . . . *Cowboys, Mountain Men & Grizzly Bears* puts the reader right in the middle of the action. Mayo is a writer to keep a lookout for."

—Larry D. Sweazy, Spur Award winner and
author of The Rattlesnake Season

"[Mayo] is a consummate storyteller with a lively, entertaining voice. . . . *Bootleggers, Lobstermen & Lumberjacks* is American history at its most violent and authentic."

—Howard Frank Mosher, award-winning author of A Stranger in the
Kingdom, Where the Rivers Flow North, *and* Walking to Gatlinburg

"Matthew P. Mayo, a prolific author of Western fiction, pulls out all the stops of his pulp style. . . ."

*—*The Boston Globe

"Mayo's Grittiest Moments books read like Loren D. Estleman and Jim Thompson got together to rewrite a Stephen Ambrose history book."

—Jeremy L. C. Jones, Booklifenow.com

ALSO BY MATTHEW P. MAYO

Cowboys, Mountain Men & Grizzly Bears: Fifty of the Grittiest Moments in the History of the Wild West

Bootleggers, Lobstermen & Lumberjacks: Fifty of the Grittiest Moments in the History of Hardscrabble New England

Sourdoughs, Claim Jumpers & Dry Gulchers: Fifty of the Grittiest Moments in the History of Frontier Prospecting

Haunted Old West: Phantom Cowboys, Spirit-Filled Saloons, Mystical Mine Camps, and Spectral Indians

Speaking Ill of the Dead: Jerks in New England History

Myths and Mysteries of New Hampshire: True Stories of the Unsolved and Unexplained

Maine Icons: 50 Classic Symbols of the Pine Tree State
(with Jennifer Smith-Mayo)

Vermont Icons: 50 Classic Symbols of the Green Mountain State
(with Jennifer Smith-Mayo)

New Hampshire Icons: 50 Classic Symbols of the Granite State
(with Jennifer Smith-Mayo)

HORNSWOGGLERS, FOURFLUSHERS & SNAKE-OIL SALESMEN

True Tales of the Old West's Sleaziest Swindlers

MATTHEW P. MAYO

TWODOT®

GUILFORD, CONNECTICUT
HELENA, MONTANA

A · TWODOT® · BOOK

An imprint and registered trademark of Rowman & Littlefield

Distributed by NATIONAL BOOK NETWORK

British Library Cataloguing-in-Publication Information available

Library of Congress Cataloging-in-Publication Data available

ISBN 978-0-7627-8965-8 (paperback)
ISBN 978-1-4930-1804-8 (e-book)

♾™ The paper used in this publication meets the minimum requirements of American National Standard for Information Sciences—Permanence of Paper for Printed Library Materials, ANSI/NISO Z39.48-1992.

To Harold Trent and all his mad, mad schemes. . . .

"A sucker has no business with money in the first place."

—Canada Bill Jones

"There is ten times more rascality among men outside of the class they call gamblers than there is inside of it."

—George Devol

"Nobody ever went broke underestimating the intelligence of the American people."

—H. L. Mencken

CONTENTS

ACKNOWLEDGMENTS

My thanks to many people, places, and things for help in tracking down information on various cheats and swindlers, among them: Bozeman Public Library, Alaska State Library, Cave Creek Regional Park, Deadwood History, Hoofprints of the Past Museum, Kansas Historical Society, Library of Congress, National Park Service, all my chums at Western Writers of America, and to my wonderful family, for all the obvious reasons.

I give big thanks to Erin Turner, indulgent editor without equal. And thanks to the swindlers themselves, without whom I would have had a far different year. . . .

Last, but never least, my deepest heartfelt thanks to my wife and partner in crime, photographer Jennifer Smith-Mayo, for her tireless support, patience, and wisdom this past year—and always. And for conducting all the photo research and procurement for my books, and so much more! Hmm . . . how about a trip to Vegas?

—MPM

INTRODUCTION

From the raw, paint-peeling alcohol of cure-all elixirs to con-artist carpetbaggers with satchels full of shoddy goods to sleight-of-hand card sharps whose wasted outward appearance belied nimble minds and adroit fingers, the Old West teemed with shady characters out for a quick buck and a good time before disappearing to another cow town ripe for the plucking. Like everyone who headed out West, these rascals sought a better life—without having to work too hard for it. The true tales of their cunning and larceny, and their eventual comeuppance, make for riveting reading.

In this collection I present a number of petty bandits, sleazy bunco artists, and conniving con men (and women), what they did, and why they are remembered for it. Everyone loves a heel, especially from the safe distance that time provides, one to whom little was sacred and who charmed his or her way into the hearts, minds, and wallets of bumpkins and belles alike.

A quick scan of the dictionary definition of "swindler" unearths a stack of salacious synonyms: fraudster, fraud, confidence man, trickster, cheat, rogue, mountebank, charlatan, impostor, bunco, huckster, heel, hoaxer, con man, con artist, scam artist, shyster, gonif, shark, sharp, hustler, phony, crook, quack, bamboozler, and, of course . . . hornswoggler, fourflusher, and snake-oil salesman!

Why is it that the maleficents and their ill-formed ilk get all the wonderful words while the good guys (who, as we know, always finish last) get stuck with "great fella, fine family man, solid, upstanding . . ."? Hmm. . . .

The pages of Old West history are filled with examples of people who misled others unwittingly, the whole while thinking they were doing the right thing. They are not swindlers—they are merely well-intentioned rubes. They lack that certain character kink that makes them want to take advantage of their fellows. And that little flaw makes all the difference.

In the most general terms, a swindler is anyone who knowingly takes another person "for a ride," "leads them down the path," hoodwinks, hornswoggles, or outright dupes another. The key to this particular lock, as I have learned, is the word "knowingly." Truly successful swindlers are not only fully aware of their nefarious efforts, they are also unfailingly intelligent, brazen in their approach, possess enormous reserves of self-confidence, and are able, time and again, to pick themselves up, dust themselves off, and sleaze their way back into the thrill of whatever game it is they adore.

At some point in every swindler's life, someone should hold him down and shout, "You rascal! You rogue! You have done too many people wrong! You must change your ways or you'll spend time in prison!" Maybe even plant a knuckle sandwich on his kisser for good luck. But it doubtless would do any good. A swindler is a swindler is a swindler. A rascal is a rogue is a rapscallion is a rake is a . . . and there's no way to mend them once they're born. So we just have to live with them and suffer their ill effects for days, weeks, months, years, decades, and centuries to come.

What one man considers swindling another might well call opportunism. It can be difficult to define the gray area, but most of the time the determination's an easy one to make. Take Al Swearengen, Deadwood's premier baddy. He lied to women, attracted them to his Gem Variety Theater under false pretenses, and hooked them on drugs until they withered away. Then he replaced them with new, fresh-faced girls from back East lured to Deadwood by a pristine round of his grand promises. Swearengen operated in no gray area. He was a vicious thug who lied to innocent people, then duped them further.

But what of someone such as Doc Baggs, Denver's Gentleman Con Artist? He allegedly never bilked anyone who couldn't afford it—and who wasn't looking to do the same to him. Certainly there's more gray area there. Or take someone such as Umbrella Jim Miner, the Poet Gambler. He never forced anyone to bet against him or his shell game, and he always warned folks beforehand, in poetic patter, that they were about to become his victims. Surely fair warning counts in his favor. And yet, he manipulated the shells in such a way that he never lost. Those odds are too good to be true. And so, Umbrella Jim was indeed a swindler.

Astute readers will notice a distinct dearth of lady swindlers herein. That's not to say they didn't exist, but the swindlers who danced in the spotlight were by far men. That's also much the case today, where a study of deceit-related headlines shows politicians, industrialists, televangelists, infomercial hawkers, and online hucksters as primarily of the male persuasion.

However, a number of Old West women were notable gamblers, among them Lottie Deno and Kitty LeRoy. And there were numerous memorable madams, too, proprietresses of houses of ill repute, often soiled doves themselves, who gladly filched wallets and gold pokes from smiling, spent patrons.

While it's tempting to consider such amazing charlatans as James Peralta-Reavis or Death Valley Scotty as the greatest swindlers ever—and they truly were singular pieces of nasty work—such a case can never fully be made, because new swindlers pop up every day (should you have your doubts, take a look at traffic medians come election time). But the primary reason we may never know who is the greatest swindler of all time is because that person will forever remain unknown—precisely because such swindlers are so good at what they do, no one will ever find out who they are.

During the research and writing of this book, I had to ask myself a number of difficult-to-answer questions such as: Is a thief a swindler? And I came to the conclusion that while all swindlers are essentially thieves, not all thieves are swindlers. If a horse-and-cattle rustler such as Dutch Henry Born were to sell back to a man the same horse he'd stolen from him (which is exactly what he did), that qualifies as a swindle.

At various points I used poetic license by adding dialogue and supporting characters where firsthand accounts were scarce. That said, a surprising and gratifying number of accounts of our rascals in action exist in the pages of historical archives. No doubt this has everything to do with the public's perennial preoccupation with ne'er-do-wells.

This book represents a mere sampling of the huge variety of mountebanks and cheats who roved the plains and mountains and paddled the rivers and coasts of the Old West. To attempt to include them all would be impossible. And yet, there are so many more who deserve a good airing. Take Clay Wilson, a small-time con man who murdered a notorious gambler named Jim Moon. For years Wilson had been a hired goon who worked for a number of big-time con men—Doc Baggs, Soapy Smith, John Bull.

Wilson also kept a journal the entire time—no doubt planning to use it to swindle his powerful employers. The journal seemed harmless, filled as it was with indecipherable writing his colleagues referred to as "chicken scratches." Eventually the police ended up with the journal and their reaction was much the same. They turned it over to a university, where after analysis it was determined Wilson had been jotting down valuable information all along—in perfectly rendered Sanskrit. The lesson? Never judge a polecat by his chicken scratch.

It has been great fun to discover salacious facts about people who set out to take advantage of others, all the while knowing full well what they are up to is not right. There has to be a moral baseline in each of us, some level to which we recognize it is unfair, unwise, and unjust to stoop below. Does that mean we don't do so? Hardly. We all are guilty of transgressions, even the slightest, even if we only admit them to ourselves. But most of us attempt to rise above them and try not to repeat them. That is what counts, and it is one of the few things that separates us from the sleazy at heart, the swindlers, the hucksters, the opportunists willing to transgress, time and again, to make a buck, to feel the deep-down tingle success over a mark brings.

Perhaps I have thought about this overly much, but then I have spent a fair amount of time of late in the company of cheats, rascals, and rogues—even if only in a historical context. Time will tell if their oiliness has rubbed off on me. . . .

In the meantime, I offer one bit of advice I gleaned from Umbrella Jim's poetic pitch: Keep yer eyes on the pea!

—Matthew P. Mayo
Summer 2015

CHAPTER 1
NED BUNTLINE
ALL-AMERICAN HUCKSTER

He felt the flames of the angry crowd's torches licking at his thin-soled boots, heard the gabbling shrieks calling for his head, his neck, and other valued parts of his anatomy, and then Edward Zane Carroll Judson, also quite well known at the time as famed writer Ned Buntline, made a daring escape. At least that is how such a moment would play out in one of his own ripping yarns. In truth, his escape was impressive, though not in the way he might have preferred. . . .

The awning frame from which his portly form clung surrendered with a snap (perhaps under the tremendous weight of Judson's bloated ego), and he dropped three stories to the hard-packed earth, jolting his weary bones. But Buntline had little time to check on his own physical state, for law enforcement bulled through the angry congregants swarming the fallen man and hustled him off to jail.

As he stewed in his cell, rubbing his swelling ankles and gnawing his lower lip, Buntline may well have—or should have—ruminated on what event or chain of them had brought him to this lowly locale.

"How," one surmises Judson may well have wondered, "did I come to such an ignoble impasse?"

And if he were honest with himself, it wasn't much of an effort to trace back the timeline to how indeed Buntline managed to find himself alone in a dank jail cell in 1846, in Nashville, Tennessee, awaiting news of his very future. He'd been in town innocently enough, promoting the latest of his various publishing attempts, a magazine called *Ned Buntline's Own*.

It appears the charismatic and very much married Judson had been caught in mid-dalliance with one equally married Mrs. Robert Porterfield. And it was Robert Porterfield himself who caught the pair of paramours flirting. He produced a pistol and cranked off a poorly aimed shot at squealing Ned who, also armed, returned fire. Ned's shot, as one would expect from a self-proclaimed "expert marksman," found its target—somewhat—for it pierced Mr. Porterfield just above the left eye. It seems that the shot didn't lay Porterfield too low just yet, but our intrepid Buntline wisely gave himself over to the authorities.

There was a hearing the next day, and Ned pleaded that it was a pure and simple case of self-defense, something to which the wounded man's brother—along with a few of the wounded man's friends—took offense. They unholstered their own firearms and proceeded to open fire at Buntline in the courtroom.

But wait—there's more! Agitated Ned, feeling most aggrieved and not a little surrounded, took the one opportunity that presented itself—the only one he felt gave him a modicum of a chance, anyway, and dashed out of the courthouse, across the street, and into a hotel. The mob from the courthouse, as well as others following the action outside, were in hot pursuit of portly Buntline, and they rained rocks and yet more bullets at the hapless lothario. He bolted up the hotel's stairwells, all the way to the third floor. But not before he was dealt a painful wound in the chest with a rock.

With the mob closing in, Buntline jumped from a third-floor window. He aimed for the awning, it broke, and that's when he dropped like a stone to the ground many feet below, from where he was hauled off to the hoosegow.

And that's precisely when he found himself in the jail, wondering about his fate, and heard shouts—the mob again—but this time it sounded louder, closer, angrier, and more plentiful. As it turns out, the mob was all these things, and for good reason: It seems his sweetie's husband, Robert Porterfield, succumbed to the bullet wound Buntline had delivered. Incensed friends, family, and anyone else with an ax to grind and a drink in his belly, mobbed up and descended on the jail.

The seething throng wasted no time in overpowering the night guard, procured the keys to the cell, and dragged the howling, protesting Ned Buntline out. They continued to drag him until they reached the town square, where someone hastily rigged up a rope with a noose at the end, dangling from a convenient post.

Despite his screams of innocence, Buntline was strung up and hanged.

Yes, hanged. By the neck.

But in typical Ned Buntline fashion, in what could well have been a breathless escape from the pages of one of his very own pages of purple prose, he made a daring escape. As his full weight dropped down, stretching the hanging

Inveterate huckster, womanizer, temperance leader who preached whilst inebriated, and all-around rogue, Edward Zane Carroll Judson, aka Ned Buntline, "father of the dime novel," was also the highest-paid author of his day, and arguably did more than anyone else to shape modern perceptions of the Old West. *Photo by Napoleon Sarony.*

rope to capacity, the hastily worked hempen necktie snapped, as luck—and a few well-placed friends in attendance—would have it. Other versions of the story claim that his friends cut him down and smuggled him out of the hot seat, whisking him away before the crowd redoubled its bloodlust.

Either way, it makes for riveting reading, and Buntline lived to dally another day. He once again appeared in court, and, owing largely to the overly zealous crowd's vigilante activities, the judge let him go. Curiously enough, though not surprisingly, Buntline would tell audiences after the incident that the chest wound he'd received from the mob's rock was in fact a painful reminder left by an Apache arrow. And his public, aware of the truth or not, lapped it up like kittens at a bowl of cream.

In a letter to a local newspaper following the incident, Buntline made hay with the events and was able to convince himself, if not what he imagined to be a vast and admiring public, that he had suffered greater injuries and injustices than he actually had. Though considering all he underwent, it's a wonder he felt compelled to embellish the proceedings at all.

> *I hasten to tell you that I am worth ten "dead" men yet. . . . I expect to leave here for the East in three or four days. I cannot yet rise from my bed; my left arm and leg are helpless, and my whole left side is sadly bruised. Out of twenty-three shots, all within ten steps, the pistols seven times touching my body, I was slightly hit by three only. I fell forty-seven feet three inches (measured), on hard, rocky ground, and not a bone cracked! Thus God told them I was innocent. As God is my judge, I never wronged Robert Porterfield. My enemies poisoned his ears, and foully belied me. I tried to avoid harming him, and calmly talked with him while he fired three shots at me, each shot grazing my person. I did not fire till I saw that he was determined to kill me, and then I fired but once. Gross injustice has been done me in the published descriptions of the affair. . . . I shall not be tried; the grand jury have set, and no bill has been found against me. The mob was raised by and composed of men who were my enemies on other accounts than the death of Porterfield. They were the persons whom I used to score in my little paper, Ned Buntline's Own. . . . The rope did not break; it was cut by a friend. . . . Mr. Porterfield was a brave, good, but rash and hasty man; . . . His wife*

is as innocent as an angel. No proof has ever been advanced that I ever touched her hand.

None of this slowed Ned, who continued to have dalliances with women other than his wives and to whom other men were married. Some folks never learn. Others never want to. Others, such as Buntline, refuse to, probably because they're having way too much fun.

And that is but one of dozens, perhaps more, of the amazing stories that together make up the real and imagined life of one Edward Zane Carroll Judson, as Ned Buntline, at one time America's highest-paid author. Arguably he was, more than any other, the man who made the men who made the mythic West. He was undoubtedly a remarkable and a largely self-made man who led an extraordinary life. The gleam of his documented accomplishments can only be outshone by the harsh glare from his all-too-real less-than-savory exploits.

Our hero was born in Harpersfield, New York, on March 20, 1821, to Bethany and Levi Carroll Judson. When but a lad of thirteen in 1834, young Edward had a dust-up with his lawyer father. It seems that dear old dad wanted him to pursue law. Young Edward resisted and the two came to blows. Edward left home and headed straight for the sea—the very career path he'd long pined for, and one his father had ridiculed.

He ended up as a cabin boy on a ship, the first of a long list of vessels that hosted the young sailor. By the next year Judson tasted fame for the first time for a selfless act of heroism. He dove into New York's East River, with little regard for his personal safety, and helped rescue a boat's crew from drowning. In true Buntline fashion it was an incident he would later brag about—much in keeping with his lifelong lack of humility.

He ended up on a number of seagoing vessels and served in the Seminole Wars. He never got too close to combat, though during the Civil War he once again served, this time as an enlistee in the First New York Mounted Rifles. He attained the rank of sergeant before being found guilty of drunkenness, resulting in a dishonorable discharge.

In 1838 he saw publication of his first story, a tale of action, in *Knickerbocker* magazine. By 1844 he began using the byline "Ned Buntline" (*buntline* being a nautical term for a length of rope attached to the lower edge of a large, square sail).

Once back in New York, Buntline launched a number of short-lived publications of his own and experienced a taste of success with a popular serialized story called "The Mysteries and Miseries of New York." The grim read detailed the realities of life in New York's famed slum, the Bowery district.

Being of an opinionated nature, Judson was not able to hold his tongue when he recognized injustices. His true motives, however, emerged as opportunities for him to orate, to raise a hue and cry, and generally attract attention to himself. He reasoned that life's gray areas were ripe for exploitation. He famously preached for temperance, railing and rallying against strong drink. And after such fiery orations, in which he exhorted his audience to abstain from the foul effects of the devil's brew, he could be found at a local tavern hoisting a few with friends. After all, raging before a crowd was thirsty work.

He toured frequently, giving lectures and working to stay ahead of creditors. As he roved, he moved from city to city, setting up shop and launching another publication on the world. In the process he racked up mounds of debt. In 1845, following a stint in New York City, he ventured westward to Cincinnati, and started up *Western Literary Journal and Monthly Magazine*, but later that year it appeared bankruptcy was his only option out of that widening financial hole. So what did Buntline do? He skipped town, beat a retreat from the Buckeye State, made a midnight run for it, and ended up in Eddyville, Kentucky.

Then, just when he was in dire need of a wad of cash, as happened so many times in Buntline's life, chance stepped in and beckoned with a come-hither look. With no help, if we are to believe Ned's own account of the event, he tracked down and captured two murderers and claimed a $600 reward for his efforts. Instead of paying off debts, however, he thumbed through the wad of fresh greenbacks, grinned, and headed out of town. This time he made for Nashville, Tennessee, where, true to form, he once again launched a publication. This time it was called *Ned Buntline's Own*.

It was this publication that he was in the midst of running when in March 1846, he was caught up in the aforementioned duel with Robert Porterfield, who had discovered Buntline dallying with his young (teenage!) bride.

Following this near-death brush in Nashville, Buntline bolted for the big city once more, and in 1848 he relaunched *Ned Buntline's Own*, this time from the Big Apple. And this time it stuck. His popularity as a writer blossomed nationwide. He was also active in politics, and because of this he was well situated and willing to exert his increasing influence where he might.

He supported nativism, a perennially popular sentiment to restrict or prohibit immigration to the United States. The movement strongly advocated for native-born peoples' rights (never mind that the only true natives at the time were members of the various Indian tribes). The movement's rallying cry, "America for Americans!" was one Buntline would use to whip up crowds at his various lectures. Buntline's support of nativism coincided with his rapid rise in the Know Nothing Party, as well as the Patriotic Order of Sons of America, in which natives sought ways to purify the political scene in America.

His connection with this exclusionary movement led to his being an instigator and participant in 1849's Astor Place Riot, a debacle that resulted in twenty-five deaths, more than 120 injuries, and Buntline's imprisonment for a year. Some time later, he was once again a member of the Know Nothing Party, and a mover and shaker in another nativist riot, this time in St. Louis, Missouri, when a man was shot and the home of German immigrants was burned. Buntline may also have been present in Maine when a Swiss priest was tarred and feathered for providing aid to Irish immigrants.

In true Buntline fashion, one of the most famous items attached to his life story never actually existed. The Colt's Buntline Special handgun was allegedly a limited-edition special order of Samuel Colt's famous .45-caliber single-action six-gun, but with barrels four inches longer than the standard eight inches. Add to that standard hand grips and the gun would have been eighteen inches long overall.

It was said to also have had a demountable walnut rifle stock, complete with thumbscrew mounting accessory, a buckskin thong, the name "Ned" carved in the butt of the handgrip, and a hand-carved custom-made holster befitting the enhanced size of the weapon. It is said Buntline had them made so that he might present them to each of five Dodge City lawmen—Wyatt Earp, Bat Masterson, Bill Tilghman, Charles Bassett, and Neal Brown—as thank-you gifts for supplying him with so much ripe material for writing his popular Western yarns.

The story of the Buntline Special has been so well polished and admired through the years that it's become somewhat apocryphal to refute it, and yet . . . it's full of holes. As was much of what Buntline claimed about his own writing, his own life, his own prowess with a gun, the story of the Buntline Special smacks of the very ingredients that make good pulpy reading so much fun. We simply want to believe the stories because they are so great to listen to. But that doesn't mean he didn't hobnob with some of the wildest characters of the Old West. . . .

Judson smacked his pudgy hands on the counter at the train depot and waited for the clerk to turn around. "What does it take for a man to get a question answered around here?"

The man sighed and slowly turned. "What may I help you with, Mister . . .?"

The stocky man thumbed his lapels and puffed up a bit, the various gaudy medals and ribbons on his frock coat clanking and ruffling. "I, sir, am Colonel Ned Buntline. And I've heard tell that a certain colorful character is in town."

"I'm certain you are the most well known currently in North Platte, Nebraska, Mr. Buntline."

Judson puffed up a bit more at this and smiled. "Be that as it may, I have heard . . .," he glanced right and left, though they were the only people in the large room. He leaned forward, lowering his voice, and continued, "that Wild Bill Hickok himself is in town."

"You don't say?" the clerk tried to suppress a smirk.

"You know where he is, don't you?" Judson smacked a hand on the counter again. "I demand you tell me where I can find him, sir."

The clerk sighed again. "You don't need to get so worked up, Colonel. Wild Bill's whereabouts isn't any secret. He's at Fort McPherson. Playing cards, I expect." He jerked a thumb over his right shoulder. "That-a-way."

"Well then." Judson tugged the bottom of his vest—it had been riding up over his paunch—and stood straight. "That's all you needed to tell me, sir. No need to play such games. I shall rent a conveyance and proceed to the fort." He scooped up the handle of his luggage and clomped down the boardwalk, aware that his presence had caused not a few stares. Good, as it should be. He smiled as he walked toward a livery.

Once at the fort, Buntline stopped before the door where he'd been told he could find Hickok. He tugged down on the bottom of his vest once more, cleared his throat, then opened the door and stepped inside. He felt his heartbeat quicken. He would soon meet a man he could envision making famous—more famous. He would make the man a household name . . . all over the world! Why, Judson would be surprised if Hickok didn't pay him for the privilege.

As he scanned the room, a few faces turned his way, then looked back to their card games, their drinks, their conversations, and he spotted the man. There he was at the back of the room, facing the door, a plank wall behind him. The man was thin faced, with a bony nose, long hair, and drooping mustaches. Everything about the man seemed long. His low-crown hat rested atop the table by his elbow.

The excitement was too much for him, and Judson strode straight across the room toward the man.

"You, sir! You're my man! I want you!"

The shout fairly echoed across the broad, well-packed room. The voice paused shoppers and riders in their tracks. Their gazes swiveled toward the shouter, a stranger who was fairly burly, none-too-tall, and had a foolish grin below bushy mustaches, his eyes wide. And he was looking straight at William Butler "Wild Bill" Hickok.

Hickok looked none too impressed. His cheek muscles bunched, but he tried to turn back to talking with the men with whom he was playing cards. But a second shout seemed to rattle the windows of the saloon. Hickok sighed, closed his eyes briefly, and shook his head. He was used to this sort of attention.

But he surprised everyone in the room by suddenly rising to his feet, cards and chips scattering across the baize tabletop as he stepped out from behind the table.

"What is it you want, little man?" Hickok spoke as he strode fast and manfully across the room, angling straight toward the boisterous newcomer.

The man to whom he spoke halted and drew back, startled by the sudden reaction his forceful words had instigated.

"I . . . I'm," the stranger stammered briefly but quickly gathered himself. He straightened and advanced on Hickok. But instead of meeting an extended hand with his, he was confronted with a drawn revolver and a hard stare, sneering lips beneath those drooping mustaches.

"You have twenty-four hours to get on out of this town, mister." He stepped close, peeled back the hammer, and raised the deadly snout of the long pistol. "Or I will shoot you dead. Do you understand me, sir?" His voice was a low, cold thing, the small mouth barely moving from under the long mustaches. But there was no mistaking the equally icy stare. Buntline knew this was no joke, no idle threat.

He swallowed, dry and tense. Hickok did not move; his gun hand was steady. Buntline nodded, kept nodding even as he backed up a few steps, then half-turned and sidestepped to the door. But even as he hastily left the saloon, even as his heart thudded in his chest, he was beginning to grin. Hickok in person was the man Buntline had hoped he would be. Wild Bill, indeed!

As he bustled back to town, the gunman's threat echoing in his ears, Buntline smiled wide and rubbed his hands together. "If I can't yet talk to Hickok, by gum, I'll talk to people who know the man. Get his story that way. And others too!"

By the time of this less-than-successful meet-up with Wild Bill Hickok, "Colonel" Ned Buntline, as he called himself (though his military records most definitely did not indicate he'd risen to any rank close to colonel), was nonetheless quite a celebrity. He was widely known as the author of more published works than any other living writer. And his income supported this designation: At a time when most people were making a few dollars a week, Buntline's annual income was in the neighborhood of $20,000. And it was as a writer of "shilling shockers" that he earned his phenomenal fame and income.

Buntline became known as the "King of the Dime Novelists," the very readables he once skewered in the pages of his newspaper as trash literature, defending his criticisms as "a duty which the station we have assumed demands of us." His own words fell on his own deaf ears, however, because he claimed to have written one 610-page novel in sixty-two hours. And while it may not have been the highest sort of literature, it no doubt entertained the masses and earned its author a tidy sum.

Shortly after his less-than-successful meeting with Wild Bill Hickok, Buntline tracked down one William F. Cody in an effort to find Hickok's friends and get his desired information in that way. But Cody surprised him in being not only affable but a man who was also a full-blown frontier character—just the sort he'd been looking for. He traveled with Cody for a time and worked up stories about the man. He even laid claim to having invented the name "Buffalo Bill," which Cody would carry through his coming global success as a showman.

Beginning with the December 23, 1869, issue of *New York Weekly*, Buntline serialized the novel *Buffalo Bill, the King of the Border Men*. Shortly after this hugely popular novel appeared, it was turned into a play. Seeing the success of his own work as a play, Buntline became convinced he could do an even better job than the playwright. He claimed that he wrote the play, *Scouts of the Prairie*, in four hours.

The work went on to star not only Buffalo Bill Cody himself, but also Texas Jack Omohundro, another frontiersman acquaintance of Cody's. Buntline even wrote himself into the play as a hard-bitten frontier character. His acting was singled out as being particularly bad. The *New York Herald* wrote: "Ned Buntline . . . represents the part as badly as it is possible for any human being to represent it. . . . 'Buffalo Bill' is a good-looking fellow, tall and straight as an arrow, but ridiculous as an actor. . . . Ludicrous beyond the power of description is Ned Buntline's temperance address in the forest. . . . Everything was so wonderfully bad it was almost good."

The 1872 play itself was a critical failure, but audiences enjoyed it, and it toured, after its Chicago debut, to St. Louis, Cincinnati, Albany, Boston, New York, Philadelphia, and Harrisburg. Starring in the play also convinced Cody that though he was not good at remembering his lines, he very much enjoyed being in front of an audience, something he would perfect in the coming years when he devised his famed touring Wild West show.

Buntline's well-documented popularity with women was another in a long line of ironies in his life, given that he was not particularly attractive. He was of less-than-average height, chunky physique, and had a pocked face topped with bushy red hair and bushier red mustaches. He walked oddly, more so when he'd been drinking alcohol, and yet even when he was sober, his gait was one of a man in discomfort. He suffered from arthritis and an improperly healed leg fracture from his three-story jump to escape from that mob intent on lynching him, itself the result of a dalliance with a lady.

Yet for all that, Buntline was also impressively erudite for a poorly educated man. He was charming, charismatic, and very well liked, even by people to whom he had become indebted. But it seems that his charms, especially concerning women, were as transitory as his fortunes. He was married six times, had six children, and was accused of bigamy by at least one of his wives. In addition to these numerous marriages, Buntline also had a lifelong series of liaisons with other women, often women who were married.

At various times through the years, he revamped and embellished his military exploits until even he no longer was sure what he had and had not accomplished during his service years. He claimed to have sustained at least twenty wounds on the battlefield, been savaged by Apaches, been a chief of scouts in the Indian War, and so much more.

He retired to his home, the Eagle's Nest, which he had custom built for himself in Stamford, New York. He died on July 16, 1886, at the age of sixty-three, sixty-four, or perhaps sixty-five. He'd lied so often about his age that no one is certain how old he was. Owing to a lifelong lack of financial restraint, overspending, and mismanaging his finances, his wife was forced to sell the Eagle's Nest to pay debt.

In addition to being a hugely successful writer—at one time the highest-paid author in the United States—Buntline was at various times in his life a posse member, probably a murderer, a bail-jumper, a blackmailer, a bigamist, an inciter of riots, a horse and boat thief, and so much more. As a critic of certain types of sport he deemed uncivilized, he shot a man's dog so the owner would no longer hunt in such a manner.

Buntline drank heavily, yet preached temperance vehemently, sometimes inviting his audiences to join him afterward at local taverns. In print he could be particularly savage in exposing gamblers and houses of prostitution. In private, he frequented bordellos, gambled, and blackmailed others he met there lest their names appear in his publications.

Conversely, he was also reputed to be a crack shot with a rifle and pistol, a swordsman, a fine rider of horses, generous to various charitable organizations, widely read, a keen hunter and fisherman, and politically active. In other words, Edward Zane Carroll Judson, aka Colonel Ned Buntline, was a complex individual not easily categorized, but he led a fascinating life jam-packed with adventure, that much is certain.

Despite—or perhaps because of—all that, does a lifetime of tall-tale-telling and tongue wagging, of lying and cheating so habitually that even the teller came to believe his own fabrications, make Ned Buntline a swindler of the highest order? You bet. And we wouldn't want him any other way.

CHAPTER 2

SOAPY SMITH
SKAGWAY'S SLIPPERY SULTAN

In these modern times when it's become fashionable to revise history to adhere to current modes of thought and opinion, it's amusing to read the efforts of people devoted to sanding the well-earned burrs and sharp corners off the jagged, smoking hunks of legacy the various nefarious sorts have left behind. One well-sanded case in point: Jefferson Randolph "Soapy" Smith.

If the name rings a bell, it's because he's been immortalized a number of times in books, on film, in song, and more. And all because he was a societal mooch. To give the man his due credit, he was quite good at his particular brand of theft. He scammed gullible galoots out of their holdings, be it cash, gold, land, or Granny's savings. And he did it all with a smile and a friendly arm around the shoulder.

Smith was born on November 2, 1860, in Georgia. And before his untimely end at the barrel of a smoking gun thirty-seven years later, Jefferson Randolph "Soapy" Smith II would range far in his pursuit of marks. It was an effort to quell the avaricious urge that was his lifelong companion. Or perhaps the need to fleece others was a monkey on his back. If so, it was a beloved pet, for Smith roved far and wide, from Texas to Colorado to Alaska, where he became the Scourge of Skagway.

But all that was yet to come on that second day of November 1860 when he emerged, one imagines red-faced and bawling, for close inspection. And that's when I picture the man as a bearded baby, tweezering a wallet from the leaning doctor's coat pocket, the bejeweled necklace from around the neck of the busty nurse, a collection of rattles and pacifiers mounding up in his own bassinet, filched from other babies in the nursery.

The less-fanciful truth is that he grew up on his family's sprawling, well-appointed plantation in Newnan, Georgia. His family was a well-heeled, well-educated lot for which cash-flow woes didn't exist. Alas, with the end of the Civil War, as with so many similarly situated Southern families, the Smith clan's cash dried up. They trekked westward to the town of Round Rock, Texas, in

1876, and two years later young Jefferson was on hand to see notorious outlaw Sam Bass succumb to death from a gunshot by a posse member.

If this influenced young Smith, it was to impress upon him the need to not get caught. Whether he was able to follow that notion in his own shady dealings remained at the time to be seen.

Not long after, the quick-witted and quicker-fingered Smith relocated, sans family, to Fort Worth, Texas, where, in the company of rogues and scalawags, he finally found a place where he felt at home. Following his cleverly devised scams, soon enough they were doing young Smith's bidding. These were heady days for Jeff Smith, still not yet known as "Soapy," building a budding reputation as "King of the Frontier Con Men."

Always careful to keep a few light steps ahead of the law—and any citizens with vigilante leanings he might have irked—Smith and his cohorts concocted a rogues' gallery of short cons. These were swindles that took little time to set up, exercise, then dismantle, all before moving on. Such quickies included all manner of variations on the shell game, card cons, and, by the late 1870s and early 1880s, the swindle he perfected in Denver for which he earned his infamous moniker. . . .

"What you got there, bub?" The man who spoke narrowed his eyes and bent forward at the waist, his hands tucked behind his suitcoat. With an intent gaze he eyeballed the display the tall young man had been for a few short minutes setting up on the busy Denver street corner. A number of people had slowed, gazing at his wares. Thus far none had stopped, save for the old man.

"I am glad you asked, sir." The young man nodded smartly toward his inquisitor, who continued to stare at the display. "I am Jefferson Smith, purveyor of fine soaps, plain and simple. If you will but stick around for a few more minutes, I will endeavor to sell my soap to these kindly folks looking to go about their business."

"And they're all in need of soap, is that what you're saying, young fella?" The older man finally looked at him. A cake of soap in each hand, Smith paused in stacking them atop his salesman's display case balanced on a tripod.

"We all, sir, could use a good soaping now and again." He kept his gaze on the man's face. His comment had the desired effect—the older man's eyebrows arched and Smith thought he detected a faint smile there. Might be he'd have to watch this old fellow. He was shrewd. Too much so? Time would tell.

Having worn out his welcome in Colorado, con man Jefferson Randolph "Soapy" Smith II headed north to Alaska in search of easy pickings. He established himself in Skagway as unofficial mayor and bilked hundreds of miners out of their hard-earned nuggets. But it all caught up to him on July 8, 1898, at age 37, when Smith was shot dead over a con he instigated. *Courtesy Alaska State Library, Historical Collections. Photograph by Peiser.*

But then he had little time for further speculation on the point, as the curious began to gather. He knew from experience that if there were no folks sniffing out the possibility of getting something for nothing, he may as well call it quits, pack up, and find another street corner. But this spot had all the earmarks of a prime location. He'd been eyeing it for a week and knew this was the corner for him.

As people stopped on their way by, more followed suit. The young man reached into an inside coat pocket and slipped out his long leather wallet. From it he produced a stack of paper currency of varying denominations.

As he worked, he nodded toward the soap. "That soap, my friends, may look like ordinary soap, and in many ways it behaves like ordinary soap. But having been a purveyor of fine soaps for a good many years, I can tell you without reservation that this Magical Bar Soap and Cleanse-All is a one-of-a-kind product that will leave the user cleaner and feeling better than he or she has any earthly right to feel. It is truly that good. How does it attain such lofty heights, you may well ask? Especially for something that looks so . . . let's face it, ordinary."

As he spoke he carefully wrapped the paper cash around a half-dozen bars of the soap, one at a time, using a dollar bill here, a ten there, on up to a single $100 bill that drew the crowd to a hush as he held it up. The higher the denomination, the more intent the gazes of the amassing crowd grew. This was something they wanted to see. Cash! Yes, something wild and exciting was about to take place, and they might have the chance to be part of it.

Smith first wrapped the cash around a selection of bars, then carefully wrapped each bar of soap in brown paper. What the rapt attendees saw was precisely what Smith wanted them to see—which is the same thing they wanted to see—valuable currency wrapped around bars of soap. What they didn't notice, however, was Smith's adroit hand-play. He carefully swapped the larger-denomination bills for $1 bills. Others he hid. Then, he mixed the bars supposedly containing cash in with paper-wrapped bars containing nothing but soap, and proceeded to sell the bars of soap for $1 per bar—far more than the poor-quality soap was worth.

The sight of the cash-wrapped soap bars elicited the reactions Smith had grown to expect. He fought the urge to exchange the knitted-brow look of serious concern and gravity on his long face with a big grin. Would people never learn that nothing in life was free? Oh, he hoped not.

He was, after all, about to take their money. Lots and lots of it. And not lose any of his own in the process. Again, the urge to grin had to be pushed down—until later.

As he worked the bars, he wrapped them in plain brown paper to both conceal the money and to give all the bars a uniform look once again. "You'll notice, ladies and gentlemen, that I have wrapped various of these bars of soap in paper currency with denominations ranging from $1 to $100. To prevent anyone from acting fraudulently, that is to say to keep us all honest—" He let that hang in the air, and within a second it elicited a crowd-wide laugh, as he'd hoped it would. "I have wrapped the remainder of this stack in plain brown paper, then mixed all the bars together. Now, this fine product should not really require such incentive to be appreciated, but I am willing to forego convention for the sake of excitement." As he spoke he arranged the pile to his satisfaction.

By the time he'd finished speaking, he had before him a pyramid-shaped stack of neatly wrapped bars of soap, among which he'd interspersed the bars wrapped in money. All this he did in plain sight of the onlookers, who had become curiously silent.

"I will now sell this soap to whoever is wise enough, whoever cares enough about their own skin, for $1 per cake. That's it, that's all, no other motivation on my end other than to introduce you all to the wonders of this fine product."

"I'll take one!" shouted a stout-looking fellow with a wide face and black, boiled-wool suit. A dented black derby sat perched atop the pear-shaped man's head as if it were afraid to topple off.

"Good man," said Smith as the stout man, none-too-gingerly, angled his girth through the crowd to stand before the soap sales display stand. The smiling salesman nodded and handed the man a neatly wrapped bar of soap as the man handed him a dollar bill. As the man walked back through the crowd, peeling the paper off his soap, he shouted, "Hey! Hey! Lookee here!" He ripped off the rest of the paper and waved a $5 bill in his pudgy fist above his head. "I won! I won me five dollars!"

The salesman beamed and nodded. "That's exactly what I hoped would happen! Now folks, if the soap's quality won't lure you in on its own merit, maybe the enticement of a few dollars for you to enjoy will help sweeten the deal, as the gamblers say."

But he needn't have explained, since the crowd all but drowned him out as they pressed forward, waving dollar bills and grasping for the bars of paper-wrapped soap. Soon he saw the scattering of disappointed faces as people tore off the wrapping to see nothing but a cake of soap that was worth far less than the dollar they had invested in it. But then many of those same people would gaze at their fellows, see the same results, and surmise that the other wrapped parcels must have not yet been purchased.

Just then, a happy shout bubbled up from a small, thin man to the side of the crowd near the front. "I'm a winner! A winner! Never in my life . . ." The smiling man rattled a crisp $1 bill and beamed at everybody near him.

"Here," a chorus of voices surged. "I'll take another!" They waved their dollar bills at Smith, the salesman, the purveyor of soap. After another few minutes of this flurry of activity, Smith held up his hands and with the barest of smiles said, "I have good news!"

The crowd quieted, all eyes forward.

"The $100 bill has not yet been sold. I repeat, the $100 bill is still hidden somewhere in this pile, available and ready for a new home."

The clamor to buy the remaining bars was great, but again the young man held up his large hands and slowly shook his head. "No, no folks, I cannot in all good conscience sell the remaining bars in such a manner."

"Why not?" shouted a woman from the back row, her scowl doing its best to sear a path through the air toward him.

"Because, my good madam, folks such as yourself who are not near the front would not have a fair shot at the winning cake of soap. No, I wish this harmless game to be fair to all who took the time to come out and see me and my humble yet top-notch products. The fairest way to go about this, it seems to me, is to auction off the remaining wrapped bars of soap to the highest bidders in the crowd."

The announcement, as he knew it would, drew a few groans from the crowd, mostly from folks in the front row. The rest of the gathered folks fidgeted, ready to place their bids.

All told, the "auction" drew swift response, with nearly everyone flailing a hand skyward at first. But as the figures crept ever higher, bidders backed off, irked they'd not be the one to reap the promising reward, but relieved, too, that they would not have to explain to an irate spouse why their weekly wage had dwindled noticeably between work and home.

Once the soap cakes had all been sold, Smith closed his display suitcase, folded the supporting tripod, and, doffing his hat to the various lingerers in the crowd, made his way down the sidewalk, turning left, right, left . . . before ducking into a side-street saloon where everyone knew his name.

Shortly, in walked the fat man who had won a $5 bill, followed by the thin man who had also won money wrapped around soap. They flanked the soap salesman at the bar and soon all three were exchanging looks, giggling, then elbowing each other and chuckling.

"Worked like a charm," said the thin man.

Smith nodded. "Just like last time. And the time before."

"Hey, Jeff, you read what the Denver paper is calling you?"

"Calling me?" said Smith, raising his dark eyebrows as he quaffed the foamy head off his beer.

"Yep, they're calling you Soapy Smith."

The tall, dark-haired man knitted his brows a moment, then smiled wide and nodded. "Yes sir, I'd guess that's about right. I'd say I earned that name. What do you think, boys?"

The other two men nodded. "Drink up," he said. "Soapy's buying!"

Over the next few months and years, Soapy Smith concentrated his ample efforts on exploiting the wide-open, free-for-all market that was Denver, Colorado. The town offered few restrictions on games of chance. Short cons such as his so-called "Prize Package Soap Sell" were merely a means to an end, some would say a way for Soapy to stay sharp. But they also provided a vital flow of always-useful cash that helped fund the more elaborate setups of his larger cons that included, at various times, sales of "stocks."

These stocks were anything but, as were the "offices" where one might go to place bets or gamble the lottery. With Soapy Smith at the helm, a gambler was guaranteed to come out on the short end of the stick. But in Denver in the latter decades of the nineteenth century, anything went, and for a time, most of it "went" to Soapy Smith. By 1879 he and his ever-growing gang had laid well-earned claim to the role of kings of the city's criminal undertakings.

How was he able to work out in the open, largely unharried by city government? Smith did what had always come easy to him. He paid off, threatened, blackmailed, and cajoled persons of official nature in Denver. He paid bribe money to a number of business owners—those he wasn't shaking down, that is—so that he and his men might operate unmolested in the relative safety of those establishments. He was so well-connected with the city's overseers that local newspapers referred to the triumvirate of Soapy, Denver's Mayor Londoner, and police chief Farley as "the firm of Londoner, Farley, and Smith."

Soapy wasn't wholly without heart, though. As he gained in reputation as a swindler, so he gained a reputation for fierce devotion to anyone who was likewise devoted to him. If a member of his gang needed help, and that member had proved himself of worth to the organization, Soapy went out of his way to ensure that man was provided with whatever he might require, be that help in a fight, a wee loan (with interest, of course), or with a bail bond should the hapless thug land in the jailhouse.

Likewise, Smith was careful not to drain the local population of cash, instead concentrating on milking travelers—businessmen, people just passing through on their way elsewhere. Shrewdest of all his kindly moves might well have been his not-so-private support of various charitable institutions, notably churches and the town's impoverished.

By 1888 Soapy Smith had assumed ownership of a number of properties, among them several drinking establishments. And chief among those was the Tivoli Club Saloon and Gambling Hall. Here was a spot fit for Soapy Smith to hold court, to direct the comings and goings of those in his employ, as well as the various nefarious dealings in his town.

Smith wasn't by any stretch dour in his business dealings, however. The man also had a funny bone, as evidenced in the sign above the door to the Tivoli that read, "Caveat Emptor," Latin for "Buyer Beware." Fair warning, indeed.

Ol' Soapy wasn't alone in his filching ways, however. His younger brother, Bascomb, joined him in this thriving family business, adding his own twist by running a cigar store that was anything but. Turns out the establishment soon gained a reputation as a joint where the games in the back room were rigged—what a shock!

Soapy was often portrayed in the press as an affable, aw-shucks character. And while he was considered a good-natured gent, generous in his donations to charities—though only to those he could ultimately benefit from—Soapy Smith was also a man who harbored unusually dark moods and a temperament to match. His black moods only increased as he gained more power in the city.

When the *Rocky Mountain News* exposed Soapy for the huckster and thief he was, Smith happened to be vacationing with his family in Idaho Springs. The paper made the rounds, however, and soon Soapy's family was snubbed by the high-society folks with whom they'd been hobnobbing. Soapy returned to Denver and, along with one of his thugs, a big brute of a man named Banjo Parker, braced Colonel John Arkins, owner-operator of the very newspaper that Soapy had perceived as maligning him.

Soapy gave vent to a litany of oaths and accusations at the well-liked Arkins, then, still in full fury, proceeded to bash the man atop the head with his cane. Arkins came away with a fractured skull and a headline for his next day's release: "Soapy the Assassin."

Soon, Soapy and his crew found that their accustomed stomping grounds of Denver had all but dried up for them, so incensed had the locals become at his presence.

He sold his holdings in Denver, skedaddled from that town, and encamped in Creede, Colorado, a raw, anything-goes mining boomtown brimming with gold dust and tired but happy miners. Soapy and his gang swooped in, set up shop, and proceeded to separate those miners from their hard-earned money. While there he also used one of his most unusual employees, one "McGinty," a petrified corpse of a miner that he exhibited for a viewing fee of ten cents. McGinty became quite an attraction and lured folks into his establishment, the Orleans Club, where they spent freely and lost a boodle to his various rigged games, including shell games and three-card monte.

Eventually, Creede's boom petered out and Soapy and his gang—McGinty included—caromed back to Denver. He enjoyed a few solid months of swindling, but soon it became apparent that the town had, in his absence, grown fond of not having him around. Various other shady characters had moved into greater positions of power, including his old nemesis, Lou Blonger.

Despite the tremendous amount of infamy he acquired during his time in the contiguous lower states, most notably in Colorado, swindling left, right, and center, Soapy Smith decided it was time to move on just before the turn of the century. It was probably a wise decision since he had largely worn out his welcome in Colorado. His decision to uproot and move on may also have had something to do with the fact that the law had become less tolerant of Smith and his ilk. What's a notorious swindler to do? Look to more promising pastures, of course.

Finding them at the time was no difficult task. One need only glance at newspaper headlines and listen in on the bar-top scuttlebutt to hear all about the fortunes being made way up north in Alaska.

Soon after the Klondike Gold Rush kicked off in 1897, Soapy relocated to Alaska. But all did not begin well for him there. As he and his men scammed their way along the famed White Pass Trail, working the crowds with their time-tested games of chance, three-card monte, and shell games, his increasing wealth began to contrast sharply with the men he'd been fleecing.

Soon, Soapy was convinced by various hardworking miners that it would be in his best interest to get the heck out of Dodge, as it were. And so he did, and he embarked on an extended journey that took him from St. Louis to the nation's capital, before returning—early in the next year, 1898—this time to the towns of Dyea and Skagway, Alaska.

Soapy and his boys entrenched themselves as boulders in a stream around which all water must flow. No matter who came in or out, traveling through the gateway town of Skagway, it seemed they had some sort of experience with Soapy and his gang.

It didn't take him long to figure out that Skagway, while still a rough cob of a town, was also a pulsing, promising nexus of commerce, a bustling if muddy little burg, through which nearly all trade in or out of the interior, conveniently for Smith, had to pass. His first order of business was to lay claim on a choice lot in town where he established his own public drinking establishment-cum-headquarters, aptly named Jeff Smith's Parlor, in March 1898. It was from here that he ensured that the law, such as it was, was tucked neatly into his back pocket by paying bribe money to the local US marshal.

From his spiffy new saloon, Smith established a number of cons, the most notorious being a telegraph office out back. Trouble was, the very notion of telegraph wires running to Skagway was at the time a distant and laughable dream. Establishment of a proper telegraph office in Skagway wouldn't come to fruition until 1901. But that didn't stop Soapy.

What dewy-eyed newcomers didn't know wouldn't hurt them. And so the wires of Smith's telegraph ended at the wall. Soapy assured the senders, newly minted miners, he was sending their heartfelt messages back East to their families. He'd collect their money—an exorbitant fee per message—lick the tip of a pencil, and diligently take down the touching telegram messages, before disappearing into the back, to "send" the message. Of course the missives never went beyond Soapy's notepad.

And while the newcomers waited for their messages to be sent, Smith made sure they were invited to sit in for a few hands of friendly poker with his regular players. And more often than not, these fresh-faced miners would limp on out of there, light in the wallet, wondering how they were going to buy the supplies they'd so carefully saved for, their heads in a daze of befuddlement.

Another favored scam, and one that his men loved to try in infinite variation, was to liberate greenhorns from their hard-earned stakes. Soapy's men would often outright pick the pockets of the men, or if they were feeling generous, they might pose as a trusted individual—often a man of the cloth. The gullible newcomer would soon end up losing great sums and be in such a financial hole that his salvation required someone to step in and rescue him. Cue Soapy Smith, often called on to pay the man's way back to his family. Which he often did, coming out looking like a decent bloke, despite the fact that he was the very man responsible for the greenhorn's desperate situation.

Within months of arriving Soapy had set himself up as the boss of Skagway, and the town's fragile new government could do little to change that. He had most cash and credit dealings locked up tight. But not everyone in town was pleased with this development—and he couldn't care less. It was this dedication to criminal pursuits that would bring about Soapy Smith's ignoble end. When it became apparent that their own local law enforcement agency was in the pocket of Soapy and others of his ilk, the townsfolk of Skagway established the "Committee of 101," a vigilance group.

The group was largely composed of Skagway citizens not inclined to see the world as Soapy Smith and his cohorts did—a wide-open, unguarded purse brimming with riches earned by others, just aching to be picked. Members of the vigilance committee were more interested in creating a community in which they might raise their children unmolested by jackals looking for impressionable, young, nimble-fingered recruits to do their bidding. They wanted a town in which they wouldn't be forced to pay protection fees to thugs in the employ of a bigger thug.

Ever shrewd, and capitalizing on his success and stature in the community, Smith formed his own similar committee, audaciously naming it the "law and order society." Its membership was triple that of the legitimate group, showing Smith's extensive reach and influence. Despite this, Soapy and his minions began to feel pressure from the town's more honest folks, people who had begun to tire of his heavy-handed thievery.

In a relatively short time, Skagway had taken on the reputation as a place to be avoided at all costs unless you didn't mind being separated from your purse. It was referred to as a "hell on earth," even by people who lived there.

Other lesser con men drifted away from Skagway instead of risking the wrath of a legitimate vigilante group composed of increasingly disgusted citizens. Sensing a unique opportunity, Smith worked double time to curry favor with the local populace in an effort to make himself appear legitimate and respectable.

In 1898 he wrote to President William McKinley and was granted official status for a volunteer army company he formed in light of the Spanish-American War. He rode as marshal of the town's Fourth of July parade and was included on the grandstand with various officials, including the territorial governor.

But Soapy was a two-sided devil and kept his swindling up day and night as his vast network of weasels continued to bilk innocents. And it all came to a head on July 7, 1898, when his men snatched a sack of gold from miner John Douglas Stewart, who had just scored big in the Klondike and found himself roped into a rigged game of three-card monte. He lost, naturally, and when Soapy's men demanded payment, Stewart refused, knowing he'd been duped. That didn't stop them from taking his money, though.

The Committee of 101 came to the man's aid and demanded that Soapy return the lost gold. But Soapy said no go, a bet's a bet, a deal's a deal. The episode devolved quickly into what has become known as the Shootout on Juneau Wharf.

On the evening of July 8, 1898, a group of incensed Skagway citizens met to hear what the recently robbed John Douglas Stewart had to say. After much wrangling, bickering, and arm waving, it was decided they'd meet on the Juneau Wharf to discuss the matter further.

Soapy Smith and a few of his closest cohorts heard of this meeting and made their way there. Soapy had grown increasingly incensed that these formerly malleable, mewling creatures under his control should suddenly show a distinct stiffening of the spine. He intended to put a stop to the outrage once and for all. Before he left his saloon, he snatched up his Winchester rifle and thumbed in shells, saying, "I will put a stop to these shenanigans once and for all, by God."

It didn't take long for Soapy and his men, all armed, to stomp their way through the hard-packed dirt street to the waterfront at Juneau Wharf.

Frank H. Reid, by trade a surveyor, and one of Smith's most outspoken opponents in town, was one of the first men Soapy came up against as he strode onto the wharf.

"Halt there, I say!"

"Frank Reid, I'd know that voice in a dark room anywhere. What in the name of all that is sacred are you doing?" Smith's words cut through the still air.

Despite his cool talk, Smith did halt. In the coming gloom of evening, he made out four armed men looking stern and intent to block his path.

"I say halt and stop your talking. You are not welcome here. This is a meeting about you, but it is not *for* you. You understand?"

"Why, you . . . how dare you and your unlawful gang of vigilantes, criminals all, talk to me like that. And in my town!" Within a second the incensed Smith shifted his rifle from his shoulder to a low position of play and covered the few remaining paces that separated him from his nemesis, Frank Reid, that perennial burr under his saddle. The men hated each other with an anger that sizzled the air between them. Their verbal exchange was merely foreplay to an incident each had long anticipated.

As Soapy stomped forward, his boot heels clacking hard against the wood, he brought his Winchester up, leveled square and close-in on Reid's chest.

But the seething surveyor was no wilting daisy. He jerked his arm at the barrel as if to knock it away, hammering down hard with his forearm, all the while raising his own firearm. As in any gunfight, the point of no return had finally been reached. Smith pushed in hard on Reid, and the surveyor reacted out of instinct. Given those elements, what happened next is hardly a surprise.

Witnesses claimed Smith shouted, "My God, don't shoot!" Though it is doubtful that Smith could not have expected gunplay, armed and angry as he was.

As if in mutual agreement, the two combatants each pulled a trigger on his respective gun, the cracks of shots split the cooling night, and the men stiffened, convulsing with the first sudden realization that their lives had changed with eyeblink speed. Then the pain set in as the men collapsed on each other, flopping away.

A shot—Frank Reid's or, other witnesses said, one delivered by another of the four guards, Jesse Murphy—had pierced Soapy Smith square in the heart, killing him almost at once. It was later learned that Smith had also received a shot to the left leg and another in the left elbow. Clearly Reid hadn't been the only man to fire a shot into Soapy Smith, though given the outcome, desired by many in town, it matters little who fired the killing shot.

It is said the king of con men was dead when he dropped to the warped boards of the pier. But just before that, his last conscious act was to trigger a death-dealing shot to Reid's gut. As with everything in Soapy Smith's life that led him to that point, this last action was not straightforward and direct, but sneaky and roundabout.

It took the gut-shot Reid a full twelve days of wallowing in agony before he succumbed to his wounds, including a shot to the leg and another in the groin.

But their mutual shooting didn't put an end to that evening's hellish events. They merely provided the impetus for action, especially for the fed-up citizens of Skagway, those in the majority who had long endured Smith's underhanded, heavy-handed tactics. No doubt feeling the sudden promise of freedom offered them, the citizenry ran riot throughout Skagway, rounding up Smith's minions. Anyone who had even been suspected of being affiliated with Smith, no matter how remotely, was nabbed.

The worst of the lot, eleven in all, were arrested and shipped to Sitka to stand trial. So well had Smith and his men covered their tracks through the years that the numerous alleged murders they committed, let alone the many thievings they undertook collectively and individually, could not be supported with the evidence necessary to sustain the deserved punishments a court of law would have delivered upon them. In the end the eleven received little more than light sentences.

Skagway rebounded and thrived once Smith's legacy of thievery and taint had been swept away. In the year following the decisive gunfight on the wharf, proper town council and schools were established, and most revealing of all, the town's crime rate plummeted.

In a telling footnote, the two men who shot each other dead, Soapy Smith and Frank Reid, were buried in Skagway's cemetery but a short distance from each other. For all his wily ways, or perhaps because of them—and because we all love a good (or bad) swindler—Soapy Smith's grave sees far more visitors than does Frank Reid's.

CHAPTER 3

THE GREAT DIAMOND HOAX OF 1872
DIAMONDS ARE FOR SWINDLERS

Ah, Kentucky . . . home of tasty whiskey and birthplace of two cousins with more audacity in their pinky fingers than most folks gain their entire lives.

They are also the fathers of what's considered the most infamous grift in the history of the United States. Philip Arnold and John Slack, cousins with long experience prospecting for gold and other valuable minerals and metals, were but two of thousands of people following the 1848 California gold rush to view America's vast West as one big ol' mother lode just waiting to be unearthed, exposed, and exploited. After a few decades, however, it began to become clear to such hopeful grubbers and speculators that this vast region of unlimited potential for instant and easy wealth was a well with a distinct bottom.

But for natural-born opportunists such as Arnold and Slack, a lack of nature's compliance posed little problem. It was Arnold who first came up with what seemed like a surefire way to cash in, and in a big way. And true to con man form, it came to fruition as a scam, one they never imagined would become the biggest in US history, one that quickly gained the name the Great Diamond Hoax.

The incredible level of bravado and bold demeanor it took these two garden-variety con men to pull off this infamous hoax is staggering. Even today, nearly a century and a half after the dust of the event settled, the names of the people who were duped still raise eyebrows. They are none other than global captains of industry and finance, politicians, and lawyers. How did they do it? Simple: by appealing to that most base of desires, the yearning for money. And how they did it is a most entertaining tale.

Though his hands were more used to physical toil, those of a man adept at swinging a pick, grasping a shovel, and hauling raw rock, in the past few months Philip Arnold had found employment in San Francisco working for the Diamond Drill Company.

While there he'd been pleasantly surprised to learn that uncut raw diamonds were employed for industrial use by the bagful on the tips of drill bits. He'd heard of diamonds' ability to cut through just about anything thrown at them, but it had still come as a shock to learn that his employer had vast amounts of these low-grade, poor-quality, uncut diamonds stored for use on his products.

And then it hit Arnold—square in the forehead like a nine-pound rock sledge. Why not make such diamonds work for him? Surely there must be a way. Arnold was no stranger to the notion of salting a claim. But the efforts he'd heard of often involved gold or silver melted down and fired into the ground with a shotgun. How would one go about salting a diamond mine?

By not mining for them, of course! By making them part of the landscape, by sprinkling them here and there as a chef would seasoning. From there it had been but a short bit of thinking to further the plan. Why stop at diamonds? Why not really make the possibilities exciting for . . . whom? Whom was he going to impress? Whom was he going to try to convince that gemstones could be found on the ground in the middle of nowhere?

Why, men with money, of course. They were the only ones he was interested in impressing. And how was he going to go about this? By salting a claim somewhere, that's how. But first he needed to sweeten the deal. He didn't have to venture far to find what he was after: garnets, sapphires, and rubies. They were more of the same—uncut stones that would attract the eye and the wallet and provide a perfect rainbow of contrasting, sparkling colors for anyone interested in making a fortune.

But he would need a confidante, someone who could help him with the various tasks such an undertaking would demand. And who better than someone he knew and trusted?

"Tell me, John," said Philip Arnold, smiling across the table at his cousin from back home in Kentucky. "You see what I see?"

"They real?" said Slack, still not closing his mouth or taking his eyes from the wide-open buckskin bag that offered so much promise. "I thought you said

In 1872, confidence man Philip Arnold, and his cousin, John Slack, salted Wyoming scrubland with poor-quality diamonds, rubies, emeralds, and sapphires—then bilked high-profile investors including Horace Greeley, Charles Tiffany, and Baron von Rothschild for more than half a million dollars. One of the swindled bigwigs, Asbury Harpending (above), later detailed the impressive con in his book, *The Great Diamond Hoax.* The Great Diamond Hoax and Other Stirring Incidents in the Life of Asbury Harpending, *edited by James H. Wilkins. By A. Harpending, 1913. Published by The James H. Barry Co., San Francisco.*

you had just had about enough with digging in the dirt. That you was done with mining, prospecting, that sort of thing."

Arnold nodded, still smiling as his fingers swirled around in the puddle of jewels in the open bag. "We're going to let these fine stones do all the digging for us."

"Whatever you do, Mr. Ralston," Philip Arnold said while looking around him, even though other than his partner, cousin John Slack, no one else was in sight. He leaned in closer. "Tell no one what we're about to reveal. We're swearing you to secrecy now."

Mere minutes before these two men had dropped in on William Ralston, a man who'd struck it big from earnings on the Comstock and had subsequently established a bank in San Francisco, the Bank of California, and was noted, among other accomplishments, as "the man who built San Francisco." (This, of course, is hyperbole, but Ralston did spend much effort in risking all to make his own personal fortunes—and if those efforts helped promote his favorite city, so much the better.)

Ralston knitted his brows. "Yes, yes, of course. You have my word. Now what is it you want?" The banker looked at them appraisingly and did not particularly like what he saw. In fact, he would have cause to regret that he had ever opened the door. It was after all, night, well past the time when he wished to be home. But he knew work's demands did not heed clocks. And now here were two haggard men, looking as if they had just been blown across a raw, parched landscape by fierce, unforgiving winds.

Arnold reached into his ratty wool overcoat, startling Ralston monetarily, until the man pulled out a small bulging bit of cloth, a sack perhaps, the sort of rough-cloth sack that might contain . . . anything. Gold? Had the men struck something and now needed his professional expertise? Ralston's eyes took on a sheen.

Philip Arnold carefully uncinched the top of the bulging sack, reached in, and said, "Now, what I'm about to tell you can't be told to another living soul, mind you."

"Fine, but what's this all about?" He leaned over the desk, eyeing the sack.

Arnold and then Slack both yawned. "Pardon," said the first. "We've been dogging it hard for hours." He leaned over toward Ralston. "And when you see what we got, you'll know why."

Before Ralston could reply, Arnold, with Slack close by his elbow, unfurled the wide mouth of the crude sack, then spilled the contents onto the desktop's leather blotter.

What Ralston saw pulled his breath in a barely audible gasp, from deep in his throat. There before him was a fortune in uncut diamonds, large ones, small ones, all of them glinting in the yellow lamplight.

He tried to speak, found his throat dry, swallowed, and tried again. "What is it you men would like from me?" What he really wanted to know was if they might tell him where they found them. Diamonds? In North America? Too good to be true, but yet here they were, proof beyond proof.

"We're looking for help, Mr. Ralston. And that's the truth of it. We need sleep, we need rest. And we can't get that so long as we're lugging this around with us."

"I see."

Slack nodded, picked up where his partner left off. "Yes, so we wonder if you have a safe you could lock these up in for the night?"

Ralston found himself nodding. "Dogging it for hours, what did you mean by that?" He felt sure now that these men might well be thieves. Should he call the authorities? And yet . . . what if they were not? What if they really had found . . . a diamond field?

Arnold's head snapped back as if Ralston had slapped him. "Why, I should think that would be obvious." He leaned forward again, his voice lowered though there was no need, as they were the only three in the room. "With a cargo such as this, we could likely be killed for it at any time. If only the scoundrels out there knew."

Ralston nodded promptly, then peppered them with questions, carefully presented, but questions nonetheless. But they were apparently so dog-tired that they could only yawn, shrug, and then say finally that their diamond field, known only to them, was off somewhere, maybe in Arizona. Beyond that they revealed little more.

"We'll call again soon, but we figured that you being a banker, reputable and all, would be our best bet to keep all this safe. We'll take a receipt for the lot, then come back when we're more alert. We got to get some rest."

Ralston was about to speak again when Arnold weakly held up a hand. "Whatever you do, though, we ask that you keep this secret. Just between us. Don't tell another living soul. You being a banker and all, we expect your word's a bond."

Ralston stood unblinking a moment, then hastily nodded. He spoke very little as they took their receipt and watched him as he carefully secreted the diamonds into the safe.

Once outside again on the near-empty sidewalk, Slack turned to his partner. "Why did you tell him that?"

"What?" said Arnold, not really paying attention to Slack, and rubbing his thumb across the smooth paper of the receipt in his pocket.

"By telling him to keep it all a secret, you know, that business about not telling another living soul!" Slack raised his hands and let them flop to his sides.

Finally, Arnold looked at him. "You don't see it, do you?" Then he smiled and shook his head slowly. "John, we have been cousins for quite some time now. Is that not correct?"

Slack scrunched his eyes. "Philip, you know the answer to that as well as I do—we've been cousins as long as we've both been alive, for Pete's sake."

"Yes, yes, but that's not what I'm talking about. Look," he said, not smiling, and raking his hand through his close-cropped hair. "We're experienced in a number of undertakings, correct?"

"Again, correct." Slack folded his arms across his chest, not sure where his always inscrutable cousin was headed with this line of thought. "I'd appreciate you getting to the point, Philip."

"Fine. My point is simply this: If you are half as sick and tired as I am of working hard for little pay, then what better way to spread the word about our recently discovered diamond field than to prevent someone from speaking of it."

Slack's eyebrows drew even tighter together.

Arnold sighed and walked slowly along the sidewalk. "Look, John. Have you ever kept a secret? I mean a big one, a really big one?"

"Well, sure. I am a proud Kentucky man after all."

"So am I. But really, when push comes to shove, people are about as liable to keep their mouths shut as an egg-sucking hound is to mind his own business in a hen house."

"Oh, I get what you're on about. You hope that sooner or later that banker is going to run off at the mouth and tell his friends the very thing we told him not to."

"Not only am I hoping on it, cousin. I'm counting on it. And much sooner than later."

"But how can you be so sure of it?"

Arnold put his arm around Slack's shoulder. "He's human, ain't he?" Then he laughed and laughed all the way to the corner. "Come on, I'll buy you a whiskey . . . *partner*." He winked and their guffaws echoed down the bustling street, mixing with the other noises of San Francisco at night.

All the way north, to their land in what seemed to Slack as the most lost hill country in all of Wyoming, he kept up a string of questions, some of which he asked several times. Along about the third time for most of the questions, Arnold paused and sighed. "John, if you were any dimmer, I'd be worried for my own safety."

"What do you mean by that?"

"I mean, cousin, that this is how we're going to do it. We've got to spend money to make money."

"But you were saving for land back home."

"And I shall buy land—more than we ever imagined buying. But first I need to invest some of that money and make it into more money. It's called an investment."

"Your wife ain't going to take kindly to this idea."

Philip Arnold's jaw muscles bunched and he leaned close to his cousin's face. "You damn right she wouldn't. But that's the good thing about it—she will never know. And if she does find out about this scheme of ours, why then I'll know just who told her, won't I?"

"Aw, you don't have to worry about me, Philip."

"Good," said Arnold, his smile slowly returning. "Now, let's get these burros loaded up so we can get on out there and plant these seeds!" He patted the side of his coat, up high, where Slack knew one of the sacks of gems had been safely tucked. There were many others.

Arnold had told him it would be just like sowing seeds, and that's exactly what it turned out to be.

The two men reached the site by midday, and set about carefully distributing the gems on the gravelly earth, wedging some in rocky crevices, others they poked into the ground with the end of a stick.

Within a day of being instructed not to blab, Ralston sent a cable to one Asbury Harpending, a banker friend in London. He told his friend that he had good information, the very best, in fact, that somewhere in the vast West of America there was a diamond field. Its worth, he said, was easily $50 million, perhaps far more. And more to the point, Ralston strongly intimated that he was riding point on the deal. And then Ralston had asked if Harpending would be willing to come on over and help manage it.

Oddly enough, the London banker initially refused. He would later have cause to regret not trusting in those initial bankerly instincts. But soon Harpending could not help himself. He was in a state of awe, primarily wondering if his old friend Ralston was losing his marbles, when another cable from Ralston all but begged him to get the lead out. He arrived in San Francisco by ship in May 1872.

Before Harpending arrived, however, Arnold and Slack dropped in again on Ralston, and Ralston pressed them for further information, not willing to accept their toe-dragging this time. He offered financial help in developing their find into a secure and professional setup. Would they be interested in such?

Arnold, who it appeared was the primary talker of the two, scratched his stubbled chin, pooched his lips, and drawled that they might be interested in something like that, yes. Just didn't know what that might be, now did they?

Ralston offered a hundred thousand in cash in return for a nominal percentage of the venture. But Arnold called his bluff, and after a slow quiet talk with his cohort, Slack, he said they'd need that money up front. Right then and there.

Ralston once again pulled in quick breath. "That amount of money, my friends, will require that we, that is to say I and the men I have talked with . . ."

Arnold nodded, having already covered the ground concerning the fact that Ralston had admitted, not but an hour before, the fact that he'd blabbed to a handful of people. It was exactly what Arnold wanted, of course, so he didn't push his belligerence act too hard.

"That is to say we'll need to take a look at the property."

The men conferred, not looking too worried. "We'll take two men, your choice, but you understand," said Arnold. "We're going to have to blindfold them for much of the trip. Safety, you know. We got to be careful."

"Of course, of course," said Ralston, relieved that there didn't seem to be any real impediments.

Weeks later, when Ralston's two men returned from this secretive trek, they bore smiles, nods of affirmation, and diamonds—and rubies—in their pockets. Along about this time, when Ralston was fit to burst, the two hillbillies seemed more wide open than ever to making a deal, allowing more of their find to be divvied up. And within days, Harpending landed and strode ashore onto the docks of San Francisco.

Soon, Arnold and Slack showed up, once again exhausted and trembling with fatigue, and holding their latest estimable haul—a sack brimming with a fortune in uncut gems. And then they told their rapidly growing circle of "trusted" potential investors—by now a handful of wealthy men whose eyes were wide and lips were wet—that while exploring their diamond field, they had discovered an even larger parcel glistening with bigger diamonds.

But the bag they brought back, at peril of death through raw territory brimming with all manner of banditti, had lost a goodly portion when crossing a swollen river. Still, it took Ralston, Harpending, and their giddy cohorts much persuasion before Slack and Arnold would deign to show them the fruits of their latest diamond-field endeavors. They spread the jewels out on a billiard table and stood back, basking in the gasps of the big-money men. There on the table were not only diamonds but emeralds and sapphires.

If there were doubts before then as to the verity of the two yokels or their find, all that doubt was wiped away. The money men pressed Arnold and Slack and finally struck a deal, signing an agreement that gave them $600,000, for which they gave up three-fourths of their diamond field to their new partners.

Their investors, now armed with what they felt was a deal that gave them a significant advantage over the two hillbillies from Kentucky, set up a corporation with stock of $10 million. They also allowed a few close friends, including Horace Greeley and Baron von Rothschild, the opportunity to get in on the action. One of the men happened to know Charles Tiffany, and they wasted no time, somewhat glowing and puffed with their wondrous new success, in asking his professional estimation.

Harpending later wrote what Tiffany said as he held up the uncut gems to the light: "Gentlemen, these are beyond question precious stones of enormous value. But before I give you an exact appraisement, I must submit them to my lapidary."

And his trusted gem examiner proceeded to agree with Tiffany. The gems were real, indeed.

Next they hired a mining expert, Henry Janin, a professional with a long track record in the business, to trek to the diamond field and provide an assessment. Arnold at this time began kicking up a bit of a fuss. He had yet to receive the significant payment they'd agreed upon. The investors insisted he lead a group of their representatives, among them mine examiner Janin, to the diamond field. At this point, it would be natural to assume that Arnold and Slack would balk, hit the trail, and vamoose with the small sum they'd already been given.

Nonetheless, in an effort to emphasize their legitimacy, Arnold agreed to show Janin and a few select others to the diamond field. Then, he said, he wanted cash to seal the deal. And so, Arnold and Slack led the group to Rawlins Spring, Wyoming, where the party rented pack mules and mounts and trekked into a bold landscape.

For several days of rough travel, they ventured deeper into the mountains. And then without ceremony on the sixth day, Arnold halted the party and pointed. "There, you see that basin yonder?"

His extended arm directed their gaze to a broad scoop in the mountainside, a boulder field strewn with rubble and bisected by a stream. He and Slack looked unconcerned, for all the world as men with no worries and certainly with nothing to hide.

Janin and his men dismounted, set to work with picks and shovels, and within minutes the first shout bubbled up, quickly followed by others. Diamonds, rubies, emeralds, sapphires—it was too good to be true! And the man, Janin, who should have known better, was not overly suspicious, so entranced was he by the sight of all that potential fortune. He should have wondered how it was at all possible.

Harpending was there, too, and rummaged along the hillside, quivering with excitement. Janin was more reserved, engaged as he was with his examinations. His team required three days, digging feverishly, examining their finds, performing tests, and scouting the surrounding countryside for more wondrous gems. Finally, he and his men, marveling at their luck, went away with smiles on their faces.

He was charging the consortium top dollar for his skills. But he was known to be among the best in the world at assessing the viability of mines. Janin had roughly six hundred past mines successfully examined to his credit, after all. But of this odd discovery, he emerged from the hills convinced of its legitimacy. And so it was that they all headed for civilization, giddy with the possibilities that newfound wealth brings.

How did Arnold—for he was the brains of the two-man outfit—do it? Simple, really. He resorted to the age-old and time-tested method of making a bad claim into a natural wonder: He salted it. It is estimated he used $40,000 worth of real uncut gems. And how could he fool a noted expert such as Henry Janin? Simply because Janin, while a noted mining engineer and expert in assessing gold and silver mines, was not an expert in assessing the worth of gems, especially in the rough. Not many people were, in fact.

Arnold and Slack were paid the last $300,000, a far cry from the $40,000 they had invested, plus their time and effort, naturally. And then they simply disappeared.

But it seems no one noticed or cared . . . yet. Harpending wasted no time in letting his friends know that his man Janin was "wildly enthusiastic" about the prospect of the field being a force to be reckoned with. He also said that the diamond field "would certainly control the gem market of the world."

And that's what started the global head swinging. So grand and promising was it that big-money folks the world over were thrusting cash at Harpending and his small group just to get in on the deal. Investors clamored for entry into the scheme and paid $200,000 cash for a share and a promise of 20 percent of Harpending and Ralston's parent company.

Fanciful newspaper articles told the world of the wonders of this great new find. And though they were grossly misinformed, that didn't stop the reporters from spinning tales out of whole cloth about the diamond fields. The *New York Sun* placed the locale in southeastern Arizona and made the bold, amazing claim that there was found one gem alone "larger than a pigeon's egg, of matchless purity of color, worth at a low estimate $500,000."

And while this massive ego balloon filled, a famous engineer and geologist named Clarence King, a geologist for the US government, paid a visit to the field, heading his own expedition. He and his team spent days examining the entire region. And on November 11, 1872, he wired Harpending with the news that the claim was, beyond all doubt, a well-salted hoax.

King wrote that the stones they found "bore the plain marks of the lapidary's art." In other words, he saw what others had failed to note, or admit—even Tiffany's lapidary—that the gems were rough-split stones purchased from a lapidary. Which is exactly what Arnold had done, of course.

King went on to explain that he and his team had found holes poked in the ground with a stick, into which diamonds had been jammed. They had found diamonds and rubies stuffed into the crevices of rocks. There were spots where it was quite obvious to anyone who knew much of anything about geology that the stones would in no way have been formed there naturally.

By the end of the month, the world knew of the fraud. The diamonds that had been found, to add insult to such severe injury, were low-grade rocks from South African diamond fields. Arnold had bought them from someone who normally sold them for industrial purposes, so low was their value.

To his credit, Harpending later wrote a biography in which he detailed the entire affair, naming names in his hard criticism. In *The Great Diamond Hoax and Other Stirring Incidents in the Life of Asbury Harpending*, he writes, "That diamonds, rubies, emeralds, and sapphires were found associated together—gems found elsewhere in the world under widely different geological conditions—was a fact that ought to have made a goat do some responsible thinking. But it seems to have been entirely overlooked by Tiffany, by Janin, by the House of Rothschild, to say nothing of Ralston, Sam Barlow, General McClellan, General Butler, William M. Lent, General Dodge, and the twenty-five hard-headed business men of San Francisco." Oddly enough, he didn't add his own name to the list.

And of Philip Arnold and John Slack? Which prison did they serve their time in? None, as it turns out. The enraged investors hired detectives to dog them and found Arnold comfortably holed up in Kentucky. They put liens on his property, and Arnold, acting shocked and stunned by this rough treatment, defended the $550,000 in his bank account, plus his home and various other real estate investments, saying they were the result of hard work and nothing but.

When pressed about the obviously salted diamond field, he feigned astonishment, said if that land had been tampered with and salted, it had to have happened after he and Slack last saw it. As proof and supporting materials, he offered his copies of the initial report from Tiffany, as well as Janin's assessment. Clever man to the last, he turned the deal on its head and blamed the blamers. And then he took up an occupation he seemed perfectly suited to: He became a banker. Eventually he was wounded in a shootout, and in his weakened state succumbed to a bout of pneumonia that killed him.

It seems poor John Slack did not end up with much of the money, after all. He moved to White Oaks, New Mexico, and became a casket maker and undertaker before dying at age seventy-six in 1896.

Despite the fact that the entire affair was proven an indisputable hoax, the peak in Wyoming directly behind the once well-salted butte is still known as Diamond Peak. To date no one has found a native rare gem, or anything resembling one, on or around its slopes.

CHAPTER 4

DOC BAGGS
DENVER'S HIGH-END HUCKSTER

If someone walked up to you on a shaded sidewalk outside a bank, held out what looked to be a genuine brick of solid gold, and said, "Just a moment, my good man. . . ." Wouldn't you halt, even for a moment, your curiosity piqued? Yep. And apparently so did a whole lot of folks in Denver back in the early 1880s. And to a person, they ended up wishing they'd just kept on walking. Because they'd just had a run-in with the singularly slippery Charles L. "Doc" Baggs, also known as King of the Confidence Men. Though in Baggs's case, the only confiding people did was in unwittingly divulging the contents of their wallets.

In addition to being known as King Con, Doc Baggs earned the epithet "Father of the Big Store," an elaborate con reserved for high rollers willing to risk a big chunk of change on a too-good-to-be-true scheme. These were his preferred marks, or targets, though his word for them was invariably "suckers."

Baggs reserved a special sneer for swindlers such as Soapy Smith, with whom he shared a town but in his estimation little else. In sharp contrast to Soapy's small-time shenanigans, Doc Baggs felt it took no more effort to fleece a single wealthy mark than one hundred poor working stiffs. Doc was much more interested in making a great pile from one wealthy sucker who, he felt, deserved to be fleeced.

Baggs famously went to great lengths perfecting big, elaborately staged cons, all with the potential for large payoffs. And that brings us back to one of Doc's favorite and most remembered scams, the gold brick con. . . .

"Señor?"

The well-dressed man stopped on the sidewalk, glanced down at the plainly impoverished man who had dared to tug his sleeve. "Yes? What do you want?"

The tugger didn't respond. He wore a look of alarm on his dark face, and he glanced about as if someone might leap out at him from the shadows at any second. A thin man of average height, he was dressed in togs that once may have been a natural white but now bore sweat stains and begrimed creases.

Denver's Doc Baggs was best known for his "big store" cons involving detailed deceptions and false shopfronts that could easily be folded up and lugged off should the police arrive unexpectedly. But he was also inventor of the gold-brick scam, in which he would sell a greedy mark a brick of "gold" at cut-rate prices. Unlike the gold bricks in this photo of one bank's holdings, in 1906 in Nome, Alaska, Doc Baggs's bricks, as his victims soon found out, were made of lead. *Courtesy Library of Congress. Photo by Lomen Bros., 1906.*

Yes, the portly businessman could see now, the man was one of those Mexican beggars, no doubt looking for a coin or two. "Now see here, I have no time for this sort of thing. I'm a very busy man, In fact, I'm on my way to . . ."

Suddenly, a new stranger stopped, stepped close. He fixed the portly businessman with a kindly gaze and spoke in a low, precise voice. "Sir, if I may allay your fears." The man was tall, dressed in a smart gray wool suit, high collar, and silk necktie of a gentleman. He wore impeccably trimmed mustaches and a beard, and atop his head perched a fine black hat with a matching silk band. On his hands he wore gray gloves with a polished ebony cane gripped in one.

"Who the devil are you?" said the businessman. Despite the new fellow's dapper appearance, he was truly busy and in no mood to be accosted here in Denver, or anywhere else for that matter.

The dandy leaned in. "I am, sir, at the moment, donating my services as this unfortunate man's translator."

"How's that? Why? What is it he wants of me?"

Now the dapper man smiled. "In fact, sir, he would like to do you a favor, if you'll permit me but a moment or two of your time."

"A favor? I don't need favors." But the businessman lingered a moment or two. The Mexican was a sad-looking case, to be sure—what could he possibly offer?

The dapper man nodded to the swarthy little Mexican, who lifted a grimy sack that contained something of obvious heft. He and the dapper man glanced at each other conspiratorially, the dapper man nodded again, then spoke a brief phrase in Spanish. "It's fine, Miguel. He's anxious to see what you have there." He pointed a gloved finger at the sack. "Open it," he said in English.

The man must have understood, for he rolled the top of the sack down to reveal something that caused the businessman to gasp and widen his eyes. "Is that . . . ?"

The dapper man nodded vigorously, said, "Shhh, yes. It is what it appears to be." He leaned closer. "A brick of solid gold."

A few moments passed while the businessman gazed, lost in honest admiration of the dully beautiful object. Then he regained his composure. "I . . . I don't understand. Why are you showing this to me?" He mimicked the other two men and spoke in a lowered voice as he glanced around at the nearly empty sidewalk.

The dapper man said, "To be blunt, sir. He needs to sell it."

"Sell? No offense intended, but what's a fellow like that doing with it in the first place? And why me? Why not you?"

"I am afraid I am not at liberty at present to take advantage of his kind offer. But perhaps we could talk somewhere a little more, um, private."

"Very good."

In a few moments, the oddly matched trio made their way to a quiet alley entrance. The Mexican placed the brick of gold, unbidden, in the businessman's fat, sweating hands. It was a heavy thing, and he grunted and almost lost his grip on it.

Almost.

"You can tell by the heft, sir, that it is pure gold."

"The only thing I can tell you is that it is worth far more than what he is willing to sell it for. Far more."

The fat businessman pooched his lips and hefted the thing close to his face. He sniffed at it, glanced at the two men watching him, and realized gold would have no discernible smell. He scratched at it with his fingernail. It was soft, as he supposed such things should be. And it did have the weight he'd heard blocks of solid gold should bear. It was roughly the same width and length of a regular brick, but with half the height and seemingly more weight. Hmm. He flipped it over and stared at it. No markings of any sort that might track it back to some crime, which he supposed was the reason for this fire sale.

"I am interested, provided we bring it to an assayer's office for verification. You don't mind, do you?"

The dapper man, still looking amused and slightly bored, shrugged, then spoke in a low voice to the worried-looking Mexican.

"It's just that I don't normally carry much money, so I would like to be assured as much as is possible, you see. I am a businessman, after all, and I am used to conducting my affairs in a lawful and legitimate manner." The fat man straightened up with that last declaration. *Let them know my intentions from the start*, he thought. *That I'm no one to be trifled with.*

"Absolutely, sir. And since you are from out of town, would you like me to suggest an assay office? One is as good as another."

The fat man paused.

"Of course, if you'd rather have one of your own choosing to perform the inspection, by all means." The dapper man smoothed his mustaches. "Or if we are, as they say, barking up the wrong tree, we will leave you in peace and bid you a good day."

The Mexican gently took the brick back and stuffed it into the sack.

"No, no, no, don't misread me, my good man. I am happy to go with your suggested office, being as I am a stranger here, as you so aptly pointed out."

"Excellent. Then let us not idle here any longer here. Follow me, sir. Follow me."

The three once more made their way up the sidewalk, the dapper man in the lead. What the fat man didn't notice was the thin smile barely showing on the dapper man's trim countenance.

In short minutes they arrived at a narrow, plain storefront with a sign out front reading, "Charles Dinsdale, Assayer."

They pushed in and a small brass bell at the top of the door dinged their entrance.

"Mr. Dinsdale? Are you in?" The dapper man stepped inside the shop and motioned for the Mexican to follow him. "Come on in, Miguel, and . . . er, sir," said the dapper man. "I realize I don't even know your name."

The fat out-of-towner nodded. "Yes, yes, well, given the nature of this venture we have in the offing, I find I don't mind that prospect in the least."

"As you like." The dapper man smiled as a man dressed in a leather smock stepped through a curtain partitioning off a back room from the front. The assay office itself was filled with the usual clutter of equipment, including scales, sacks of ore bearing tags, and various bits of scientific-looking apparatus the fat man had never seen before.

"Mr. Dinsdale," the dapper man leaned over the counter. "We have need of your services."

"Oh?" said the assayer. "I certainly hope so. Otherwise, I'd be wondering just what it is you're doing here." He smiled and looked at each of the three men in turn.

"My acquaintance here would like to know if this brick of gold is indeed the real thing, the genuine article." As he spoke he nodded to the Mexican to set the precious bagged commodity on the counter.

"I trust you will be discreet?"

"If that means will I keep my mouth shut about what it is you're showing me, well yes, I will. I wouldn't be in business all that long if I couldn't, now would I?"

"Very good." To the fat man the dapper man said, "He'll have to cut out a portion of the brick in order to test it accordingly."

The fat man nodded in agreement to these terms, and the man behind the counter carved out a chunk of gold from the brick, then went through the chemical process required of the assayer's art. The piece tested high—the quality, it seemed, was as good as the gold bar's looks led the quivering rube to believe.

The fat man didn't catch himself doing it, but the dandy saw the out-of-town businessman lick his lips. The dandy suppressed a smile, knowing the hook was set, the fish was almost landed, and soon, one of them would be richer, and one poorer.

Within the hour, the dapper gent had kindly escorted the portly visitor to Denver to a bank where he was able to retrieve cash, borrowed against his reputation as owner of a rather large freighting concern.

It wasn't until the fat man was on the train and nearly back to his home town of Wichita that he discerned his wonderful bar of gold was little more than a painted bar of carefully shaped stone. He suppressed a groan, closed his eyes, feeling a throbbing in his temples and a tightening deep in his gut as he thought back on the entire episode. He'd given a great wad of cash to a man he'd met in the street, and all for something that was too good to be true. Oh, but he should have known better.

By the time Charles L. "Doc" Baggs had perfected the gold-brick scam—which he is credited with inventing—he was one of the best bunco operators of his day. And in the nineteenth-century West, that was saying something.

Charles L. Baggs was born in Soda Bay, New York, on February 11, 1843. When he was sixteen he joined the rush to Pikes Peak, and had already decided that a life of office-bound drudgery was not only boring but painful. He'd recently lost a finger to the maw of a printing press while working in Illinois as a postal clerk. Baggs spent two months rummaging in and around the mines near Boulder, then decamped to Denver in early June 1859.

He went on to serve in the US Army as a quartermaster before agenting for the Overland Stage Company. From there he ventured north to Virginia City, Montana Territory, where his attorney father, Charles Sr., was busy lawyering and serving as a member of the territorial Council. Ever droll, Baggs the younger was, years later, quoted as saying, while on the stand at a murder trial (as a mere witness), that of the three years he spent up north, toiling under his father's thumb, he had worked a total of "several days," and that the only swindling he had engaged in was "selling mines."

For a man who, by his own admission, was arrested "about a thousand times"—and who are we to not believe the claims of such a fine, upstanding citizen?—Doc Baggs was never convicted of a single bunco crime.

As with many of his conniving cohorts in the field of swindling, Baggs was indefatigable, bouncing back time after time, arrest after arrest, conjuring deceits of greater daring and loftier planning, increasingly complex and oddly successful. So what kept him—and for that matter, so many of his ilk—returning perennially to fleece the sheep, as dupes were considered? Baggs once famously and quite candidly addressed this very point:

"I defy the newspapers to put their hands on a single man I ever beat that was not financially able to stand it. I am emotionally insane. Whenever I see anyone looking in a jewelry store, thinking how they would like to get away with the diamonds, an irresistible desire comes over me to skin them. I feel like drowning them if I can."

That said, the man was also quick to point out that he was himself a fine, upstanding chap: "I don't drink, smoke, chew, or cheat poor people. I pay my debts."

A famous instance illustrating Baggs's impressive self-confidence took place in court one day shortly after he was arrested by Denver lawman Michael Spangler on the not-uncommon charge of "bunco steering," or sleight-of-hand swindling. Not only did Baggs act as his own attorney, but standing before the court, immaculately dressed as always, Baggs refuted the charges against him, then went on to successfully debunk the very charge of bunco steering itself.

"Gentlemen," we can picture him thumbing the lapels of his immaculate suitcoat and stepping slowly back and forth, a gentrified rooster explaining barnyard etiquette to a bunch of upstart cockerels. "How might I possibly be guilty of a charge that does not even appear in the statutes defining criminal acts? Indeed, no such term as 'bunco steerer' appears there."

He let those words hover in the hushed air of the court for a moment. "Indeed," said he again, flipping open a massive dictionary he'd thoughtfully brought with him for just this moment. Baggs made a quick, deliberate show of thumbing through the mighty tome's pages before driving an imperious forefinger in the midst of a page. "It would appear that this very dictionary, a most revered work in itself, does not even hold the term 'bunco steerer.'"

His bold gaze met that of the judge, eyebrows raised. The dictionary was checked, the statutes were checked and double-checked. And then the judge dismissed the case. One can only assume Spangler the lawman reddened and worked his jaw muscles as he watched the dapper form of Doc Baggs exit the courtroom, whistling as he strolled down the sidewalk, free and easy.

As high theater as were his various courtroom antics, Doc Baggs's grandest productions were his infamous "big-store" scams. Elaborate to the extreme, these involved setups became his signature swindles, emulated to this day.

The big-store scam was, as the name implied, a storefront setup, often a grand and expensive design for the express purpose of bilking a wealthy mark out of a large sum of money. Baggs's shops were full-blown offices filled with bustling workers and grand furnishings, and anchoring the scene was a massive built-in vault. The door would be partially open to allow visitors—marks—a glimpse inside. And what they saw would go a long way toward convincing them that this was an office to be trusted.

Even the oak railings and counters were designed such that they would collapse and be hauled off or stashed away in hidden compartments in the event that the setup was rumbled by the police. And this would happen now and again. But naturally, Doc had that angle covered as well.

On the occasion that a sucker would haul a marshal to the spot where less than an hour before he'd been bilked, he'd not find the same bustling office. Instead, Doc and his team would have disassembled the entire affair, then decked out the room to resemble a boudoir, and hired a Chinese woman to explain that her employer, the missing lady of the house, was not in. The mark would go away sore and vowing he'd find that shop, if it was the last thing he did....

What they didn't know was that the vault, along with everything in the place, was a ruse. The interior of the safe was little more than an optical illusion cleverly painted on silk to resemble the interior and exterior of a safe. But it was enough to get the job done, the job being to convince whomever had been marked for bilking that the place was most legitimate.

These elaborate scams took in a number of wealthy folks, who often also happened to be high-profile society types. This factor often worked in Doc's favor as the famous marks were not apt to want their names outed in the press should they complain to the police. And so they frequently kept quiet, preferring anonymity to revenge through law.

A prime example of one of Doc Baggs's big-store scams is also one of the most famous, notably for the high-profile name of the mark and his soon-to-be-famous son.

In 1882, wealthy Las Vegas, New Mexico, businessman Miguel Otero Sr. traveled to Denver in part to take in the spectacle that was a visiting Oscar Wilde, Irish writer, dandy, and bon vivant. While there, Otero Sr., just leaving his Denver hotel's lobby for a stroll alone, happened to bump into a harmless-looking man who claimed to be an old acquaintance. This acquaintance/steerer said in low tones that he'd just been onto a sure thing, a can't-lose proposition, and that he was headed to a local "policy shop" (a legitimate business at the time engaged in state-sanctioned lotteries). And why didn't Otero tag along to see if his ticket was a winner?

As luck would have it, on the street they bumped into a chum of the Denver man who, oddly enough, also possessed a lottery ticket. But this chap winked and allowed as how he had a particular system for besting the game. Otero, at this point, was amused and curious, still sensing no reason for alarm.

The policy shop was run by a trim, middle-aged man with brown hair and beard and green glasses, and curiously, he sported a space where a finger should be on his right hand. The next draw took place, and though Otero's "friend from back home" came up duds, his chum from the street, true to his word, scored $100 with his "system."

He won the next drawing as well. His repeated claims that he knew how to best the game were, apparently, quite true. Otero was intrigued enough that when the young man, short of cash but eager to press on, inquired sheepishly if Don Miguel might fund the venture for a fifty-fifty split, the elder moneyman agreed. After all, he reasoned to himself, this was a sure-fire way to make a spot of easy money.

Soon enough it appeared Don Miguel's investment was to be a worthy one. But there was a problem: The shop operator, he of the missing digit, informed them that he would only pay that much cash if the gamblers, Otero and young sure-thing, could establish their credit. To do so they had to prove their veracity by offering the same amount, proving that from the start they were legitimate bettors, in the event they had lost the game of chance.

Naturally the young man pulled a worried look and sheepishly once again looked to Don Miguel Otero Sr., who also happened to be a bank president as well as a former railroad executive. Yes, Don Miguel smiled benignly, he would gladly proffer a five-day note covering the $2,400. He signed it over and was told to return the next day to collect the winnings. All sounded quite aboveboard and legitimate. This was, after all, a state-sanctioned, run-of-the-mill policy shop.

When he returned the next day, however, there was nothing but a locked door and no sign of the shop. Hmm. He next went to the bank to inquire as to the whereabouts of his note and was told that the young man, his "friend," had taken receipt of it. Otero was left holding the bag, or rather an empty one.

The only bag involved was Doc Baggs, who amazingly enough admitted to the scam the next day in the newspaper: "I'm a poor man and Otero is rich. I need the money and he can afford to lose it. He dares not squeal or have me arrested for he is a businessman, has served several terms in Congress and is afraid of publicity."

In truth, the check made its way to a banker named Pliny Rice, who paid Baggs a percentage of its worth. The banker intended then to cash it himself for full value.

True to Baggs's guess, Otero wanted no part of the publicity his lapse in good judgment would bring, so he failed to show up in court to testify against the bunco king. But not so with Otero the younger, who was traveling with his father at the time. When he learned of his old man's woeful skinning, he vowed to retrieve the money and get someone to pay for the crime. Papa cried no, but the son bulled ahead.

He stopped payment at the bank, then recruited a lawman, who threatened to arrest Doc Baggs, and ended up negotiating for the return of the purloined check—for a fee, naturally. Enter banker Pliny Rice, again, who took $1,000 for Otero Sr.'s check. As the check and cash were proffered for exchange, bold young Otero grabbed the check.

Alas, Pliny (or perhaps Baggs?) had the last laugh, as the snatched check turned out to be a fake. The nerve! Once more, a meeting took place at a Denver bank. Pliny swore the check, this time, was the real deal. Once again a swap happened, but Otero Jr. took no chances and had an undercover Denver police officer descend on Pliny Rice. Rice blustered that he would sue Otero for the missing $1,000. It's a safe bet that Otero didn't pay up.

Curiously enough, Miguel Antonio Otero II became a prominent politician, as was his father before him. He also wrote a number of popular books about Western history and lore, though he did not go into great detail about his father's bilking at the hands of Doc Baggs.

Predictably, Doc Baggs was nowhere to be found following the younger Otero's attempts to recover his father's money. Though the Denver police force tried for several days to run him aground, they turned up empty-handed. When asked later what he thought of the matter, Baggs himself, never short of opinion or words, replied:

> Why don't the papers pitch into bad places and try to break them up, and also go for "tin-horn" gamblers, who are robbing the poor laboring man of his last dollar. Here are all these keno and faro rooms running night after night and no one says "stop them." Many a poor laboring man who has been robbed of his few dollars of hard-earned money has come to me for help and I always help them in such cases. I have often found a poor devil of a clerk gambling away $25 of his employer's money and I have taken him to one side and said: "Look here, you are bracing yourself against a game that I can't beat, smart as I am. Here is $25, take it, fix matters straight and never bet on a game again." There are many young men that I have thus saved from ruin. I never try to rob these poor fellows, but now because of an ex-member of Congress, who told me that he knew all about finance and was the smartest man in this whole Western country, starts out with me and gets robbed of $2,400, at least they say he was, the press all began to attack me. I look down with supreme contempt on all these "tin-horn" gamblers, and I will give $350 toward suppressing them and driving them out of town. But I will tell you one thing: We want a chief of police that can see a trick when it is turned, and who won't let a sucker be skinned before his face and eyes.

Throughout his many years as King of the Confidence Men, Doc Baggs was always busy with one scam or another and likely enjoyed every minute of it. He was known for his snappy mode of dress, his kindly voice, and for not using off-color language. Instead he got his jollies conning people and indulging in a theatrical bent. He played many roles in his various cons, among them ranchers, miners, bankers, and ministers, and he sported elaborate costumes and disguises for each.

By 1915 it was reported in a Denver newspaper that the dishonorable Doc Baggs had bilked his last mark in Denver, a doozy of a con netting him $100,000. It is believed that Baggs, by then in his seventies, took his newfound mountain of cash and retired to his ranch in California.

CHAPTER 5
CLARK STANLEY
THE RATTLE-SNAKE KING (AND OTHERS OF THE SNAKE-OIL SET)

The dictionary tells us that a *nostrum* is a "medicine, especially one that is not considered effective, prepared by an unqualified person." Well, in the latter half of the nineteenth century, it was a good bet that the majority of tinctures, tonics, liniments, and compounds pedaled over hill and dale were of dubious effectiveness, especially when they contained significant amounts of alcohol. No wonder the users provided glowing reviews.

But who is to say that many were prepared by unqualified hands? This was in the days before government regulation and oversight of the medical field, after all. A time when most folks relied on themselves or a wise elder to minister with trusted folk remedies passed down in families for centuries. In such a context, it is difficult to judge the qualifications of a homegrown healer, someone who learned how to treat a chest cold with comfrey leaves or bruising with arnica.

All that changed when opportunists saw the promise of easy money to be made by preying on the fears of the masses. After all, they intoned to their rapt crowds, if you don't have your health, what do you have? In the nineteenth century there were thousands of hucksters working their tenuous trade, rolling from town to town, farm to farm. They brimmed with confidence and spewed outlandish claims about their particular product, whether they were merely selling someone else's tincture or they themselves had concocted it.

Among the popular derivation tales explaining where the term "snake oil" came from is one attributed to early European settlers who had seen native peoples of what is now the northeastern United States gather naturally occurring oil seeps for use in treating wounds. The practice was attributed to the Seneca tribe of the Iroquois, and the Europeans, ever on the make, bottled and labeled the goop as a cure-all-ills salve. The name "Seneca oil" eventually became bastardized through mispronunciation and laziness to "snake oil."

SNAKE OIL LINIMENT

GLARK STANLEY'S

SNAKE OIL LINIMENT.

THE STRONGEST AND BEST LINIMENT KNOWN FOR THE CURE OF ALL PAIN AND LAMENESS.

USED EXTERNAL ONLY. FOR

RHEUMATISM
NEURALGIA
SCIATICA
LAME BACK
LUMBAGO
CONTRACTED
MUSCLES
TOOTHACHE
SPRAINS
SWELLINGS
ETC.

TRADE MARK

CURES
FROST BITES
CHILL BLAINS
BRUISES
SORE THROAT
BITES OF
ANIMALS
INSECTS AND
REPTILES.

IT GIVES
IMMEDIATE
RELIEF

IS GOOD
FOR
EVERYTHING
A LINIMENT
OUGHT
TO BE
GOOD FOR

Manufactured by
CLARK STANLEY
Snake Oil Liniment
Company
Providence, R. I.

Hatched in Abilene, Texas, in 1854, Clark Stanley grew up to become America's "Rattle-Snake King." Decked out in garish cowboy garb, Stanley traveled the US, butchering hundreds of live rattlesnakes for their oil in front of rapt crowds. With claims that it could cure everything from frostbite and rheumatism to all manner of critter bites, "Clark's Snake Oil Liniment" sold like gangbusters. Too bad that in 1917 the federal government found his "snake oil" was mostly mineral oil.   The life and adventures of the American cow-boy: Life in the Far West *by Clark Stanley, better known as the Rattle-Snake King. Published by Clark Stanley, 1897.*

This possibility seems far less plausible than the commonly accepted derivation of the term, which came from the healing lotion Chinese laborers concocted in part from Chinese water snakes. They rubbed the salve into their aching limbs after working long, inhumane hours laying track on the First Transcontinental Railroad. Eventually they shared their soothing balm with their European comrades and thus an industry was born.

In time, the shady but likable character so familiar in Western movies—the one who wheels into town atop a fancy-painted wagon with bold claims painted on the sides—became a fixture throughout the West. This was in the days long before the federal government had established oversight that protected citizens from swindlers bilking them of their money in exchange for shoddy goods and services. Until the landmark 1906 Pure Food and Drug Act, the United States was a-crawl with peddlers, mostly up to little good, hawking tonics, tinctures, lotions, salves, and creams, claiming they could cure anything from headaches to cancers.

All these products really ever did was lighten the wallets of the poor sots who purchased them. The sad part of such transactions is that often the buyer suffered from a genuine affliction, one often exacerbated instead of relieved by the fake medicine. The only real creative element of the salesman's product was his over-the-top trumpeting proclaiming his product to be the very thing the world had been waiting for.

These peddlers often billed themselves as doctors, offered inscrutable or untraceable credentials when pressed, and could rattle off a litany of scientific-sounding jargon to seal the deal. The very best of them could whip up crowds into a frenzy of need, whether or not they had a genuine affliction.

Often a ringer or shill would work with the "doctor," circulating through the crowd, corroborating the doctor's claims with outlandish claims of his or her own, purporting to have been cured recently by the very same product the good doc was offering for a mere pittance.

But wait! Who hasn't heard that phrase, say, when an infomercial comes on and you're about to change the channel, but there's something . . . something that compels you to stay your hand, just a moment, then a moment more. And before you know it, you're dialing the phone, getting in on the last-minute opportunity to buy that miracle cleaning product that you really didn't need. But then again, it does such a good job, surely you'll need it. And then there's that offer—two, wait, three bottles for the price of one! How can they afford to practically give away their products?!

These modern hucksters learned from the best, their predecessors: those charlatans roaming the byways of America's yesterday. One of the most famous of these roving shysters was Clark Stanley, self-proclaimed "Rattle-Snake King." He not only was a snake-oil peddler, he was *the* snake-oil peddler ... until the US government shut him down. But we're getting ahead of ourselves.

Hatched in Abilene, Texas, in 1854, Clark Stanley grew up to become a cowboy never quite satisfied with the day-to-day drudgery of ranch life. Stanley had an idea that there was more to life than staying put and working for peanuts. As with most other hucksters of his (or any other) age, he seems to have been born with an innate urge to make his mark—and his fortune—in a grand way. The big, vague things he thought he might like to pursue in life would require money to accomplish, of that much he was certain. His penchant for big bucks—any way he could get them—led him to sniff out possibilities and opportunities that might lead to money.

Stanley followed along a well-trod trail for young men in Texas at the time and became a ranch hand. He must have enjoyed aspects of it, for he spent eleven years at it. But unlike many of his colleagues of the saddle, Stanley's searching mind led him to study traditional Hopi medicine for two years under a Moki pueblo medicine man at Walpi, Arizona. It was there, at the Hopi village to the east of the Grand Canyon, that he learned the intricacies of gathering ingredients for natural remedies.

Clark Stanley was also, from an early age, charismatic and wholly slippery. And at a time rife with people clogging the back roads and byways, well-trammeled routes, and main streets all over America, peddling cure-alls for ailments most folks had no idea they had—until they heard the hucksters' patter—Clark Stanley stood out among them. Indeed, he is arguably the most famous snake-oil salesman of them all. So much so, it is said, that he is the man for whom that very phrase is coined.

In true huckster fashion, Stanley was most often a one-man band, coming up with his own product, hawking it himself—and working hard doing so—conjuring the advertising lingo, which was as creative in its claims as was Stanley's outlandish Western garb.

As we've learned with any good huckster, Clark Stanley showed no shortage of self-confidence. In 1897, primarily as a vehicle for selling his tonic, Stanley penned an odd, forty-one page publication, part autobiography, part lesson plan for would-be cowboys, and one-third compendium of advertisements for Stanley's liniment, touting its wonders and revealing tall-tale claims of healing.

The first edition contained a number of cowboy songs he had collected from his years as a ranch hand, and by including them in his book it has become one of the earliest, perhaps *the* earliest, published collection of cowboy ditties. Stanley used the book as a selling tool in his shows. It had the effect of showing him as a learned man, but not so much as to distance himself from his primary clientele, the average laborer looking for relief from a real or imagined illness. He revised and added to the pamphlet a number of times over the coming years, including personal anecdotes, more history, and most importantly for him, glowing testimonials from users of his magic snake potion.

During his heyday in the 1890s, Stanley toured the country as a celebrated showman-huckster and claimed his "Snake Oil Liniment" was "good for man and beast." He also said that his snake oil was "the strongest and best liniment known for the cure of all pain and lameness" and that it was an excellent curative for "rheumatism, neuralgia, sciatica, lame back, lumbago, contracted muscles, toothache, sprains, swellings, etc."

But wait—there's more! He also claimed it "cures frost bites, chill blains, bruises, sore throat, bites of animals, insects and reptiles" . . . and if that didn't convince the average attendee, he sealed the deal with the vow that it would afford the user "immediate relief" and that it was "good for every thing a liniment should be good for." All that for a mere 50 cents a bottle. Who could possibly resist? Not many, as it turns out.

So how did our man Stanley create this magic topical tincture? If he was to be believed—and everything he said should be ingested with copious helpings of skepticism—Stanley gleaned his super-secret recipe from that ancient medicine man of the Moki Pueblo tribe under whom he studied. This claim is thought to be true, at least in part because various Native American tribes were known for making a soothing balm of grease squeezed from rattlesnake carcasses. . . .

With a confident downward slicing motion, the man who called himself "the Rattle-Snake King" dispatched yet another long serpent. The deadly, jaw-popping head, now separated from the curling, writhing body, nonetheless continued to snap and bite harmlessly at the air, reflexively and brutally.

Yet the man who wielded the blood-smeared blade smiled as though he had just been informed he was the recipient of a vast fortune.

"You are a long way from Texas, cowboy!" someone shouted.

"You bet I am," said the tall, handsome, smiling cowboy as he stood over a large crate to one side of a low wooden stage. He was dressed in a flamboyant, well-appointed suit, topped with a fine hat. His attire was most appropriate, he felt, given the grand venue he found himself in: The World's Columbian Exposition of Chicago in the year 1893.

His face wore a perpetual wide-eyed look, as if daring anyone he came in contact with to ask him what was wrong. And talk he did—at the drop of a well-worn trail hat, Stanley would launch into a nonstop patter proclaiming the wonders of his liniment, pausing only long enough to snatch hold of yet another rattlesnake from his seemingly bottomless crate full of writhing serpents.

"It's as the bottle says, ladies and gentlemen, a wonderful pain-destroying compound composed of the very thing you would suspect would cause nothing but pain and grief. Yes, folks, I am referring to the oil of rattlesnakes! And do you know what?" Clark Stanley held his right hand, outstretched, palm down, scanning the crowd as if the arm were itself a snake.

"No? Then I will tell you, for I have no secrets, no fears save one, ladies and gents, and that one fear is that a soul in need, just one, I tell you, will leave here today without a bottle of Clark Stanley's Snake-Oil Liniment in their hand, and go on home to a sad, dreary existence filled with the torment of never-ending pain, pain that, I tell you folks, can be lessened and eventually eradicated, given repeated doses, with what I know without a doubt to be the strongest and best liniment known for the cure of all pain—yes, all pain—and all manner of lameness, too!

"Now, I know a number of you are standing there saying, 'But Mr. Clark Stanley, how is that even possible?' I will tell you just how. For I happen to know that we have in our presence a special treat—a satisfied customer is here today, folks. So why take my word for it? Take the words of this wonderful young woman."

He nodded toward a girl who had begun to walk forward toward the low stage. ". . . who when I met her was little more than a fledgling, wasting away in bed, unable to raise a hand to help her dear family.

"So lame was she by a deathly crippling case of rheumatism, but not just any run-of-the-mill case, no, this poor young woman was born afflicted and spent the first eighteen years of her days on God's earth as a bent, crippled, and stooped young woman looking far older than her years for far too long.

"Every moment awake was an agony for her, and every moment asleep was a double-threat—for she did not know if she would awaken the next morning. In fact, she told me she secretly hoped that she might not wake one fine day, so tired was she of spending her life in the throes of agony. But don't take my word for it, ladies and gentlemen, take hers!"

The packed crowd gathered before the low stage on which Dr. Stanley trod back and forth, all the while holding a writhing rattlesnake in each hand, the rattles clacking and vibrating and buzzing, the bodies twisting and curling, writhing around his gesticulating arms. But those gathered had momentarily lost interest in this bizarre sight as their gaze swiveled to take in the pretty young woman walking confidently forward as the crowd parted before her.

Even Clark Stanley paused momentarily. Luckily she was in his employ, if momentarily. He suppressed a wry smile, felt the snakes twisting on his arm, the sinewy muscles twitching and writhing, and came back to himself.

He was always careful to avoid the very thing that could put him right out of business. For a bite from a rattlesnake would dictate that he treat himself with his own medicine, and though he claimed it was good for healing snake-bites, he didn't want to test that thin theory. He knew that if he all but died before his adoring public, they would have a difficult time buying his patter ever after.

During a show later that day Stanley patiently answered a series of questions from a man who looked as if he never believed anything anyone ever told him.

"As I said, my patent liniment comes from the purest oil of snakes, sure as shootin'." Stanley stood there looking down at the man who'd questioned him, his eyebrows pulled together as if he wasn't sure, but maybe he hadn't heard the man correctly. Maybe the man hadn't seen what he was doing right there in front of him.

Stanley held up the still-writhing body of the snake. The head lay at his feet, the eyes beginning to glaze, but a slow reflexive opening and closing of its jaws showed that, even in death, the snake was still determined to defend itself.

The man who'd questioned him stood as he had throughout the grisly proceedings, his arms wrapped tight about himself, the sleeves of his wool jacket pulled tight about his fat arms. His face wore a smirk, a knowing look that said he was anything but a believer. He was, yes sir, a skeptic.

Stanley had seen his kind before, and he found them amusing. He also liked the challenge of bringing them around to a point where he might introduce doubt in their skepticism, if not outright belief in his product.

Stanley faced the crowd once again. "My assistant and I will now render down these snake bodies into a fine oil that is more valuable than all the gold in the West. Do you doubt it, friends? I do not, and once you see the amazing curative effects this precious liquid can have on a body fatigued by pain, crippled by overwork, and agonized by ill-tended injury, why then, my friends, you shall see the power of Clark Stanley's Rattle-Snake Oil. Or I am not the Rattle-Snake King!"

With that, the flamboyantly dressed cowboy washed his hands and proceeded down to his favorite part of the show—selling his bottles of oil and taking money in exchange.

While it is possible that Clark Stanley began his snake-oil venture with the purest snaky ingredients and the best of intentions, by 1917 he was finally investigated by the federal government, which seized a large shipment of his product. Predictably, when tests were run, his Snake Oil Liniment was found to contain a creative blend of a number of benign ingredients including mineral oil, 1 percent fatty oil (determined to be beef fat), red pepper, turpentine, and camphor.

None of these ingredients, in any combination or amount, could even remotely be responsible for curing much more than a bad case of heavy wallet. The other determination was that the primary ingredient was good old mineral oil, with not a whiff of oil or fat derived from honest-to-goodness rattlesnakes.

Because of the 1906 Pure Food and Drug Act, the US government was able to bring a lawsuit against Stanley for unlawful branding and misrepresentation of his product. Unsurprisingly, the feds won. Alas Stanley was fined a mere $20. But the lawsuit's real benefit helped give the term "snake oil" a well-earned taint among the American public. Soon the term "snake-oil salesman" meant little more than someone up to no good, a huckster with a shoddy product spouting false claims. There were many imitators, but there was only one Clark Stanley, the Rattle-Snake King.

BUILT ON CLAY

Leila P. Irish, of Cave Creek, Arizona, made a worthless gold mine pay, and pay handsomely. She bought the Clay Mine but found, much to her consternation, that it was nearly useless and produced no gold. It did prove, however, to be a gold mine in a wholly unexpected way. No slouch, Ms. Irish discovered the mine was rich in clay deposits. In an effort to recover some smidgen of her investment in the paltry mine, Ms. Irish mixed her mined clay with water. She bottled the result and sold it as a cure-all-ailments elixir called "Apache, a Perfect Mineral Drink," though she wasn't entirely sure what it might be used to cure.

It turns out it really did ease one ill—the gut-wrenching ailment known as dysentery, rampant throughout the West at the time and caused primarily by the drinking of tainted water. It turns out that mixing clay with water, an old remedy, had the desired effect of "stoppering" the offending flow.

No one was more astounded than Ms. Irish when she made a fortune off the stuff, money from which her heirs are still enjoying today.

DOC AND THE STINGER

Joseph "Yellow Kid" Weil lived from 1877 to 1976 and gained prominence throughout the United States by stealing more than $8 million throughout his life in a series of over-the-top cons. But he got his start hawking his mentor's patent medicine, "Doc Meriwether's Elixir," to the hopeful. Said to have incredible healing powers, the shoddy tonic was composed chiefly of rainwater. But Weil's life and exploits, the basis for the Hollywood movie *The Sting*, were most effective.

HADACOL!

Heck, even silver-screen stalwart Mickey Rooney wasn't above shilling for dubious products. In 1950, at a low point in his career, he was so cash-strapped that he toured the South with the Hadacol Goodwill Caravan, a roving variety show sponsored by Hadacol, a supposed vitamin supplement. And for just one box top from the packaging a bottle of Hadacol came in, you could gain admission to the show. Hadacol was the brainchild of Dudley J. LeBlanc, Louisiana state senator, who *Time* magazine described as "a stem-winding salesman who knows every razzle-dazzle switch in the pitchman's trade."

Alas, the product, as with so many before and since, proved too good to be true. The US government said no-go when Hadacol was found to contain upward of 26 percent alcohol and little else of a redemptive, helpful nature.

As we all know, Rooney, indefatigable as ever, made his way back to Tinseltown and continued to wow fans for decades to come. No word on whether Hadacol had anything to do with it.

Yesterday's snake oils are merely today's unlicensed, over-the-counter, non-prescription remedies, often called "alternative medicines." And these tonics, tinctures, liniments, and lotions can trace their lineage back to eighteenth-century Britain, where "patent" medicines were born. As with those old-time remedies, some of today's offerings work wonders, and some are pure snake-oil hokum. Only the inventors know for certain, and they're not talking.

CHAPTER 6

GEORGE DEVOL
KING OF THE RIVERBOAT GAMBLERS (PLUS CANADA BILL!)

G iven his childhood predilection for schoolyard fisticuffs and roguish behavior, it's a good guess that people who knew George H. Devol as a child might well have predicted the young upstart would live an interesting, if not particularly long, life. As to his pugilistic tendencies, he maintained a life-long fondness for a good fight. And as to his longevity, he lasted a good many years longer than most who knew him in his youth would have guessed. In the process, he came to be regarded as the most famous gambling man of his day, known up and down the Big Muddy as King of the Riverboat Gamblers. But he didn't earn that title without working a few cons along the way.

It's also probable that much of his life's praise is due, at least in part, to his autobiography, *Forty Years a Gambler on the Mississippi*, which he wrote at the end of his career, when he was fifty-eight, in 1887. No matter the truth of the tales therein, it's a fun read that provides interesting insights to life during the heyday of gambling aboard riverboats on the Mississippi. Devol led a long, fascinating, and largely successful life doing what he loved and loving what he did.

Born on August 1, 1829, in the little river town of Marietta, Ohio, George was the youngest of six children. With a ship's carpenter for a father gone from home for long periods of time, as a tot Devol showed signs of independence and belligerence where authority was concerned. He wasn't particularly keen on attending school and frequently bunked out, preferring to roughhouse and engage in fisticuffs with other boys. It must have been a secret relief to his mother when the hard-headed handful ran away from home at the tender age of ten.

He became a cabin boy on the river steamer the *Wacousta*. He soon traded up to a better position on a ship called *Walnut Hills*, then the *Cicero*. While on this ship, George began his education in the fine arts of card play, bluffing, and

George H. Devol is regarded as the Mississippi River's greatest riverboat gambler, and he was equally well-known as a master con man who loved a good fight. By the age of 30 he had made hundreds of thousands of dollars working riverboats and railroad lines. Though he earned in excess of $2,000,000 in his career, Devol died a pauper in Hot Springs, Arkansas, in 1903. His autobiography, *Forty Years a Gambler on the Mississippi*, is an eye-opening read.
Courtesy Library of Congress, 1887.

sleight of hand. His goal? To emulate the high-falutin' lives of the gamblers who plied their trade onboard.

Before long, war with Mexico reared its head and George felt he had to dip his oar. He landed a job as a barkeep aboard a ship bound for the Rio Grande.

As a soldier, he perfected his playing-card trickery and fleeced fellow warriors out of their cash.

By the time he'd had his fill with the army, George H. Devol was seventeen and had earned $3,000, a fortune in those days, a fair chunk of change for a lad who should have been more concerned with girls than gambling. But then again, Devol never could be considered normal.

Within a few short years of working paddlewheel steamers, of getting into scrapes and never backing down from a bare-knuckle dustup whether he was in the right or wrong, Devol cemented his reputation as a hardheaded man with a penchant for gaming that often exceeded the bounds of being on the up-and-up.

By the age of thirty, Devol had made hundreds of thousands of dollars working southern riverboats. During the Mexican-American War and the War Between the States, he gladly fleeced soldiers and fellow gamblers alike, offering legitimate games when possible, but he was not above rigging the deck, dealing from the bottom and seconds, palming cards, and recovering the cut—all invaluable skills to a man in his line of work. He learned these skills as a youth working aboard the riverboats, from older, wise hands who took the bright, eager young man, always large for his age, under their wings. Little did they know that in a few short years Devol would exceed their skills and teachings.

As shrewd and adroit as he was, Devol admitted that part of his success he owed to his imposing physique. In his autobiography, Devol mentions that he was on the large side, weighing in at more than two hundred pounds. He was proud of his sizable hands, claiming the ability to "hold one deck in the palm of my hand and shuffle up another."

But it was his clever head's substantial mass that he was most proud of:

I don't know (and I guess I never will while I'm alive) just how thick my old skull is, but I do know that it is pretty thick, or it would have been cracked many years ago, for I have been struck some terrible blows on my head with iron dray-pins, pokers, clubs, stone-coal, and bowlders, which would have split any man's skull wide open unless it was pretty thick. Doctors have often told me that my skull was nearly an inch in thickness over my forehead.

This rather odd trait seems to have served Devol well during a lifetime of indulging in fistfights and out-and-out brawling whenever the urge gripped him, an urge that appeared to overcome him with some frequency. The man loved a good fight and was noted for head-butting his adversaries with that bull-thick skull . . . when he wasn't drawing down on them with his gun, that is—another skill he had reason to cultivate, given his dicey line of work. It must have been a trait that stood him in good stead all those years, four decades plying his trade, the good, the bad, and the nefarious sides of it, up and down the great rivers of the West, as well as in cowtowns and along rail lines. He worked the deck anywhere he could scare up a good or bad game.

In all those years as a professional gambler, Devol won vast fortunes, and he spent them, too. And though he cheated untold numbers of folks out of their hard-earned cash, he also won as much money in honest games of chance. As with so many others of his ilk, he claimed that he never peeled the wad from anyone who wasn't also looking to do the same from him. Maybe not an admirable quality, but a commendable one.

After the Civil War he gambled along the budding railroad lines, stopping to fleece out-of-their-depth cowpokes and miners from Kansas City to Cheyenne. It was while he was engaged in gambling in the Gold Room Saloon in Cheyenne that he first met the infamous Wild Bill Hickok. Though he was not the gunman's dealer, Devol cheerfully recounted the scene: Hickok placed a $50 bet, promptly lost it, then placed another $50 bet. This time he won. But the dealer only gave him $25 in return.

Hickok was fit to be tied and made it plainly known.

To which the dealer replied: "The house limit is $25, sir."

Hickok stood, his chair squawking backward on the plank floor. "But you took fifty when I lost!"

The dealer smirked. "Fifty when you lose, sir."

With the speed for which he was known, Wild Bill delivered a quick striking blow not with a revolver but with his walking stick, straight to the dealer's gleaming pate. Then the famed gunman upended the games table and snatched the entirety of the till, filling his pockets. No one protested. Devol shifted the cigar in his mouth and smiled, flicking his eyes back to his own cards. He was not about to waste the opportunity this unexpected and unguarded moment presented to glance at the cards of his opponents, once again demonstrating he was merely an opportunist looking for an angle.

For all his cunning, Devol could at times be his own worst enemy. Never more so than one evening when he worked the Cheyenne-to-Omaha route, enjoying what for him was turning out to be an excellent game onboard the Missouri Railroad.

One by one the other men at the table dropped out, and his florid opponent, a well-dressed man whose name he did not yet know, became more flustered as the game crawled on. But Devol was in his element. He indulged in a moment taking in details of the scene: The clackety-clack of the gently swaying train, the slight movement of the brocade curtain's gold tassels as the train surged along gentle curves through a pretty landscape, and a fine game made even better by a man who was so far gone into his impending loss that he took no pains to hide his discomfort.

Soon enough, the reddening man watched as a wryly smiling Devol shifted the cigar to the other side of his mouth and laid out an unbeatable hand.

"That's . . . that's . . ." the man's face fairly shook with rage.

"That's poker, my friend." Devol offered a sympathetic look, then quietly slid the pot to himself.

"You cheated, sir. Of that I am sure!"

Devol's eyes narrowed and he left the money, chips, and cards where they lay on the baize surface. "And you, sir, are a poor loser." His big voice rumbled low and menacing. "If there was trickery involved in this game, I can assure you it was not on my part." He shifted his bull-headed, indignant gaze to the three other men who had dropped out of the game, but none dared voice complaint.

The rest of the gambling car had grown silent, yet the losing player did not seem to notice, or perhaps didn't care.

"But I lost $1,200!"

"Yes," said Devol. "Yes, you did. And no one told you to bet. I saw no gun placed to your temple."

"I know well who you are, Devol," said the man, standing, rage quivering his lips and shaking his outthrust finger. "And do you know who I am, sir?"

"I've no idea," said Devol, doing his best to not smile too broadly.

"I am a director with this railroad, and from this moment on there will be no gambling on our trains. Do you hear me, Devol? I will see to it! Ha!"

Devol sat in silence, said nothing. Finally he looked up at the angry man and slowly shook his head, keeping up the appearance of righteous indignation. But inside he knew he'd potentially ruined a good thing, not only for himself but for all those other gamblers with whom he was acquainted. A few of them wouldn't blame him, of course. But there were a good many who relied on the rail routes to earn their keep. And he had just single-handedly nipped that in the bud. He would not be popular with them.

The sore loser stomped off, brusquely brushing past a waiter and two men entering the car full of stunned passengers.

It would be but a few days before Devol saw the handbills the man had had printed up and hung in his railroad's cars. They prohibited gambling onboard and threatened conductors with loss of jobs should they allow such aboard their trains. Devol's chum also informed him that the railroad had hired Pinkerton Detectives to patrol its lines, on the scout for professional gamblers. With a regretful shrug, Devol shifted his attentions to other train lines and back to the riverboats.

One of Devol's peculiarities involved the fleecing of men of the cloth. Apparently the ubiquity of gambling on the frontier was such that even the Godly were not unaffected by the allure of the wager. But never let it be said that Devol was a less-than-charitable gambler. . . .

George H. Devol sipped his drink, set it down, and studied his cards. He didn't need to, for he knew just what his opening move would be. But it pleased him to make a show of this, one of his most cherished pastimes—that of gambling against a minister. "I see by your manner of dress and by your pious countenance that you, sir, are a man of the cloth."

The others at the table raised eyebrows, two of them barely concealed smirks. They were all-too-familiar with Devol's peculiar habit and had, imperceptibly but between the pair of them, nodded to each other, placing a silent bet as to whether Devol would or would not succeed in fleecing the preacher. And now the little saga had commenced.

"I too am a man of the cloth, you see," said Devol. "The green cloth, that is." He smiled broadly and dragged a chubby hand across the baize surface before him. "But it all amounts to the same in the end, doesn't it, Padre?"

The man had reddened considerably since he'd been outed as a minister. "Why, yes, yes, I . . . I am privileged to have been called upon to spread the Good Word, as it were. But . . ."

Devol's head cocked and his eyebrows arched out of curiosity. "Yes?"

"Only, I wonder how it is you came to know I am a man of God?"

Devol kept his eyes on the paste boards pinched in his hand. He looked as though he were giving the matter mighty thought. What he really was doing was concentrating on the purpose of the game. Finally he laid down a face card, said, "Hold," and flashed his eyes briefly about the table. He recognized the almost imperceptible shadows of doom cross the faces of his fellows. Not a good hand between the lot of them, he guessed. Then Devol addressed the minister once again. "You might say that you wear your occupation not unlike a wine stain. No matter what you do, it will not wash out."

"I'm not sure quite how to take that, sir."

"Any way you like, though I assure you it was meant in the highest regard for your profession."

No more was said on the matter as play continued, gaining intensity and fervor until one by one the men dropped away and the two who remained were, naturally, Devol and the minister. The latter tried to suppress a smile but could not. The confidence he had in his cards was clear.

Devol pooched his lips and set his cigar down. He channeled concern through his face, well-trimmed beard and thick features topped with slicked-back hair lightly scented with lavender. With a small flourish of his pink hand, Devol laid his cards down.

"But . . . but, how can that be?" the minister pushed back from the table, hands still visible, shaking and pale, as was his face. "That simply cannot be."

Devol curled a thick finger around his cigar, fixed the man with a beetle-brow stare, and said, "I assure you it can be. Indeed, it is. And any further chatter about how I could not have won a simple card game, a game of chance, I might remind you, would intimate to me and all others gathered here and within earshot—for your cries have attracted unwanted attentions from nearby tables—that I had somehow contrived to win by any means necessary, perhaps even through chicanery."

"Oh, no, no, I don't mean that at all, sir. I was referring to my own foolishness. For you see I am broke, having gambled the entire wad that was to have sustained me on my journey to St. Louis and back again."

Devol poked the cigar back into his mouth, regarded the fretting man a moment more, then stood and raked his haul into an assembled stack. He looked down once more at the glaze-eyed minister, who himself sat staring at the meager hand he had laid down moments before with such confidence.

Devol once again plucked the cigar from his mouth, proffered the folded cash before the minister's face, and in a voice loud enough for much of the large, crowded room to hear, said, "Now, go forth and sin no more."

As Devol threaded his way through the crowd toward the bar, a few of his fellows patted him lightly on the shoulder as he passed. It was a good feeling, and he offered slight nods of appreciation. He also didn't have to stand himself a drink for the next hour.

"He's one of a kind," said one of the two other men at the table, privy to Devol's ultimately kindly treatment of the man.

"How do you figure that?"

They headed toward the door, onto the deck of the big thrumming riverboat to take in fresh air before the evening's play commenced.

"Because I know he always says that to the men of the cloth and makes a big show of it and all." He fished his cigar case from an inner pocket. "But you'll never see him cut slack to farmers, businessmen, salesmen, soldiers, or the like."

"And definitely not with other gamblers!"

"Don't I know it," said the man, touching flame to his cigar. "Thanks for reminding me."

Though he earned in excess of $2,000,000 in forty years of gambling throughout the South and West, sixty-seven-year-old Devol, at the request of his wife, retired from his life's work as a professional gambler in 1896. He had seen the end coming for some time anyway.

The heyday of the great riverboats steaming up and down the mighty Mississippi River and sumptuous gambling cars aboard railroads were all but gone. Instead, Devol hawked his memoir, which he had written a few years before. The book proved to be a crafty blend of fact, fiction, tall tale, and outright balderdash—not unlike his claims of being an honest gambler. When he died in 1903, in Hot Springs, Arkansas, George H. Devol, King of the Riverboat Gamblers, was a man poor in wealth but rich in memories.

BOOM . . . BUST:
WILLIAM "CANADA BILL" JONES

A good friend, confidante, and frequent partner of George H. Devol was William "Canada Bill" Jones, considered one of the all-time top card sharps. Devol spent considerable time in his own memoir describing Canada Bill, who, contrary to his nickname, was no Canadian but arrived there from his birthplace of Yorkshire, England, as a young man. He brought with him a long litany of scams—and left in his wake many fleeced victims, which leads one to wonder about his motives behind emigrating to Canada.

He made his way south and found a ready-made situation for men such as himself aboard the riverboats. For several years he worked as one-quarter of a foursome of gamblers, each with his own specialty, among them Holly Chappell, Tom Brown, and George Devol. Rumor has it that before the quartet whittled down to just Jones and Devol, Canada Bill's take alone from the team's mutual efforts was $240,000.

In time the team reduced to the duo of George Devol and Canada Bill, who worked successfully together for several years. Eventually, the two men fell out, each claiming to have caught the other cheating him. (Did they really think otherwise?) Devol's version of the events tells that Jones was the first to cheat, so Devol merely returned the favor.

Of his old friend, Devol said:

> Canada Bill was a character one might travel the length and breadth
> of the land and never see his match, or run across his equal. Imagine a
> medium-sized, chicken-headed, tow-haired sort of a man with mild blue
> eyes, and a mouth nearly from ear to ear, who walked with a shuffling,
> half-apologetic sort of a gait, and who, when his countenance was in
> repose, resembled an idiot. For hours he would sit in his chair, twisting
> his hair in little ringlets. His clothes were always several sizes too large,
> and his face as smooth as a woman's and never had a particle of hair
> on it. Canada was a slick one. He had a squeaking, boyish voice, and
> awkward, gawky manners, and a way of asking fool questions and
> putting on a good-natured sort of a grin, that led everybody to believe
> that he was the rankest kind of a sucker—the greenest sort of a country
> jake. Woe to the man who picked him up, though.

That glowing sketch came far too late for a lifetime's worth of marks that the squeaking, dolt-like man led down the lane and fleeced. Though he was adept at a number of games, including poker, as were all his cronies, Canada Bill's game of choice was three-card monte. He learned this inherently crooked, house-stacked, and rigged game from Dick Cady, another famous gambler con man. Play kicks off when the dealer shows three cards to another player, places them face-down, rearranges them, then points to the player and tells him to find just one of the cards shown to him.

Another grifter, Dutch Charlie, teamed with Canada Bill in Kansas City following the war. They cleaned up, earning $200,000 before moving westward on trains. It wasn't long before people began complaining about their losses due to the monte players on the rail lines. Officials on the Union Pacific Railway began a rout of the offenders, so Canada Bill tried to head off the trouble before he lost out on his good thing. He famously wrote to the superintendent of the line and offered $10,000 a year for the guarantee of exclusive rights to run a three-card monte game on their trains. Alas, he was turned down.

Canada Bill was also in love with the notoriously house-stacked game of faro. So much so that despite his enormous success at three-card monte, Bill routinely dumped his ill-gotten gains straight into faro, at which he was not so good at "evening the odds."

Sadly, at the age of forty in 1880, Canada Bill died of consumption, broke and homeless, in Reading, Pennsylvania, and was buried in a pauper's grave. When his old gambling chums heard of his untimely passing and sad resting place, they chipped in, paid the city of Reading for its expenses, and bought a proper marker for Canada Bill, King of Three-Card Monte. Though he relished "snaking in the greenhorns," Canada Bill was also remembered as being a generous soul, often peeling off cash for a Sister of Charity he'd meet on the sidewalk.

There are a number of snappy quotes attributed to Canada Bill, among them "A Smith & Wesson beats four aces!" and "Nobody ever went bowlegged carrying away the money they won from me." But perhaps the most famous: When told by Devol that a faro game Canada Bill wished to play in was rigged, Bill said: "I know it's crooked, but it's the only game in town!" Now that's dedication to one's craft.

CHAPTER 7

JAMES ADDISON PERALTA-REAVIS
ARIZONA'S LORD OF FRAUD

One fine day in 1871, twenty-eight-year-old James Addison Reavis sat at the desk in his small real estate office in St. Louis, Missouri. He had just finished altering a title to a parcel of property that would otherwise go unsold. A slight amendment to the wording was required or the entire deal would end up hamstrung, barely reaching probate court. And all because it lacked a few slight inky flourishes to make it a saleable transaction in which the seller would be pleased, the buyer would be pleased, and Reavis himself would be pleased, for he would earn his commission.

What then is the harm, he asked himself, in altering the moldy old documents ever so slightly to enable all involved to get what they want? With a final satisfied sigh, Reavis set down the last page and leaned back in his desk chair. His client would be none the wiser. In fact, no one would.

Surely, he mused, there had to be a way to make more efficient use of his talents than merely helping others by ushering their own land purchases through the sometimes-hairy process of acquisition. Granted, he was rather good at it and it was something that he enjoyed. The challenges were just enough to keep his interest sparked, and they held much more appeal to him than any of the numerous jobs he had held up to that point.

Reavis folded his long hands behind his head and mused on the path that brought him to this point—owning his own, albeit modest, real estate brokerage firm. Yes, it was a one-man shop, to be sure, but it beat all to heck clerking in retail establishments, roving from place to place as a salesman. Lord, but that had been a slog. As with most things he'd turned his hands to, he had been good at it, better than most, in fact, but at what cost? The worst job, of course, even though it, too, had elements that he had enjoyed, had been as a streetcar conductor in St. Louis.

"Not bad for a man with scant schooling," he said softly as he looked about the empty office. And all the while he had slogged through those various jobs,

In 1883, James Addison "Peralta" Reavis laid claim to twelve million acres of Arizona and New Mexico, due to his possession of an Old Spanish Grant—backed by the US government. He collected millions of dollars before it was noticed his ancient documents dating from 1748 contained numerous errors and discrepancies. Turns out Reavis was a forger and swindler of the highest order. He went to prison for fraud in 1896 and died penniless in 1914.

The Land of Sunshine, *Vol. 8, No. 3, February 1898. Published by Land of Sunshine Publishing Co.*

he kept in mind that they helped provide him with the means to better himself. He was not interested, never had been, in fact, with behaving as so many of his fellows did. Squandering his hard-earned money on foolishness, on frippery and frivolity.

Sure, he enjoyed fine things in life, enjoyed slipping out for a cool glass of beer now and then, in fact, but he was not interested in frittering his money away and having little at the end of his days to show for it. He wanted real amounts of money, and all the fineries it could bring. And so while he slogged through his days at jobs he did not care for, he had padded his nest by purchasing real estate.

It went slowly at first, as he taught himself how such things happened, how the intricacies of land transactions occurred, what they required of all sides, and he kept his eyes open. He began to realize in the process that not only could he make more money conducting such transactions, but that he didn't have to expend as much effort for a more harmonious outcome. And part of that meant more money for him.

Who could have predicted that the forgery skills he had honed over the years and put to excellent use in the army crafting passes for himself and his fellows would also come into such excellent play? He smiled again and indulged in another long, satisfied sigh.

And on that day in 1871, that was how George M. Willing Jr. found James Reavis when he entered the small real estate agency's front door. And from that initial meeting to the end of his days, James Reavis's entire life would never again be the same. It would contain all the excitement, fame, riches, and more that he dreamed of. Too much so, as it turned out.

Willing had once upon a time been a physician, but the allure of possibility out among the rocks of the Southwest proved too tempting and he left his practice to become a prospector. He did, however, retain enough semblance of his former profession to enable him to sell patent medicines, bottled cure-alls likely containing more alcohol than anything curative. Willing had the opportunity to visit Reavis on the advice of a friend, Colonel Byser, who had used the creative documentation skills of Reavis some time earlier. Willing told Reavis that he had recently purchased a Spanish land grant from a broken and down-on-his-luck prospector named Miguel Peralta.

The mention of a land grant that was within reach was something of great interest to most people at the time, and Reavis was no different. According to the Treaty of Guadalupe Hidalgo (1848) and the Gadsden Purchase of 1854, any Spanish land grants posited by either the Mexican or Spanish governments were to be honored by the US government. And anyone possessing a land grant stood a good chance of gaining real wealth; untold to be sure, but the potential was there, nonetheless. Reavis leaned forward, eager to hear more of Willing's tale.

The good doctor admitted proudly that he had paid $20,000 in gold dust as well as all the equipment and mules an ever-hopeful prospector could want. For his part, Willing was only too glad to see those vestiges of prospecting leave, as he held out great hope that the land grant would be the answer to all his future money woes.

Willing's deal with Peralta took place at a mine southeast of Prescott, Arizona Territory, in Black Canyon, on October 20, 1864. The agreement came together in an informal and unorthodox—some might even say suspect— manner: "When the trade was made, I had no paper on which to write the deed, so I scouted the camp and found a sheet of greasy, pencil-marked camp paper upon which I wrote . . . and as there were no justices or notaries present I had it acknowledged before witnesses."

Willing did what few of us would do were we holding the keys to a potentially lucrative land grant—he waited three years, making it to Prescott by 1867, to have the odd transaction officially recorded. Perhaps the man was a slow walker.

Once he arrived in town, and finding he was, as always, low on cash, Willing revealed his inner swindler to the stable owner. He proposed that should the man purchase rights to half the land grant, the two of them could strike it rich immediately by demanding local mine owners pay them for the land on which they operated. Instead of the excited, greedy response he expected, Willing was verbally threatened by angry locals. He left town early the next day.

And that's the story Willing fed Reavis, the budding title tweaker, on their first meeting. Reavis, intrigued but wary, asked Willing to leave the documents with him so that Reavis might read through them and become familiar with the details. Willing, probably sensing a fellow shyster, said, "Nothing doing, pal," but did promise to return.

And return he did, with yet a third sleazy swindler in tow, in the form of one William W. Gitt, also known as the "Old Spanish Land Title Lawyer," who had spent twenty years in Mexico dodging a stateside arrest warrant for his part in shady real estate transactions.

Never were there three more ideally suited partners. The men spent time each week together, poring over the various papers pertaining to Willing's land grant. There was enough substance to them that they continued exploring the possibilities. In addition to the hasty deed, Willing's sheaf of documents contained the all-important *expediente*, which is a copy of all documents known to exist about the land grant. An 1853 letter signed by Mexican President Antonio López de Santa Anna stated that all possible effort had gone into procuring the relevant documentation pertaining to the land grant.

This was an exciting time for young Reavis, a time of much free education, when he acquired skills needed to research the confusing and intricate world of Mexican and Spanish land documents. Eventually Willing and Reavis formed a partnership in order to continue promoting and exploring the land grant's claim.

On May 5, 1874, Reavis married for the first time, to Ada Pope. Then he headed west, first to California to retrieve various documents Willing had left years before with a merchant to secure a loan he'd taken with the man. Reavis also didn't return to his wife . . . for six years. She grew fed up—who can blame her?—and in 1883 was granted a divorce due to desertion by her husband. Reavis, for his part, didn't care. He was like a bloodhound on the heady scent of potential riches and importance, no matter it would at best be mere fabrication.

Willing returned to Prescott, Arizona, in March 1874, and no sooner did he finally file his official claim in the Yavapai County Courthouse than he breathed his last. He was found dead in his room the next morning, and though nefarious causes, including poison and other strange situations, were suspected, Willing's death instigated no official investigation. News of his partner's demise reached Reavis in San Francisco. And he was giddy, for that left Reavis, as Willing's partner, in dire need of those papers that Willing had in his possession.

As desperate as he must have been for them, he was too poor and sickly on his arrival in California to do much about it. He had to build up his health and his bank balance, so Reavis took on the job of schoolteacher in Downey, California, during 1875–76. Then, oddly enough, he headed north to work as a journalist for two Frisco newspapers.

Reavis eventually made his way to Arizona Territory in May 1880. He roved the Phoenix region, then hopped a stagecoach to Prescott. He was armed with a letter from Willing's widow that authorized Reavis, as Willing's partner, to take ownership of the dead man's possessions, held in a safe place by the probate judge who had overseen the case of Willing's death.

Reavis headed back to California with his precious paperwork. And that's when his efforts slipped into top speed. The first thing Reavis did was to transform the land grant from a "floater" to one that was based, or fixed, to a specific location. In this case, Reavis claimed a sizable spread measuring 49.5 miles by 149.5 miles that later metastasized to a mammoth hunk of real estate measuring 78.8 by 236.49 miles. It seems Reavis's boldness knew few bounds, as his grant's reach claimed the burgs of Phoenix, Tempe, Florence, Casa Grande, Globe, and even eastward to Silver City, New Mexico, as well as the land on which resided the famous Silver King Mine and a sizable portion of the Southern Pacific Railroad.

Then Reavis headed eastward to Washington, DC, to examine a rare record book on loan from the Mission San Xavier del Bac, in southern Arizona Territory. He headed west once more, and in 1881 spent three months, from September through November, rummaging in the archives in Guadalajara and Mexico City. He stole documents, altered others, inserted still more—forgeries all—and made copies of more yet, using seals and other official-looking aspects to suit his needs.

From there he headed back to California, befriending archivists in Los Angeles and San Francisco, giving him unprecedented access to all manner of obscure and rare materials. From there he went to Kentucky to see his dead partner's widow, and on May 1, 1882, he obtained full possession of the grant, persuading her to sign over her interest in exchange for $30,000, which he swore to pay to her over time.

And all this time he created a full and stunning, legitimate-sounding family lineage—steeped in old money, naturally—to which he and he alone would have claim. While "studying" the archives of Mexico and Spain, he craftily smuggled out documents, altered them, then smuggled them back in. He also altered various entries, interspersing his fabricated family's name and titles, forever altering old and precious documents.

Reavis also amassed a huge amount of paperwork, stolen, real, old, and new—but made to look old—all in an effort to support what would be a tremendous claim that would establish him as the sole hereditary Baron of Arizona, making him heir to all the holdings his expanding and fictitious Spanish land grant contained. He was engaged in nothing less than creating an empire out of thin air (and his considerable skills as a forger). Everything had to be in place before he unveiled his masterwork.

In San Francisco Reavis used his journalistic experience and credits to pen a number of anonymous articles for the *San Francisco Examiner* in which he claimed "irrefutable evidence" that the Peralta land grant was legitimate. It was his official opening salvo, a shot across the bow to all with whom he would soon begin negotiating.

Among those he engaged in negotiations were Southern Pacific Railroad executives. And it worked—he was ultimately given $10,000 for the railroad's right to an easement across his land. He finally filed his first official claim on March 27, 1883, in Tucson. Part of the process involved him supplying copies of the various papers he had collected, which amounted to two steamer trunks filled with documentation.

Once the claim was filed, Reavis decamped to a town called Arizola, near Casa Grande, location of famous historic ruins tracing back to the thirteenth century. Reavis, however, claimed that they were the ruins of the home, La Hacienda de Peralta, occupied by his fictional forebears, the first Baron of Peralta. Reavis laid claim to the site and, hiring builders, commenced construction on a mansion with servant quarters, a stable, and more.

Filled with righteous self-confidence, he hired a number of individuals to act on his behalf as agents and rent collectors, and he sent them throughout the vast region he had laid claim to and began offering quit-claim deeds to settlers, of whom there were many, in exchange for sums ranging from a free meal to $1,000. Most of those approached were suspicious but not quite sure enough to argue. Many of them had been living there for generations, on land they had bought and paid for. They were threatened with litigation and few of them could afford to go up against Reavis and his men.

Especially not when they began reading notices Reavis had posted throughout the entirety of his claim. Those residents were told they must contact Reavis's lawyer "for registering tenancy and signing agreements, or regard themselves liable to litigation for trespassing and expulsion when the Peralta Grant is, as it must be, validated by the US government." He even hired publicists to trumpet the news that the all-important water and mineral rights were his as well.

These were small fry compared with Reavis's negotiations with the owner of the Silver King Mining Company, James M. Barney. Incensed but convinced that Reavis had some semblance of veracity to his claims, Barney ended up paying $25,000 for a quit-claim deed. Reavis laughed all the way to the bank, especially once he nailed into place payments from both the Silver King Mine and the Southern Pacific Railroad, all but guaranteeing that naysayers and holdouts had better not go against Reavis or his minions when they came calling.

Many settlers, so convinced that his claims were legitimate and iron clad, and unable to pay potential fees in exchange for the quit-claim deed he was offering, packed up their possessions and abandoned their homesteads.

Two voices of reason, however, Phoenix-based newspapers the *Herald* and the *Gazette*, urged local residents to refrain from buying quit-claim deeds from Reavis, at least until further legitimacy could be proven. A slight setback came when it was found that the owner of the *Herald*, Homer McNeil, had secretly purchased a quit-claim from Reavis. There was public outcry, and McNeil made a public show of renouncing his quit-claim purchase.

Soon enough, holes began to appear in the intricate weave of deception Reavis had so carefully crafted. Various signatures could not be verified, and complaints arose that some documents had not initially been given enough attention to verify authenticity. Reavis was forced to announce publicly that his claim hadn't actually been confirmed by the government just yet. But, he claimed, it was merely a matter of time.

In an effort to quell the rapidly bubbling rumors of fraud, he circulated falsehoods intimating that no less than the US government had all but offered to pay him $100 million for full claim to the grant. Instead of shutting his mouth, Reavis did the opposite and continued to expand the reach of his quit-claim attacks.

Meanwhile, newspaper editors continued their instigation of insurrection against Reavis, resulting in a handful of organized opposition groups in towns such as Florence, Phoenix, Tempe, and Globe.

At this point in the epic, unfolding drama, it's fair to ask what Reavis hoped to gain by altering ancient and official government and church documents, by potentially displacing thousands of settlers, by fouling masses of real estate transactions for years to come, and damaging no less than the fragile and still-budding formation of United States territories and statehoods?

As with so many men whose very core is corrupt and bent, it appears Reavis wanted far more than wealth. He wanted power, and he enjoyed the very real thrill he got from making all his nefarious plans fall into place. Should he pull it all off, and he wholly believed he would, then James Reavis would be known soon and forevermore as James Addison Peralta-Reavis, Baron of Arizona.

By the mid-1880s, however, Reavis and his mighty minions were all but halted in their tracks by a pair of lawsuits. The first, a claim by his dead partner's father, George Willing Sr., petered out due to lack of finances on Willing's part. But the second lawsuit, brought by Territorial Attorney General Clark Churchill, was much more substantial. In it, Churchill held fast to what he believed were his own personal properties.

In effect it was a challenge to Reavis to offer the goods, to make a case for his land grant's legitimacy. It was a challenge Reavis could not afford to ignore, but his February 1884 deposition revealed a number of chinks in his armor. Among them were questions about his finances and how he came to possess the land grant. Reavis grew defensive, arguing that the territorial court had no right to question the validity of his grant. The court said, "Not so fast," and sided with Attorney General Churchill. This would prove a major victory for opponents of the increasingly wary Reavis.

Verification research being conducted by the Land Office and Surveyor General was halted, all but killing in its tracks Reavis's claim. As if to prove his detractors correct, Reavis tucked his thieving tail between his legs and ran for California. But he wasn't done. Not by a long shot.

The entire time he'd spent dashing all over the map accumulating information, forging, filching, altering, and stealing documents, Reavis had also been accumulating information about possible descendants of the Peralta line to which his claim was attached. He learned that there may be some descendants in California. On a train there some years before, he met a woman whom he decided resembled the fictional second baroness of his claim. This young thing, all but a peasant, was engaged as a servant. To have a handsome stranger tell her that she might well be heiress to a substantial fortune was no doubt overwhelming to her.

Fortunately for Reavis, the young woman possessed no documents as to her lineage. Not a problem—Reavis was nothing if not a conjurer of such papers. And conjure he did. Following a correspondence-based courtship, they married on December 31, 1882. Then, so confident was he that his claim was to be a raving success, he sent her to a convent school so that she might gain the manners of a lady.

Following the thrashing he took in court in Arizona, the chastened Reavis made his way back to California and managed to accumulate an impressive stack of letters of introduction from well-placed contacts in California. Reavis, along with his wife, who outwardly traveled as his ward, headed to New York City, where they used their letters to meet senators, congressmen, men of high finance, and most importantly, John W. Mackay, a man who had made a fortune in silver in the Comstock Lode. Mackay was so thoroughly taken in by Reavis's impressive mass of documentation substantiating his claim that he offered Reavis $500 a month as a stipend so that Reavis might continue digging deeper to substantiate his claims.

This financial boon enabled Reavis and his wife to travel to Spain to foul archives in Seville and Madrid with his forgeries, thefts, and alterations. Reavis was so crafty and convincing that Spanish families with names he'd connected to his grant gladly entertained the couple.

By the fall of 1886, they made their way back to the United States, where Reavis had a line of high-profile politicians and businessmen falling over themselves to acknowledge his refreshed claim to the land grant and its holdings. This only goes to illustrate how excellent Reavis was at making seem legitimate his entire package—forged paperwork, phony old portraits of claimed descendants, and even his wife.

In August 1887 the emboldened couple returned to Arizona Territory. He had taken to calling himself James Addison Peralta-Reavis, and his wife, for whom he filed a claim, was known as Doña Sophia Micaela Maso Reavis y Peralta de la Cordoba, third Baroness of Arizona. Once back in Arizona, they took a carriage ride into the mountains southwest of Phoenix, where they "happened upon" what he claimed was the Peralta land grant's original southwest corner marker. In reality, it was a known boulder covered in ancient petroglyphs.

Showing no shame, next to these petroglyphs Reavis chipped in a rectangular figure he called the "Inicial Monument." Then he took a photograph of his wife standing beside the markings.

With this new establishment of the legitimacy of his claim, and with the backing of so many high-profile movers and shakers of industry and finance, Reavis no longer monkeyed with selling quit-claim deeds. Instead he used his new contacts to develop corporations, three in all, that would offer shares, the sales of which would ostensibly develop the construction of railways, dams, roads, and numerous other improvements. He would also lease water rights— no small consideration in that arid region.

His investors plied him with money while his plans were received by Arizona Territory residents with anger, scorn, and outright hostility, so much so that he and his wife left Arizona and roved between their residences established in St. Louis, New York City, and San Francisco. They dined at the finest eateries, wore the very best of fashions, and entertained all their well-heeled society friends.

They bought an estate in Chihuahua, Mexico, and there Reavis was treated with the respect he felt he deserved, particularly after he funded a hospital and a home for the blind. He even commissioned a monument to be built of his wife's nonexistent ancestor, Don Miguel de Peralta. But all this largesse was coming to an end.

Following the 1888 presidential election, new inquiries into the Peralta Land Grant were made by the Arizona Territory's reappointed surveyor general, Royal Johnson. He'd long been a critic of the Reavis claim and had, while out of office, kept up with his investigations of its legitimacy. On October 12, 1889, he released his official findings in a document titled *Adverse report of the Surveyor General of Arizona, Royal A. Johnson, upon the alleged Peralta Grant: a complete expose of its fraudulent character.*

In it, numerous errors, problems, and inconsistencies were found, among them that a number of the eighteenth-century documents bore distinct evidence of having been written not with the more historically accurate quill, but with steel-nibbed pens, a rarity of the time. Various samples of printing were shown to bear inconsistencies with other similarly aged documents, and there were many instances of grammatical and spelling errors, not something expected in documents derived from the Spanish Royal Court.

Despite the initial excitement and happy relief residents of Arizona Territory expressed, it would take the powers that be in Washington, DC, until early 1890 to respond. The Commissioner of the Land Office instructed Johnson to remove Reavis's claim from all consideration. This effectively dismissed the Peralta Land Grant from further consideration as legitimate. Though he was given the opportunity to appeal, it would have been wise of Reavis to leave well enough alone and slink off into the night, recouping whatever finances he might still have within his grasp. Alas, Reavis was never a man to give up a fight.

Instead of appealing to the Secretary of the Interior, Reavis sued . . . the government of the United States. He accused the government of thieving from him 1.5 million acres, and more. He demanded $11 million in damages he had thus far incurred and made provisions for "further relief and costs" should he incur other financial costs. He wasn't flying blind, however, as he was being represented by the attorney for Southern Pacific Railroad, along with notable assistants.

A number of stalling tactics, governmental delays, and fact-finding trips abroad postponed the trial's commencement until June 3, 1895. Reavis and his attorneys failed to show for the first seven days. The government's case proceeded nonetheless, and stacks of problems were presented with relation to Reavis's accumulated Peralta documents, among them entire pages he'd forged, then inserted into old official books of documents. This was but one of dozens of blatant examples revealing the shameless depths of his chicanery.

Nonetheless the case continued, with Reavis finally appearing on June 10, acting as his own counsel. By this time he was nearly destitute, having spent all his money in frantic travels all over the map in efforts to cover his earlier tracks and put out various incriminating fires. The case dragged on with the government's lawyers poking holes in Reavis's increasingly flimsy defense. He resorted to showing portraits of his wife's alleged long-dead relations, trying in vain to establish a family resemblance between his own twin sons (born two years before) and his wife's "ancestors." His efforts were, at best, feeble—so much so that the government waived its right to a closing argument.

Reavis was arrested, charged with forgery, presenting false documents to the Court of Private Land Claims, and with conspiracy to defraud the United States government. The forty-two-count indictment left little room for doubt as to his guilt.

He spent a year in jail awaiting his criminal trial, which commenced on June 27, 1896. All the old evidence was dredged up, with Reavis maintaining his innocence in firm and full indignation. Nonetheless, three days later, on

June 30, 1896, he was found guilty, and two weeks later was sentenced to two years in prison and a fine of $5,000.

He was released on April 18, 1898, his good behavior in the clink earning him a three-month reduction. Though a broken man, he did his best to stir up interest in various schemes he'd cooked up about developing large-scale irrigation in Arizona. Not surprisingly he met with no success. His wife and sons had relocated to Denver, Colorado, while he was in prison. He stayed with them for a time, but by 1902 his wife filed for divorce.

In 1913 he was living in a Los Angeles poor house, and the following year he died in Denver and ended up in a pauper's grave. Hollywood has made much hay of the life of James Reavis, including numerous television shows and a 1950 film starring Vincent Price called *The Baron of Arizona*.

In the span of a few years, James Reavis had forged more signatures and documents—including in excess of two hundred Spanish documents alone—than most of us write in a lifetime. Various amateur mistakes aside, he was an amazingly talented man, especially considering his abilities were wholly home-grown. Imagine if he had used his innate skills and quick mind for purposes benefiting more than just himself and his own ego.

Instead, Reavis attempted to take ownership of more than 18,600 square miles of land in Arizona Territory and western New Mexico Territory. He frightened thousands of residents, scared hundreds off their land and out of their homes, and bilked a number of high-profile investors, people who were among the top tier of the day's financiers and titans of business. He took from them $5.3 million (equal roughly to $150 million today). And through it all he maintained his innocence, even while he moldered in prison.

CHAPTER 8

ALEXANDER MCKENZIE
BIGGEST CLAIM-JUMPER EVER

Known as the "senator maker" through the long halls of the federal government, North Dakota behind-the-scenes politico Alexander McKenzie preferred to stay out of the limelight and instead influence legislation through carefully placed handpicked candidates. He was so successful with this gambit that he was the Republican party's national committeeman for nearly two decades, all the while placing his own hand-selected representatives and senators. He skirted serious trouble with the law a number of times, and he and his hired goons were accused frequently of buying votes and physically attacking those who opposed him, including voters and opposing candidates.

In 1900 he placed candidates he'd personally selected for the positions of federal district attorney, Joseph K. Wood of Montana, and federal judge, Minneapolis lawyer Arthur H. Noyes, along with a handful of other choice positions in Nome, Alaska, which at the time was in the midst of a gold-rush boom.

Behind this was a bill McKenzie helped shove through Congress that effectively stripped out the language protecting the rights of aliens to own US land. With that seemingly trivial, overlooked, and innocuous bit of language missing, Alexander McKenzie proceeded to the next step in his plan. His bought-and-paid-for federal team proceeded to "legally" take a number of lucrative mines from their owners—who all happened to be foreigners whose mines were bought and paid for with their own sweat and blood.

McKenzie orchestrated the entire affair, naturally, and then went to Nome himself and personally oversaw removals of rightful mine owners, then saw to it that "his mines" were worked for himself, by his own selected miners. McKenzie took possession of everything at the mines when his thugs "escorted" the men off their own property, along with their tools, clothes, and food. The ample profits from the mines went straight into his personal vault in Nome.

"You can't be serious." The corner of Red's whiskered mouth rose in a half smirk. He shook his head as he sunk his spade once more, levering out an irksome head-size stone. He didn't glance again at his partner, Duncan (most folks called him Dunk), a reedy drink of water whose neck was all Adam's apple rising and falling as he talked, like a float in a water gauge. The man's face fared no better—it was all rough whiskers and back-sloped forehead that came together in a long, big-nostriled nose.

Finally Red stopped, and still wearing a smile, he looked again at his pal. "You know, Dunk, we been partners at this claim for what? Six, seven months? And I will say that between the two of us we make one decent miner. And fortunately for us one's all this claim needs. We been lucky."

Dunk nodded, his Adam's apple bobbing in counterpoint to the action. "What're you sayin', Red?"

"My point is you're always coming up with fanciful tales and whatnot."

"So? I thought you liked my chatter. You told me yourself that it helped pass the time."

"And so I did, yes sir. But this time you've outdone yourself. I'm used to you running off at the mouth all hot and bothered because you heard some rumor in town that we'll all be kicked off'n our claims. But this one takes the cake."

The skinny man screwed his begrimed cap down tight onto his head and squared off, as if he were a pugilist before a mirror. "Now see here, Red. You got no right to call me a liar. I may be a lot of things, but I ain't lying. I'm telling you the truth."

Red stared at his partner as if he'd not seen him in a long time, as if he'd not broken bread with the man every day for the past eleven months. As if he'd not shared the same dingy little cabin no bigger than the inside of a Conestoga wagon for the same stretch of time. Red didn't think that if they'd met anywhere but here in Nome, Alaska, each needing a partner in order to work a claim efficiently, they'd ever have been friends.

"You really do believe in the bull you're shoveling at me, so help me, don't you, Dunk?"

The thin man merely nodded. He was not one to gloat. Though it was true he was prone to pushing and pulling a story to make it even better when necessary. "Never let the truth get in the way of a good story," his Pap had once said.

In what is considered the largest case of claim jumping in US history, behind-the-scenes political boss Alexander "Senator Maker" McKenzie, of North Dakota, forced laws that allowed him to fleece hundreds of miners in Nome, Alaska, of their mines and earnings in 1900. He was sentenced to a year in prison and served three months before being pardoned by President McKinley. McKenzie died many years later, a very wealthy man.
Courtesy Library of Congress. Photo by Lomen Bros.

But this one time he didn't have to do a thing except run back to the claim with the sack of corn meal and tin of milk and tell Red just what he'd heard.

"Now say it again, but slower this time. If you're telling the truth, and so help me I guess you are—though I wish you wasn't—we'd better think on this thing."

"Yep, but we can't think too long, you know."

"Why? It's our claim, ain't it?"

Dunk shook his head. "Not for long. Them two fellas, the Pole and the Swede, down the hill? They been evicted. I talked with Jabert and he told me he seen the Swede put up a fight—you know how big the Swede is—and by God if they didn't leave and come back with the law, put shackles on the man's big ol' wrists, led him off." Dunk pantomimed the action, his long bony legs high-stepping a few paces away, his own hands clasped behind his back.

"But what danger are we in? We have our papers, our deed, all in order. We made doubly sure of that."

"Yep, but it don't matter. This politician named McKenzie, I think it was." He rubbed his whisker stubble on his chin, then nodded and snapped a finger. "Yep, Alexander McKenzie, that's the man. He represents, oh, I don't know just who. . . ."

"Himself, that's who," said Red. "I heard all about him. Just didn't think there was teeth enough in the story to worry about it."

"You heard about him and you didn't tell me?"

"I just said it didn't seem like anything we needed to worry about, didn't I?"

"So what do we do now?"

"How bad is it?"

"Bad enough. I hear tell McKenzie won't actually own the mines, but he's the one who'll operate them while the people who own the mines, you and me, for instance, and all our friends up and down the valley here, are booted off our own property."

"How come it's only the foreigners?"

"Speak for yourself, Red."

"No, I'm serious. You weren't born of the United States, were you?"

"Well, no."

"And neither was I. And the Swede and the Pole? Nah, nor the two Russian brothers. But you take that other fellow, the one who keeps to himself, John Quinton is his name. He's not been molested yet, has he?"

"I don't think so."

"So what should we do?"

"We should go to town, see what we can make of this with the law."

"But Red, from what I've heard, he is the law. Or at least he owns it. He's the man who got all them appointed to their positions."

"Well this can't just happen. Has to be somebody who can help us. I tell you what. You help me gather up what we can. We have to stash it somewhere, then I'll go to town, see if I can figure out who to meet with. Got to be somebody who can help us."

"Why you?"

"Because we need someone to stay at the diggins', else we're sunk before we float."

Dunk thought about it a moment. The logic addled him, but he nodded. Red always seemed to know the right thing to do right quick, whereas he had to take his time and mull things over a spell before a solution came to him, right or no. Maybe his mammy, God rest her, was right—she had once told him he was a blessedly simple creature.

The broad-waisted man drummed fat fingers on the worsted-wool vest stretched drum tight on his ample midsection. An aroma he recognized immediately tickled his conditioned nostrils. Here was a warm feast not long from the stovetop. A civilized meal while out and about making the rounds with his security force—now here was a treat. And all his!

"Sir, that's the man's supper." The man who spoke abruptly shut his mouth and backed a pace toward the door when his employer fixed him with a steely stare. He didn't dare say another word as he watched the fat man, Alexander McKenzie, settle himself down at the table and tuck into the hapless mine owner's afternoon meal.

Despite himself, the hireling had licked his lips. The meal smelled good and looked even better. He bet it tasted even better than that. Corn bread, thick stew—spuds and carrots and hunks of beef all piping hot. Real beef? Nah, had to have been moose or venison. But still. . . .

Fact was, he was beginning to regret ever taking on this job. The rest of the boys were numb enough between the ears that they'd follow along lock-step with McKenzie's orders, but he was growing increasingly distressed as time wore on. Half the men he had "arrested" were fellows he knew. Good, honest, hard-working gents who sent most of what they mined back home to their families. Or else saved up to buy bigger stakes. And he had begun to have serious doubts about the legality of Alexander McKenzie's claims on these men's holdings.

"I know what you're thinking," said McKenzie in between chews and swallows and gulps of the absent man's rapidly disappearing hot meal.

Now here was McKenzie, with the gall to tell him he knew what he was thinking? "Oh?" He folded his arms. "And what's that?"

McKenzie dragged his cuff across his mouth and said, "First of all, when I speak to you, you address me as Mr. McKenzie. And second of all, I don't like your tone. But I'm going to tell you what I was thinking anyway. You think all this business of appropriating those mines that are rightfully mine is somehow a seedy business, don't you? You are becoming disillusioned with it all. You think that you have discovered some truth, some hidden morsel that makes you feel holier than high, don't you?"

"No, no sir." The hireling reddened and felt this face heat up. How did McKenzie know what he'd been thinking?

McKenzie resumed eating. Presently he spoke again. "You're not the first, you know. Nor will you be the last. But I tell you," he wagged the knife, gravy dripped from the point, hit the floor. "The law is the law and a man has to make his own way in this world, else he'll be nothing but somebody else's rube. You hear me?" He gulped wine. "I hired you because you seemed to have a head on your broad shoulders, which doesn't hurt, and now I see that maybe I made a mistake."

"Oh no, sir. Mr. McKenzie. I didn't mean that. I . . ."

"That you what?" McKenzie smiled. "Never back up. Never give them an opening. Keep moving forward. And believe in what you're doing."

Even if it's wrong? He watched his employer gobble down the rest of the man's meal. Before the afternoon was gone he'd watch McKenzie do the same to three more meals miners had prepared for themselves.

Knowing they would not get a fair shake in Nome, and finding themselves without mines or much in the way of personal property, the miners, many of them Swedes, ventured all the way to San Francisco to the Ninth Circuit Court of Appeals. The judge there saw McKenzie's duplicity for what it was and overturned the decision of the corrupt, handpicked judge in Nome.

The outraged McKenzie refused to acknowledge the validity of such an action. This proved to be the turning point in the case—the fabled "McKenzie's Machine" had flouted the law a little too aggressively. While McKenzie stayed on in Nome and continued to rummage with his fat hands in the rich diggings he'd stolen, the judge from San Francisco readied two federal marshals to travel north to Alaska to arrest him.

"If I didn't know you to be the most honest judge in all of San Francisco, heck, in all of California, I'd swear what you're saying just can't be true." The federal marshal tapped a forefinger against his tight-set lips, and shook his head.

"Oh, and if I didn't know you to be a lawman who'd seen more chicanery than most, I'd think you were buttering me up for something." The judge winked and set his ebony fountain pen down neatly beside the sheaf of papers he'd just finished signing. He rubbed a thumb and forefinger along the bridge of his nose where his spectacles rested, then turned bleary eyes on the two marshals.

He sighed and scooped up the papers, handing them to the senior of the two. Not yet letting go of the documents, he said, "Never let it be said that the lowly Ninth Circuit Court of Appeals is an impotent little setup." As he said it he smiled, releasing his hold on the papers.

"We'll get that scoundrel McKenzie, judge. Or we'll . . ."

But the judge held up his hands. "I don't want to know about the execution of your task, I just want to be assured that you'll follow the letter of the law in doing so. We're closer than we've ever been to nailing his scurvy hide to the barn wall. We can't risk it going wrong now. And besides," he fixed each of the men with a hard stare, "those miners are counting on us. Now, go arrest McKenzie and bring him back for trial. Good luck and God speed, gents. It's a long journey and you'll not have another chance to get a boat so late in the year. I assume you've made the necessary reservations to get you there?"

"Indeed we have, sir. We were able to book passage on the very last ship of the season heading north before ice-up. Our route takes us through Norton Sound to Nome."

After the two eager lawmen left, the judge sat down heavily and stared at the closed door of his office. Forty-five hundred miles. He didn't envy those two men the trip they were embarking on. And with winter coming. But he knew they were up to the task. Any man with a sense of decency and justice would do the same.

He slowly filled the bowl of his favorite briar pipe, thumbed down fragrant flakes of tobacco, and set fire to it, drawing deeply several times, then puffing like a train on an uphill grade. He leaned back in his chair, smoking with closed eyes, and ruminated on the rascal who'd occupied much of his and his staff's time these last weeks.

Alexander McKenzie. Most folks knew of him or were affected by his machinations in one way or another, even if they were unaware of it. For all his powerful plays, the fat McKenzie had gone out of his way to place others in public office, preferring himself to remain in shadow, tugging strings and feathering his own ample nest with the gains of hardworking, innocent citizens.

The judge sent a blue plume of smoke billowing toward the ceiling. How was it a man could become so perverted? So consumed by a thirst for control and a craving for money that he would allow himself to ruin the lives of hundreds, likely thousands, in his quest. Those miners were wronged and the perverted political machine that McKenzie ran had overstepped itself for the last time. He ignored us once, flouting the law with his own handpicked judge and lawyer, but not this time. This time, thought the judge, we have risen to the bait and will drag McKenzie overboard when we tug that line.

The judge knew he had to believe that. Otherwise the ramifications would be severe and far-reaching. He didn't for one moment think that McKenzie's reach was limited. Rumor had it that even President McKinley was beholden to McKenzie.

"I'll be glad when we can get McKenzie in cuffs and hustle him southward to stand trial. This place might well be beautiful, but I am a California man and I have no intention of spending months on end socked in here until it thaws enough to let us leave."

"Then we have just a few hours, if what the captain told me is correct. His is the last boat of the season headed southward. So let's go."

"We know where he's holed up?"

His companion smiled, nodded. "Same place he is every day at this time. Captain told me."

"Captain knows a lot, eh?"

"He does indeed."

"So where are we headed?"

"The Golden Gate Hotel. Specifically, the dining room. He holds court there, and eats."

"From what I've heard, that's one man who can eat."

The two federal marshals asked for directions of a woman they passed on the sidewalk in the otherwise surprisingly quiet burg of Nome, Alaska.

"There he is," said the younger marshal, glancing through the front window. They pushed through the big double doors and scanned the busy dining room. The air was thick with cigar and pipe smoke, but the din of chatting voices, of laughter, of clinks and clanks of glasses and china and cutlery abated somewhat as eyes turned to see who these two newcomers were who'd let in the draft of cold air.

The two men paid them no heed. They scanned the room and finally settled on the fat man seated alone at a large table in the back center of the room. He, too, met their stare. He mopped his mouth as he looked them up and down. The men approached, and as the older man in the lead took off his fur hat and reached with his other hand to unbutton his overcoat, McKenzie saw the glint of a badge.

The rage on the man's already florid face became even more evident the closer the two men drew to his laden table.

"I see you already ate," said the marshal.

"Yes, indeed I have." McKenzie balled up the voluminous napkin and threw it on the gristly remains of the steak on his plate. He belched once, his cheek fluttering, and guzzled a glass of wine. He belched again, then said, "And who are you two supposed to be?"

"We're not supposed to be anything, but we are your new escorts."

"Escorts, eh?"

The older of the two lawmen leaned down, put both hands on the table, and said, in a lowered but level, menacing voice, "Listen, Mr. McKenzie, we can haul you out of here kicking and screaming and causing a big loud fuss, or you can go peacefully, even amiably. Same ends, so it doesn't matter to me."

The portly diner glanced around at the dozens of faces of his fellow diners, all of whom were trained on him, unabashed. This was big news in Nome, and Lord knew when they might get another such round of excitement, given that the cold months were all but upon them.

"Do you have any idea who I am, lawdog?" McKenzie spat the words through clenched teeth. Hs jaw muscles jounced under their fat sags and he glowered at the men.

"Why, yes, Mr. McKenzie. You're the man we're here to arrest." He slid a hand into an inner pocket and lifted free the neatly folded and signed warrant for McKenzie's arrest.

McKenzie made a lunge for it, but the marshal pulled back. "Ah ah, now, now, Mr. McKenzie. Remember what I told you about playing nice? I'll gladly let you see it when we're out of here, safe and sound away from prying eyes. And any hoodlums you may have in your employ."

Minutes later they were standing outside, watching the fat man shrug himself into his tight wool overcoat. The younger of the lawmen made sure they were well away from the bright lights of the hotel's dining room. The windows cast wavering squares of gold light on the boardwalk as shadows of peeking heads thrust in and out of the light. "Looks like there are a whole load of folks in there just aching for a chance to see you hauled off in chains. Why do you suppose that is, Mr. McKenzie?"

"You two lawdogs will answer for this. Mark my words. I am a big wheel and not just in this two-bit town. I own half the Congress, I've made and broke more senators than you bumpkins will ever vote for, and I daresay you and your families will regret crossing. . . ."

"Now Mr. McKenzie," said the older marshal, leaning close enough that his straight nose tip almost touched the fleshy bulb of McKenzie's. "You can tell us about your credentials all night long. I'm sure it will prove illuminating to the judge. But you dare not threaten my family or his, or there will be legal ramifications. Do you understand me?"

Once the federal marshals caught up with McKenzie in Nome, they forced him to open his vault and turn over the $600,000 in gold he had removed from the mines in the absence of their rightful owners. The mines and their earnings were eventually returned to those owners.

As for Alexander McKenzie, as with so many swindlers, he did not suffer horribly in the short or long term. He was convicted on conspiracy charges and sentenced to one year in prison. He served three months before President McKinley pardoned him in May 1901. He went on to amass even greater wealth and had two towns and a county in North Dakota named after him. Books, plays, and films have been made of Alexander McKenzie and specifically about his blatant, thieving ways in Nome at the turn of the century. He died a wealthy man in St. Paul, Minnesota, in 1922. Who says crime doesn't pay?

CHAPTER 9

UNHELPFUL GUIDES
UNTESTED, UNTRUE, UNWORTHY!

This chapter could easily be titled "Beware Self-Proclaimed Authorities," for they often know far less than they believe they do. During the early decades—the 1840s through the 1850s—of overland travel by masses of emigrants seeking better lives out West, there were precious few experts around, people who could claim to have made the trip West and come back to tell about it. Of the few who did, how many had the ability to re-create in a useful form, via maps and journals, the most viable routes through all manner of treacherous terrain?

Almost simultaneously with the hue-and-cry over the discovery of gold at Sutter's Mill, a flood of guidebooks poured out to the masses seemingly overnight with such fashionably windy titles as *California: Her Wealth and Resources* and *California, from its Discovery by the Spaniards to the Present Time, with a Brief Description of the Gold Region.*

The titles alone were barely able to contain the authors' zeal for the jaw-dropping wonders potential emigrants could expect should they venture westward. In truth, most of the guidebook authors were deskbound ink wranglers in cities back East, men who had never been west of their neighborhood bars. What they did do was rummage through newspaper files to pillage the few available verified reports from people who had actually traveled the overland trails to the West and back again.

The guidebook authors leaned heavily on accounts by the few men who'd been there and back, among them Colonel Richard Mason and Consul Thomas Larkin, and from legitimate travel journals by Richard Henry Dana and John C. Fremont.

But the facts they pulled from firsthand accounts paled on the page with their own fanciful fillers: baloney, fiction, balderdash, and chicanery—with added sprinklings of fact for flavor. A prime example is the bestselling *Emigrant's Guide to the Gold Mines*, whose author actually wrote of riverbeds "paved with gold to the thickness of a hand." Of such ubiquitous California rivers, he went on to write that "twenty to fifty thousand dollars of gold" could easily be "picked out almost instantly."

And if the journey was long and the information contained within those pages proved too tempting to buoy flagging spirits, publishers often included poems and ditties to be sung along the trail—all revolving around the wonders of California and its awaiting fortunes in gold. Who wouldn't want to head west, a copy of this guidebook tucked under one arm, leading an amiable mule towing an empty wagon ready to be filled with easily plucked riches?

It says something of the caliber of journalism of the day, and of the influence over the masses of the media (little seems to have changed), that one guidebook well regarded for its alleged allegiance to fact was the best-selling 1849 *Emigrants' Guide to California* by Joseph E. Ware. At the time of its writing, the author had not actually been out West. In the publishing fashion of the times, the book bore the windy yet informative subtitle "Containing every point of information for the emigrant—including routes, distances, water, grass, timber, crossing of rivers, passes, altitudes with a large map of routes and profile of country . . . with full directions for testing and assaying gold and other ores." No one could accuse the author of shirking on topics.

The book was a compilation of choice chunks of practical trail wisdom, including such hopefully well-researched nuggets as "Start at 4—travel till the sun gets high—camp till the heat is over. Then start again and travel till dark." And "After the upper Platte Ford, for over fifty miles, the water is impregnated with poisonous matter. If you would avoid sickness, abandon its use." And "TRUCKIE'S PASS, You will be tried to the utmost. Pack everything over the summit, then haul your wagons up with ropes. You will certainly save time, and perhaps hundreds of dollars."

Unfortunately for the author, a few years later he attempted to follow the route he prescribed in his book but fell victim to cholera whilst on the trail.

The ever-present guidebooks were but one bit of the kit that young argonauts—those seekers of gold—were persuaded they needed for a successful journey west. Such starry-eyed rubes were frequently talked into buying tremendous amounts of gear, much of which they would discard on the journey.

"Vital" gear bundles included multiples of the following: heavy woolen trousers, jackets, vests, shirts, socks, boots, a variety of hats, underwear, candied fruits, brandy, salves, and tinctures. The recommended amount of

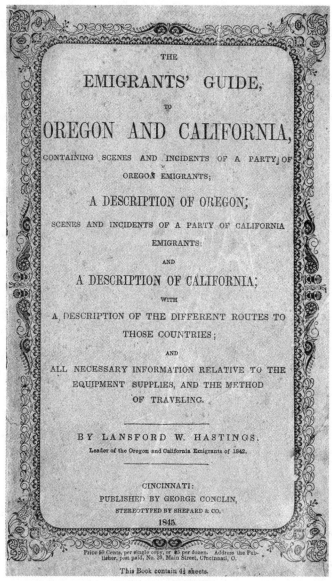

THE

EMIGRANTS' GUIDE,

TO

OREGON AND CALIFORNIA,

CONTAINING SCENES AND INCIDENTS OF A PARTY OF
OREGON EMIGRANTS;

A DESCRIPTION OF OREGON;

SCENES AND INCIDENTS OF A PARTY OF CALIFORNIA
EMIGRANTS;

AND

A DESCRIPTION OF CALIFORNIA;

WITH

A DESCRIPTION OF THE DIFFERENT ROUTES TO
THOSE COUNTRIES;

AND

ALL NECESSARY INFORMATION RELATIVE TO THE
EQUIPMENT SUPPLIES, AND THE METHOD
OF TRAVELING.

BY LANSFORD W. HASTINGS,

Leader of the Oregon and California Emigrants of 1842,

CINCINNATI:
PUBLISHED BY GEORGE CONCLIN,
STEREOTYPED BY SHEPARD & CO.
1845.

Price 50 Cents, per single copy, or $5 per dozen. Address the Publisher, post paid, No. 59, Main Street, Cincinnati, O.

This Book contain 4½ sheets.

Dozens of guidebooks relied upon by wagon train emigrants were all-too-frequently poorly written by people who had never been west of the Mississippi River. Lansford Hasting's *Emigrants' Guide* contained much useful information and suggested a shortcut that he said would save travelers hundreds of miles. But at the time he wrote it, he hadn't tried that route himself. The ill-fated Donner Party opted to try the shortcut, with tragic results. A decade later, other such untested guidebooks would again lead to horrific incidents, such as those on the "Starvation Trail" to Colorado's gold fields.   The Emigrant's Guide to Oregon and California *by Lansford W. Hastings, 1845.*

weaponry per man was impressive and included an assortment of knives, hidden and worn outwardly, plus belt revolvers, rifles, and shotguns.

They also bought journals and writing utensils by the dozen. And a good thing, too, as many of these argonauts, primarily young men, kept detailed diaries of their lives on the trail, in the goldfields, and elsewhere. These journals have become valuable and entertaining accounts of early emigrant life. Not to mention that many make mention of the fact that, at some point in their journeys, they realized their guidebooks had proven worthless.

What the guidebooks—well-intentioned versions included—agreed on was that for every enjoyable mile walking under blue skies, with a light breeze and plenty of water, there would be hazards untold along the route from the Missouri River to the Willamette Valley in Oregon. Frequent deaths occurred from an overabundance of harms awaiting the emigrants. In addition to afflictions such as cholera, scurvy, ague, and scarlet fever, hydrophobia from slavering, crazed wolves and coyotes was a concern. Not to mention crossing rain-swollen rivers, lack of water, food, and firewood, and no shortage of poisonous snakes, stinging plants, and stabbing insects.

And then there were the wagons. . . . Dismemberment and death occurred daily along the trails when wagons rolled over travelers, frequently children, who grew accustomed to hopping on and off the slowly rolling behemoths. The top-heavy conveyances also tipped over with ease. Beasts of burden frequently took ill and died, leaving families with wagons filled with their only possessions, the very things with which they hoped to renew their lives—and with no way to pull them.

The Oregon Trail was littered with pump organs, oak furniture, trunks filled with clothes, cast-iron stoves, heavy tools, anvils, wedding dresses, top hats, and finery of all sorts. Remnants of such goods are still found today, bleached and dried, popped and sprung under the vast, dry Western skies, symbols of the slowly fading ebullience of the westward-headed emigrants. They were people who put their faith and their lives in the hands of others, and frequently those others were journalists who knew less than the people they were instructing.

No emigrants of the mid-1840s are more widely known than the Donner and Reed parties. They were among the many travelers heartened by the (barely) successful journey of three hundred pioneers who chose the largely unexplored California Trail southward from Fort Hall. The route sidled up to the Humboldt River before taking travelers over the Sierra Nevada range and down into Eden, aka the Sacramento Valley. Never mind that the party almost did not make it, having faced severe privation for much of the route.

The Donner and Reed parties brimmed with confidence, armed as they were with a guidebook published in 1845 by Lansford Hastings, a man whose motivation in writing the book was to lure emigrants to California. Once there he hoped they would settle, building up a formidable enough population to wrest California from Mexico's grasp. At that point, Hastings had every intention of becoming president of this fabulous and wealthy new republic. A guidebook to lure settlers to the West was, he reasoned, a fine first step toward building that empire.

Instead of recommending to his readers that they depart from the Oregon Trail at Fort Hall, as had been done so recently, though barely, by other parties, Hastings suggested, based on no personal experience with his suggested route, that they depart from the Oregon Trail at Fort Bridger. This mud-and-pole trading post was owned by famed frontiersman Jim Bridger, himself a two-decade veteran rover of the frontier.

Hastings Shortcut, as it was soon named, took travelers on an untested route westward across the Wasatch Mountains, through the Salt Lake valley and across the Great Basin before joining the California Trail along the Humboldt River. It purported to save the travelers four hundred miles. All this sounded quite alluring to emigrants such as the Donners and Reeds.

The only trouble with the plan was that Hastings had never gone west along that route. He had followed the Oregon Trail four years earlier, in 1842. But he did travel his proposed shortcut, from west to east, in 1846, though not with winter coming on, not with overloaded wagons and draft animals and elderly and infant family members and dogs and chickens. . . . Hastings had traveled it on horseback, with pack mules, and in decent weather, arriving at Fort Bridger mere weeks before the Donner Party. While there, and emboldened by his success, he talked a wagon train of two hundred people and sixty-six wagons, led by a crusty old frontiersman, Captain George Harlan, into taking his route.

The train ran into severe difficulty in the Wasatch Mountains, where narrow gorges necessitated that the travelers move boulders and dense brush.

Then, when they could go no farther, they were forced to hoist their wagons up and over bluffs by ropes and pulleys. They came at last to the Great Basin, a vast, unforgiving salt plain without water, on which oxen died and wagons were abandoned. They all felt sure their ends had come. They finally reached the Humboldt River, where they found themselves three weeks behind others who had taken the longer Fort Hall route.

But the Donners and Reeds, arriving at Fort Bridger weeks later, could not know of the difficulties Hastings Shortcut was presenting. Their own nightmare journey would be far worse, presenting hardship almost from the first day. It all began with severely overloaded wagons. These were massive, specially equipped conveyances outfitted with built-in bunks, cookstoves, all manner of heavy gear, far too many head of livestock, plus fine foods, liquors, and wads of cash sewn into bedding. Add to this the fact that the Donner and Reed parties began their trek far too late in the season, then spent weeks playing catch-up with the last of the 1846 emigrant trains.

By the time they reached Fort Bridger, the season was waning quickly, their window of opportunity closing with each day that passed in discussion and dithering. And so they decided to try Hastings Shortcut. After all, they reasoned, hadn't they been told at Fort Bridger that Hastings himself had just taken it? And saving four hundred miles might well mean the difference between getting to California or not—between, dare they think it, life and death.

Their decision made, they set off. The details of the second half of their arduous journey read like a list of all the horrific occurrences that could befall an emigrant wagon train. Almost from the day they departed from Fort Bridger, July 31, 1846, with seventy-four people and twenty groaning wagons, life grew tougher, and each day brought new defeats. They lost time dickering on river passages, taking twenty-eight days to journey the 50 miles to Great Salt Lake.

Their trek through the desert nearly put an end to their journey—one hundred oxen died, numerous wagons were abandoned, their food supplies were nearing depletion, and they had begun grousing amongst themselves. Nonetheless, the haggard party trudged onward, losing members to starvation, exhaustion, lack of water, and infighting.

On October 20 they finally made it to the base of the Sierra Nevada mountains, gazing upward to see snow already topping the high peaks. They tried to cross over before the cold and snow settled in for the winter, but only made it as far as Truckee Lake, just below Truckee Pass—the last major obstacle between them and the promise of the Sacramento Valley far below.

A number of them tried several times to breach the pass, but most turned back exhausted. Hoping help would arrive soon, they accepted defeat and settled in at Truckee Lake for what would prove to be a living hell. By Christmas they were reduced to boiling hides of dead oxen and eating the glue-like result. Storms followed storms, a bony family dog was eaten—every bit of him— and one by one human members of the party began dying off. By early February thirteen people had succumbed to starvation. Soon enough, cannibalism of the recently deceased became commonplace and the only way those still clinging to life could survive.

By February, when rescue parties were able to breach the pass, forty-seven of eighty-one people were left alive.

Certainly all the horrors of their unfortunate journey cannot be attributed to Lansford Hastings. But it is fair to say that he and other guidebook authors had been far too flippant in their descriptions of life on the trail, painting light and airy depictions of the roads leading to the promised land. Had the majority of them been better versed and not motivated by their personal sources of greed— be they visions of empire or wads of quick cash from book sales—it is doubtful that today mere mention of the Donner Party, and all the attendant horrors those words conjure, would be such an unfortunate cultural reference point.

As the years wore on, guidebooks claiming mastery of the terrain and always-better routes proliferated, numbering more than one hundred by the time the Civil War began. Slowly, a curious change took place, as a number of these references were written by people who had actually traversed the terrain of which they spoke. And those books became dependable references used by the travelers who continued to stream west toward Oregon and California.

In 1858, a couple of thousand miles east, a prospector from Georgia named William Greeneberry "Green" Russell, along with his part-Cherokee wife and his brothers, struck gold in Colorado's Rockies. The discovery kicked off the Colorado Gold Rush, also known as the Pike's Peak Gold Rush, and the participants would be called Fifty-Niners, a reference to the Forty-Niners, gold seekers drawn to California a decade before.

Unlike numerous smaller strikes in the Colorado region throughout the 1850s, which attracted the attention of jaded miners and prospectors from California's played-out goldfields, many of the new wealth seekers came from the east. They traveled from as close as Kansas and Nebraska, and from as far away as the East Coast—New England, Virginia, and points south. Most of them had no idea exactly where the diggings were or how to get there. But they were convinced that once they arrived, they would be able to, as early, shameless newspaper reports read, "scoop up nuggets of silver and gold as one would river rocks."

In order to get to Pikes Peak from the east, the most expeditious routes involved travel through Kansas and Nebraska territories. In addition to trekking across vast stretches of unforgiving terrain, the weather could be fickle, and attacks by Plains Indians were all too common.

But the promise of vast wealth clouded the eyes of each seeker, and opportunists popped up at every turn in the road, eager to exploit the travelers' naïveté and fears, and to sell them items they didn't need. These grubbers convinced the soon-to-be prospectors that the admirable urge to seek gold and silver was not enough. It must be accompanied with vast and varied quantities of equipment, specialized gear, clothing, tinctures, tonics, foodstuffs, and more. If all this sounds familiar, that's because the same thing happened ten years earlier when California's goldfields broke wide open.

A number of these opportunists, as had their predecessors in previous years, created guidebooks filled with advice and directions to help lead travelers from where they were to where they wanted to be. In 1859 that meant getting the gold seekers safely to the goldfields. While some of the guides were written by men with firsthand knowledge of the routes they described, a good many more were penned by untraveled journalists armed with little more than a handful of crude maps. If lucky, they also unearthed interviews with hard-bitten characters who claimed knowledge of the routes, then added their own fanciful notions of what the country west of their eastern offices might well look, feel, smell, and sound like.

In other words, many of the guidebooks were still little more than poorly researched fabrications. But the eager gold seekers knew nothing of this. They laid down their hard-earned dimes and delved into their newly bought guides with gusto, regarding them often as the most vital purchase they had made in preparation for their journeys westward to imagined wealth.

Much of the promising gold-filled terrain of the Pikes Peak rush was within the boundaries of the Territory of Kansas, established in 1854, a mere five years before, a region much larger than what became the state of Kansas. So it is little surprise that more than a dozen guides and tracts of instruction were penned by residents of that territory. This obvious attempt to lure the expected vast hordes of gold seekers through their region would help residents sell all manner of goods the travelers would need to outfit themselves for their journeys—even if those travelers didn't know it yet.

A prime example of one of the earliest guidebooks for the Fifty-Niners came from the pen of William B. Parsons, an attorney from Lawrence, Kansas. Originally published in December 1858, it was written by Parsons upon his return from an extensive expedition with a number of fellow prospectors throughout the Pikes Peak area and on down into New Mexico, a trek without luck in finding promising ore. They were then tipped off by other prospectors that color had been unearthed up north at Cherry Creek, where Denver today resides.

As it turned out, the men did have some luck finding gold there, and before winter a number of the party headed back to eastern Kansas, Parsons among them. That's when he set to work on his guidebook, suspecting correctly that the region would soon become overrun with gold seekers.

By early 1859 his book, a slim forty-eight-pager, came out in a second edition in Cincinnati for 25 cents. As his guide contained a number of advertisements of Lawrence-based businesses with goods and services targeting gold seekers, it was in Parsons's best interest to make a case for Lawrence being the ideal jumping-off point for gold seekers heading to Pikes Peak.

He suggested three routes from Lawrence to the goldfields, two of which he was personally familiar with, having traveled them. The third he was not familiar with, but on a map it looked plausible. That route, the Smoky Hill Trail, was theoretically the most direct route. It would also prove to be the most problematic.

Parsons and the other guidebook authors could hardly be blamed for exuding exuberance in their claims regarding the potential for the goldfields to produce tremendous amounts of riches. Such claims were based on the early promise of gold found. But they should have used restraint in their descriptions.

Much gold was found, but not on the grand scale some of the guidebook authors professed. Their biggest crime, however, was to tout the Smoky Hill route as a viable alternative to the two longer routes.

Unfortunately, a number of subsequent guidebooks urged prospectors to consider that middle, shorter Smoky Hill route. While true that mile-wise the Smoky Hill route was the most expeditious, it was also the most untested. The guidebooks that urged use of that route were written by men who had no experience whatsoever with it.

Shortly after following this route, travelers found that not only did a trail not exist, the landmarks described in the books were nonexistent as well. Entire parties soon became hopelessly lost, and while some managed to find their way back to civilization, many did not. Stories of starvation and cannibalism eventually emerged as byproducts of the journeys of those who took the Smoky Hill trail.

Eventually newspapers reported with frequency the tragedies befalling travelers of that promoted route. The *Western Journal of Commerce* (Kansas City, Missouri) asked: "How often will it be necessary to tell the public that there is no road up the Smoky Hill?"

Another publication, the *Cherry Creek Pioneer*, wrote, "Any other route is better than the Smoky Hill Road." Another, the *Rocky Mountain News*, wrote, "Every day we meet men arriving from the States by the above route—most of them in an almost famishing condition."

And yet people kept taking it, largely because of the ease of it as described in the faulty guidebooks. In what seemed a prime illustration of the dangers of taking the now-infamous Smoky Hill trail, it was reported in a Kansas City newspaper that an expedition of one hundred men, barely alive and owing to scant luck, made it down out of the Smoky Hill route and stumbled upon the Cottonwood Crossing trading post. They set upon the owner, beat him severely, and robbed him of eighty to one hundred sacks of flour, corn, and other provisions. Thus fortified, they headed straight for the goldfields.

Still other reports filtered in from small, straggling groups that somehow made it through. They spoke in dazed, hushed tones of seeing upward of one hundred corpses along the trail, wasted from starvation. The survivors, and increasing numbers of newspapers, laid the blame at the feet of the numerous guidebook authors and others who instructed the prospective prospectors to take that route. They filled the heads of travelers with the full expectation that there would be ample food, water, shelter, and camps already set up along the way. What the travelers found was the opposite—no trail, let alone a wagon road, little to no wood, scant water, and a distance that was more than half again what was indicated they could expect.

And the reported horrors were not yet over. The story of the Blue brothers and others of their party would prove the most horrific of all the Smoky Hill sagas.

In February of 1859, Daniel, Alexander, and Charles Blue, along with two friends, left home in Illinois and made their way toward Pikes Peak. By the time they arrived at Fort Riley, their merry band had grown to sixteen. On the advice of one member who assured them he had taken that route, they took to the Smoky Hill Trail. Soon after, nine of the men stopped to hunt buffalo, while the remaining seven kept on toward the goldfields.

It was not long before they became lost, as did their pack animal, on which was loaded much of their provisions. Then a snowstorm walloped them, and the group split again. Three went on and four remained, too weak to continue. Among them were the Blue brothers and a man named Soley. Within days the last of their meager provisions were gone and they foraged with little luck, subsisting on grass and snow.

They made a pact that should one die, the others would eat his body in an attempt to regain strength enough to press on. Soley soon died. It took the Blue brothers three days before they could bring themselves to eat the man's flesh. And so it continued, with brothers eating brothers until only Daniel Blue remained. He was found, barely alive, by Arapaho Indians, who brought him to the nearest express company office. In the end only five of the original sixteen men of his party ever made it to the goldfields. Little wonder that the Smoky Hill route came to be known as the "Starvation Trail."

It is telling that not long after such woeful stories emerged, a journalist stated what would come to pass, too late to save so many so much hardship: "That route will doubtless turn out as good in the end as either the Northern or Southern. But at the time of the beginning of the Pikes Peak emigration, it was but partially explored. . . ." And that is indeed what came to pass, as the

Smoky Hill Trail would within a few years become the preferred route. But not without further effort and hardship.

Despite the numerous ill-prepared guidebooks containing misleading or erroneous material, there were a good many more that were solid efforts with well-researched information written by individuals who had traveled the described routes. They took great pains to annotate their secondhand references, and to make note of waymarks and useful sources of water and safe places to rest. These guides, as well as all manner of anecdotal and firsthand evidence and experience, often provided enough information to get people closer to their desired destinations at the diggings.

Coupled with the can-do attitudes of the thousands of emigrants who trekked west, not just for a better life but as often for a different life, the western half of the United States and its still-emerging territories slowly became populated. What would those early pilgrims think of today's western United States? What would they think of the enormous sprawling cities, of the vast highway systems and power lines connecting everyone with everyone else? Of the wonders of GPS and satellite navigation that all but guarantee a person's immunity from starvation? Perhaps that's going too far. . . .

CHAPTER 10

DEATH VALLEY SCOTTY
THAT LIKEABLE ROGUE

The man who came to be known the world over as "Death Valley Scotty" is one of those singular, quintessential American characters. It's as if he popped out of a mine shaft fully formed and ambled around for a while with that knowing half-grin on his face as he waited for the world to catch up with him.

The details of his life aren't too far off that mark. Born in Cynthiana, Kentucky, on September 20, 1872, Walter Edward Perry Scott wore, in his long life of eighty-one years, numerous hats, notable among them consummate con man; prospector; stage, screen, and film performer; surveyor; cowboy; and trick rider. Some of those hats fit him better than others.

Raised in a family that traveled hither, thither, and yon working the harness-racing circuit, young Walter showed an early proclivity toward horseback riding. He also sported a wide and long independent streak. By the time he was eleven, Scott lit out on his own, filled with dreams of becoming a top wrangler on the wide-open, alluring frontier. Already in place and living that Western dream were his two older brothers, working on a ranch near Wells, Nevada.

Those early years were doubly formative for young Walter, who indulged in all his cowboy ambitions and quickly proved himself to be a top hand. By 1884, twelve-year-old Scott was cowboying with the rest of the ranch hands. While working on a survey crew that year, he first ventured into the region that would come to define his very person, persona, life, and reputation. As it has with so many before and since, that vast and varied, arid three-thousand-square-mile terrain known as Death Valley entranced young Walter Edward Scott. Something in the seeming wasteland gripped the youth down deep, and though he would go out into the world and pursue many other ventures, Death Valley never loosened its hold on Walter. It was an early and formative experience that prodded him into realizing his talents and ambitions might be broader than cowboying would allow.

Despite his infatuation with that mysterious place, Walter Scott stuck with working as a cowboy. Within four years, at the tender age of sixteen in 1888, he was hired on as a trick rider for Buffalo Bill Cody's touring show, *The Wild West*. Scott stuck with the show for twelve years, traveling all over the United States and to Europe, performing as part of the show's vast cast for packed houses, for kings and queens, for presidents and paupers. His trick-riding skills, already formidable when he joined, became an anchoring, anticipated sensation.

By the time the new century rolled into view, the independent-minded Scott had begun to chafe under Cody's dictates. The two headstrong men— one the boss, world-famous Cody, the other, willful Walter Scott—locked horns a number of times over the years.

Finally, in 1902, on the announcement of his betrothal to Ella Josephine Milius in New York City, Cody and Scott had a final argument over money, and Scott left Cody's employ. This came at a time when the show had begun to feel the tension of increasing financial difficulties. Scott and Ella, whom he affectionately called "Jack," relocated to Cripple Creek, Colorado, site of many past successes in gold mining. Unfortunately, Scott's efforts were not sufficient enough to earn him a spot on that list.

Feeling the sting of insolvency, Scott attempted to patch up his differences with Buffalo Bill but was unsuccessful at that as well. Though he'd always had a streak of the devilish about him, and had dipped a toe now and again into the brackish waters of chicanery, it was his next venture that would earn Scott a place on the Swindler's List. On learning that he'd been turned down by Cody's touring extravaganza, Scott returned to Death Valley, a place he'd been working for years in the off-season, when Cody's show was off the road for the winter months. Scott also shifted his attentions to a well-off New York City businessman.

The silver-tongued Scott convinced his newfound patron that he need only invest in his promising gold mine and fortunes would soon follow. The man, swayed by showman Scott's ample powers of persuasion, agreed to front Scott's Death Valley diggings.

In exchange, the investor received month after month of excuse upon excuse, each more promising and frustrating than the last. Incredibly, he put up with two years of letters from Scott telling why the mine hadn't yet paid off.

The real reason Scott hadn't shipped a single ounce of ore? There was no mine. His New York City investor had been backing a complete fabrication, and all the while Scott enjoyed himself at the expense of his patron, to the tune of $5,000.

Knowing that his repeated excuses and lies had worn thin with the gullible but frustrated patron, Scott hatched yet another devilish scheme, at the same time unwittingly gaining himself the national attention he craved. Scott sent word of good news to his investor—he was headed east with a sack of gold dust, $12,000 worth, in fact. When he arrived in the Big Apple, however, he shouted high and low to anyone who would listen—especially to the press—that he'd been robbed of his precious $12,000 in gold while in transit.

Already quite a celebrity due to his time touring with Cody's *Wild West* show, Scott's misfortune aboard the train gained him wide newspaper coverage. Intrigued, Scott hatched plan after plan to gain himself fresh rounds of media exposure.

He became convinced that shameless self-promotion could only help his aims of attracting more and bigger investors in his schemes. In addition to his celebrity status, it helped that he was becoming known as Death Valley Scotty due to his fondness for the unusual place.

His earlier investor pulled stakes and moved on, finally convinced he'd been pouring money into a bottomless hole. Undeterred, by 1904 Scott found a pair of wealthy men to fill the breach. Alas, he milked them only for a few months before they, too, moved on. But in that time Scott managed to extract in excess of $4,000 from their well-off wallets.

Having learned the value of publicity, in 1905 Scott arranged a humdinger of a public spectacle. He turned his sights on the newspapers—and it worked. He rented a train in Los Angeles, dubbed it the *Scott Special*, a four-car juggernaut composed of engine, baggage car, dining car, and sleeping car—lest anyone not know it was him. His goal? To break the train-speed record for cross-country travel. He claimed he could shatter the old record of just shy of fifty-three hours, roaring from Los Angeles to Chicago. And to prove it, he took along two trainmen, himself, his wife, and a *Los Angeles Examiner* journalist. The *Scott Special* made the overland journey in a record-breaking forty-four hours, fifty-four minutes.

Once more Scott was heralded across front pages of newspapers from coast to coast. And in an even bigger twist that surely must have been both flattering and flummoxing to Scott, Buffalo Bill Cody hired a Walter Scott impersonator for his show. Cody, that consummate showman, had managed to capitalize on the attention-grabbing appeal of Death Valley Scotty without having to put up with Scott's bloated ego and constant whining for money.

Walter Edward Perry Scott, aka "Death Valley Scotty" (top, right), sweet-talked and scammed his way through a long life as a prospector, cowboy, and performer in Buffalo Bill's Wild West show. He brazenly bilked huge sums of money from investors in his non-existent gold mines. Incredibly, the man he bilked more than any other, Chicago millionaire Albert Johnson (top, left), and his wife, Bessie (top, center), were so taken by the con man, and by Death Valley itself, that they built Death Valley Ranch (bottom), more commonly known as Scotty's Castle. They even allowed Scotty to tell visitors they were his hired help.   *(Top) National Park Service. (Bottom) Jennifer Smith-Mayo, 2014.*

Throughout this period, Scott continued to attract a number of "investors" by capitalizing on his surging fame to lure them as backers of his gold-mining schemes. He had an uncanny ability to peel money from the billfolds of wealthy men while at the same time to run diversions to head off their justifiable questions. When necessary, he employed evasion tactics whenever he got wind of impending visits by current and potential investors. But as so often happens to men with too many balls in the air and not enough hands to catch them, Scott would eventually fumble in the midst of this juggling act.

Walter Scott's overinflated ego was justified in part by the fact that the media paid him all the attention he craved, and then some. Eager for ever-wider audiences, newspapers knew that the public loves a huckster, and this was the golden age of such shady showmanship. The public, and so the media, didn't seem to care one way or the other if a scheme smacked of truth; they wanted more. Scott did his best to feed the fire by conjuring ever-more fascinating publicity stunts, scams, and schemes.

Each one seemed to top the last, until in Seattle, on March, 11, 1906, Scott became the subject—and star—of a genuine stage play, *Scotty, King of the Desert Mine*. The house was packed that night with a standing-room-only crowd, all there to see Death Valley Scotty himself.

By all accounts the show was not overly impressive, but when the curtain closed that night, the lackluster play quickly became overshadowed by even bigger news: Law officers were waiting in the wings for Scotty. They clapped cuffs on him and again he made headlines, though this time not for undertakings he wished to be known for.

Earlier in the year he had finally been caught scamming men sent to investigate his mine's activities. They of course found nothing, and after repeated visits, with Scott nowhere to be found (and thus no one available to take them to the mine), investors deduced he was the fraud they had suspected.

These backers were livid, and though the ensuing trial proves them wholly correct, Scott, ever the rose in the outhouse, emerged from the trial with charges dropped. True, only on a technicality, but he was free. What did result, however, was a taint to his reputation from which he was unable to recover. For his part Scott continued to proclaim his innocence.

So what, specifically, landed him in this predicament? Earlier in the year, a group of his investors showed up at his door in Death Valley, some represented by investigators, for the express purpose of seeing the mine for themselves. Not surprisingly, they wanted concrete proof that their investments were truly supporting a functioning mining concern. How dare they....

Their arrival was not unexpected but planned well in advance. And when they showed up, Walter Scott was prepared for them. What resulted, however—the Battle of Wingate Pass—was anything but expected and would be remembered as one of Death Valley Scotty's most famous hoaxes.

The party consisted of Scotty, mining promoter A. Y. Pearl, mining engineer Daniel Owen, a potential investor named Albert Johnson (a Chicago insurance magnate who had recently learned of Scotty and became intrigued), and two of Scotty's brothers, Bill and Warner. Also tagging along were Bill Keys, a Cherokee half-breed miner and acquaintance of Scotty's, as well as miner Jack Brody.

After several days of preparation, on Friday, February 23, 1906, two wagons were loaded with ample supplies that included food, whiskey, all manner of camping gear, much fresh water, and trailed by extra horses and mules. By Sunday, the travelers reached Lone Willow Spring, fifty miles into their journey. Only Scotty and his associates knew where they were headed—vaguely toward a mine owned by Bill Keys, but more importantly straight into Wingate Pass.

Scotty had begun to act uneasy around the mine investigators, claiming they were in dangerous territory and that they should be alert. Bandits roamed the hills in these parts, he said, preying on the unsuspecting.

"What do you mean we have to be careful?" Pearl had been a pain in Scott's backside for hours.

Scotty didn't answer, but walked off beyond the campfire light, a rifle cradled in his arms, a look of concern playing on his face.

"What did he mean by that?" whispered Pearl to the others. No one knew, but if they did they kept silent.

The night passed uneventfully. In the morning, before they lit out on what the out-of-towners hoped would be the final day of their journey to the mine, Scotty told his brother, Bill, to stay at the camp with the horses and mules. He instructed Jack Brody and Bill Keys to ride ahead of the main party and scout for signs of trouble on the trail. Scotty then held the party there for a time, saying he was giving the men ample time to ensure the route was safe for them to travel.

Then they rolled out toward Wingate Pass, made it through and down the other side, southward. The day was long and dusty, and everyone's spirits were caked with alkali and rimed with salt from their sweat. They were relieved when, with dusk approaching, Scotty told them to begin searching for a decent place to pitch camp.

Sudden gunshots cracked the still, desert air. They looked up to see a rider, a stranger, hell bent, heading toward them from the north. He told them he'd just been shot at and had his pack animals run off by outlaws. Scotty was visibly shocked—this was unexpected but potentially useful to him. It's exactly what he had intended to unleash on his little band of investors. He wanted to scare them enough to dissuade them from continuing the trip.

"Let's keep it moving," said Scotty. "We'll travel a bit farther tonight before setting up camp. Put distance betwixt us and the shooters."

They made it past Dry Lake, then Scotty slid his rifle clean of its sheath and cranked off two shots at something he'd apparently seen in the distance.

"What are you shooting at?" shouted one of the men, but his words were drowned out by the bucking, dancing horses and braying, kicking mules.

Scotty's shot frightened mules pulling the lead wagon, commandeered by Warner Scott and Daniel Owen, who lost his seating and fell backward into the wagon.

Then a shot rang out, not from Scotty this time, and his brother, Warner, screamed and clutched at his groin, already welling dark-red blood.

"Warner!" Scotty shouted, reaching toward his brother, then suddenly reining his mount toward the rocky escarpment from where the shot had drilled. He galloped hard toward it, shouting, "Stop shooting! Stop shooting, I tell ya!"

The shooters did indeed stop, and a hasty camp was set up. By scant firelight they tried to close up Warner's wounds. It seemed not only had the bullet hit him in the groin, but it had passed through the leg and into his arm. Despite the wounds, it appeared as though Warner would live through the escapade. But Scotty knew they needed to get him to a doctor. And as a bonus, it would get them out of the desert without having to see the mine.

Scotty spent the night mulling over the mess the trek had become. This was exactly what was supposed to have happened, but not in the way it did. No one was supposed to be shot, least of all his own brother. And worst of all, he knew he'd blown the ruse by commanding the "outlaws" to stop shooting. Oh, what a mess.

Further troubling was the fact that the big-city mining dudes, Pearl and Owen, as well as that newcomer, Johnson, talked among themselves in low tones. There would be trouble from this, no doubt. But first things first, thought Scotty. Get Warner to a doctor, and then he had to get himself to Seattle, where his play was due to open in a few days.

The next morning they made it to the town of Daggett and loaded Warner on a train bound for Los Angeles and much-needed medical attention. All of Scotty's fear and doubts on the trail came home to roost in short order. Over the next few weeks, A. Y. Pearl, now fully convinced that Scotty had no mine at all and was instead a desperate con man, also had become convinced that Scotty had intended to have him killed while on the trip.

Pearl went to the authorities with the full story and his suppositions. Scotty was already a highly suspicious character in the eyes of the law, so it didn't take much convincing for them to issue warrants for the arrests of Scotty, Bill Keys, and Jack Brody. The latter two men failed to return to camp before the party left for Daggett, thus affirming their potential culpability.

Scotty was arrested and released on bail no fewer than four times over the next few weeks. In April he learned that his brother, Warner, who had been shot because of Scotty's scheme, was suing him for $152,000 in damages. An impressive case was building against Scotty for the false ambush gone awry, backed by deep investigations and the arrests of Keys and Brody. It looked as if Scotty might finally have come up against a case from which he couldn't wiggle free. Then, astoundingly, on April 27, four days before a preliminary hearing was to take place in San Bernardino County Court, the charges were dropped.

Once again, that luckiest of swindlers, Death Valley Scotty, had evaded big trouble. It seems questions about jurisdiction arose—the shooting had actually taken place in Inyo County, not San Bernardino County. And the authorities in Inyo County weren't interested in pursuing the case. What no one learned until many years later, in a newspaper interview published after Scotty's death, was that he had suspected jurisdictional issues might arise. So Scotty did what he did best—he sneaked out one day and moved the surveyor's post that defined the Inyo–San Bernardino County line.

Despite this spectacular failed ruse, incredibly enough, the Chicago millionaire, Albert Johnson, came away from the debacle of a trip somehow impressed with Walter Scott. Sure, he knew that Scott was a hoodwinker of the first order. But Johnson had solid instincts that had rarely let him down in the business world. He felt sure that this time, as with his other potential investments, there was meat between the bread—promise, buried however deep, in this venture.

A week later, back at his offices in Chicago, Albert Johnson addressed the man he'd summoned to work for him. Johnson detailed what he knew about Death Valley Scotty. Finally, he paused, steepled his fingers, elbows on his desktop, and said, "So you see, Mr. MacArthur, I need someone to head out to Death Valley and shadow Mr. Scott. I want his every move seen and documented. I will tell you that he is a wily creature, prone to move about night and day, a difficult man to pin down."

"Not to worry, Mr. Johnson. This sort of investigation is what I do. I bird-dog a subject until I learn everything my employer needs to know. That said, I have to tell you that from everything you've told me already, this Death Valley Scotty fellow doesn't sound like he's too interested in playing ball on the up-and-up, if you know what I mean."

Johnson smiled. "I know, but wait until you meet him before you form too much of an opinion. There's something about him that is mighty convincing."

MacArthur smiled. "The only convincing I'll need is to see that producing gold mine for myself, firsthand."

"Good. Then it sounds like I have the right man for the job."

Alfred MacArthur headed on out to Death Valley within days. Scotty saw trouble coming, so instead of growing resistant, he responded in true Death Valley Scotty fashion. He seeded an old abandoned shaft with raw gold ore. "Well, what do you think of that, Mr. MacArthur? Need much more convincing than that?"

Scotty pointed to the gold he'd dug free right in front of MacArthur. "That there," he said, holding up a nub of rock between their faces, "is gold ore, plain and simple. Just a taste of what I've been coming up with. But make no mistake, MacArthur, you want to make money in this game, you got to spend money."

He leaned close to MacArthur, and spoke in a low, conspiratorial tone. "That's what I been trying to tell these investor types like Mr. Johnson, see?

This ain't an overnight type of thing. Mining for gold takes time, it takes money, it takes dedication and investment. Plain and simple."

"From what I've seen and from what I've been told, Mr. Scott, you've had plenty of both time and investment, in the form of other people's money. What you haven't shown is that any of it is paying off. Heck, Mr. Scott—no, no, now let me finish," he held up a hand to stop the blustering Scott from stomping all over his words. "What I haven't seen hide nor hair of, Mr. Scott, is an actual working gold mine with promising ore."

"What do you call this, Mr. MacArthur?" Scott held up the recently unearthed ore. "That's gold, that is! Right here in this shaft!"

"Scott—I'll dispense with the whole 'Mr.' thing, if you don't mind, as neither of us are much into the formalities this situation does not require."

"I'm not sure I follow, Mr. MacArthur."

"What I'm saying is that I'll be informing my employer, Mr. Johnson, that you are no closer than he suspected to exhibiting proof of a working, bankable gold mine. This shaft, Scott, is an old, abandoned, useless, and spent thing. And don't try to convince me otherwise. I didn't fall off the turnip truck yesterday."

True to his word, despite numerous protestations by Walter Scott, Albert MacArthur reported back right away, via telegram, to Albert Johnson. Scott, he said, had failed at every turn to convince him not only that he had indeed struck gold but that he even had a gold mine.

In short, it seemed that Death Valley Scotty had burned the last bridge to a moneyman that he had. The one last wealthy investor who seemed to want to believe him, and believe *in* him, a man who had been kind enough to throw out a lifeline, had just been told that Scott was exactly what the press claimed he was: an outright fraud.

Incredibly, Scott was able to keep this millionaire investor, Albert Johnson, on the hook and supplying funds to keep the "mine" in operation. Even after MacArthur visited the mine and reported back that there truly was no mine at all, Johnson funded Scott's sleazy efforts.

The next year, 1907, Johnson decided to visit the mine himself. Scott decided that the only way he could keep Johnson on the hook was to make the visit particularly exhausting—not a difficult thing to do in Death Valley. He took Johnson on a grueling horseback tour through Death Valley. But Johnson surprised him, even though he suffered weak health from a train wreck he barely survived as a young man. Indeed, Johnson fell in love with the sunny, dry place and stayed for a month. He felt great and his health conditions improved. Even though it became quickly apparent he was being swindled, primarily because they never seemed to arrive at a mine, he and Scotty hit it off. It was the beginning of a lifelong friendship. And it was an odd pairing at that, Scotty being a man fond of drink and outright lies, while Johnson was a teetotaler and a pious, churchgoing man.

You'd think Scott would quit while he was ahead, but not a chance. Once a thief, always a thief. And in Scotty's case, he devolved even further, going from swindling to outright theft of physical property. The first thing he did, though, was to obtain a lease on a worthless, played-out mine in the Humboldt Mountains of northern Nevada. Then, when no one was around, Scott took to visiting various mines throughout the region. While there he pilfered substantial amounts of high-grade ore and sold it at various locations around the region, careful to not sell too much at any one location lest he arouse suspicion.

Ever the blowhard and braggart, Scott headed back to Death Valley with a lie on his lips that would land him in court, and then jail, once more. He told everyone who would listen that he had sold his mine in the Humboldts for the tidy sum of $12 million. But as clever as he claimed to be, Scott conveniently overlooked the fact that he had a lengthy string of creditors dogging his trail like hungry wolves on the scent of a fat rabbit.

Once these long-suffering former investors got wind of his supposed windfall, though surely they had their doubts about Scott's truthfulness, they sued him for nonpayment of old debts. The result was, once again, no money forthcoming from the penniless shyster. The only person in the deal to receive anything was Scott himself, who got a three-year jail sentence.

By 1915 Scotty, out of jail, was lying low, or as low as a serial swindler was able. He'd moved to the town of Twentynine Palms, California. Johnson dropped in on him and eventually forgave Scotty for being such a sleaze. Once more they roved Death Valley together, Scotty showing the man his favorite locales, and Johnson falling more in love with the ghostly place with each day. Before long he bought the Staininger Ranch in one of the most lush spots in Death Valley, Grapevine Canyon. At its heart is an oasis of trees surrounding an ample freshwater spring, used for centuries by local Indians.

The ranch consisted primarily of many acres of barren land and a few ramshackle buildings. It was enough for Johnson, and he had a modest home for Scotty built there as well. But after making a few trips to the ranch with his wife, Bessie, she made it clear that she wanted something more comfortable if he wanted her to accompany him on his Death Valley vacations. The result, begun in 1922 and continually expanded, is an estate that cost Johnson upward of $2.5 million. Johnson also added to his acreage through the years until, by 1937, he owned more than fifteen hundred acres surrounding Grapevine.

The massive, multistory Mission Revival and Spanish Colonial Revival villa is officially named Death Valley Ranch, though it is now better known as Scotty's Castle. Over the years, Johnson built Scotty a fine five-room cabin at an adjoining property, Lower Vine Ranch, which Johnson also owned. It sits five miles from the castle. The place he built for Scotty also included a number of outbuildings and room for Scotty's mules.

Despite this largesse, Scotty the Swindler could not help himself. As the never-ending castle took shape, growing more elaborate with each month, Scotty did little to dissuade people from thinking he had finally and truly struck gold in a big way. He intimated that all those negative headlines through the years were incorrect, and he went out of his way to tell everyone he was, in fact, the builder and owner of the estate. Rather than take offense, Johnson found Scotty's tall tales amusing and did nothing to spread the truth.

In fact, Johnson and his wife were so fond of the affable Scotty that they had a special bedroom made up for him in the villa, though he never used it. He would gladly drive on up to the big house from his modest ranch, entertain the Johnsons' guests, regaling them with barely believable stories of his life, then bid them adieu and head back to his own place to spend time with his dogs and mules.

The elaborate villa, a massive compound, consists of a main building with numerous guest rooms, a music room and pipe organ (with 1,121 pipes), a quarter mile of tunnels beneath the main house, a garage and stable, guest and servants' quarters, a gas station, a powerhouse, dynamo, and solar hot water heater, all designed by Johnson himself, a clock tower, a massive unfinished swimming pool, and much more. And all of it sumptuously decorated with one-of-a-kind pieces of furniture, artwork, and tiles from all over the world.

Following the stock market crash, Johnson's company slid into bank-ruptcy in 1933. Though he and his wife lived on limited means compared with their previous level of spending, they still lived quite well, traveling back and forth from Chicago to Death Valley throughout the year. Despite that, construction on the villa and various buildings ceased, though much of it was already complete.

In order to help defray the hefty costs of running the place, Scotty suggested the Johnsons take in paying guests and give tours of the exotic home. When they were not in residence, Scotty played tour guide, answering the door as if he were the man of the house. He would proceed to tell visitors that he had had it all built, that the Johnsons were actually his live-in maid and butler, and that he paid for the place with earnings from his various successful mines. Convincing as ever, people didn't doubt the homespun huckster for a moment.

Scotty and his wife, Jack, separated shortly after his son, Walter Perry Scott, was born in 1914. Scotty was, predictably, a lousy husband and father, but once again, his guardian angels, Mr. and Mrs. Johnson, stepped in to prop him up. They felt badly that though they were supporting the swindling Scotty, he was doing nothing to support his own family.

So in true benefactor fashion, the Johnsons took the boy into their lives, raised him for a few years, and even attempted to adopt him. His mother resisted the idea, so they bought Scotty's estranged wife a home in Reno, Nevada, and paid her a tidy sum each month, ranging from $100 to $150, for upkeep of herself and the boy. They even paid for young Walter to attend a military academy, and he later joined the navy. All the while Scotty did nothing on his own to help his family. He spent his time strutting the grounds of "Scotty's Castle," as if he owned the place.

On the Johnsons' passing, she in 1943, he in 1948, they willed the property to a religious foundation they had established, with the provision that Death Valley Scotty be allowed to continue residing at his place, unharried, for the rest of his days. And that's just what he did, dying there in 1954. He is buried on a hill overlooking his "castle."

CHAPTER 11

THE US GOVERNMENT
SHAME, SHAME, SHAME. . . .

For thousands of years before invaders from afar came calling, the land mass now known as North America was occupied by numerous tribes of native peoples who lived largely in tolerance with one another. When Europeans "discovered" this land of hope and possibility several centuries ago, a cycle of conflict began between oppressor and oppressed that continues to this day.

From an early meager toe-hold, Europeans established settlements in the New World, and with them their own forms of governance. British-ruled colonies transformed into the fledgling United States of America.

From that time through today, the US government has made more than five hundred treaties with Native American tribes and has in one way or another broken, altered, or nullified each, most notably for land acquisition, and most famously on the Western frontier. But long before the federal government herded Native Americans onto reservations throughout the West, they drove the First People from the East. . . .

In 1794, in an effort to quell growing unease among the Six Nations tribes, also known as the Haudenosaunee, President George Washington helped create the Canandaigua Treaty, which came about because private opportunists were cheating Native Americans of their lands. Washington worried these "jobbers, speculators, and monopolizers" were undermining his efforts to nurture his fragile young nation.

Terms of the treaty included an affirmation of the six tribes' rights to their own lands. It was hoped the pact would help establish "firm peace and friendship" among the tribes and the United States. The United States agreed to a one-time payment of $10,000 and annual tithes of $4,500 in goods, among them an annual supply of calico cloth, of which the Indians were fond.

Over the centuries, the United States government has made and then broken, altered, or nullified each of its 500-plus treaties with Native American tribes, most notably for land acquisition. Tribes such as the Navajo, the Cherokee, the Hopi, the Sioux, and many others were relocated for varying reasons including the demands of white settlers, and the discovery of gold on previously deeded tribal lands. The tribes endured forced marches over hundreds and thousands of miles, suffering starvation, illness, inclement weather, and death.

Courtesy Library of Congress. Harper's Weekly, December 26, 1868. Sketched by Theodore R. Davis.

Washington also commissioned a six-foot Wampum belt, a symbolic item to commemorate the event.

A shadow of the agreement, now referred to as the Calico Treaty, is still in place. A token payment of cloth is still sent to the tribes of the Six Nations. The once-fine calico cloth has diminished over time to lengths of cheap muslin. As to the lands owned by the tribes, they have long since been subsumed into the ever-growing republic.

Though preparations began many decades before, with proposals for "cultural transformation" made by George Washington and Henry Knox, in 1830 President Andrew Jackson helped usher passage of the Indian Removal Act through Congress. This allowed the US government to remove all title Native

Americans may have had to land in the southern states. The act freed up desirable land for white settlers, whose growing demands for property, particularly in the deep South and Southeast, were fast proving insatiable.

In 1831 the Choctaw Nation was removed and ushered westward. The Seminole fought tooth and nail but lost all, and in 1832 they were also removed. Two years later the Creek were driven out, then the Chickasaw in 1837.

In 1838 the US Army forced 16,542 Cherokee off their ancestral lands in Georgia, herding them like cattle all the way to modern-day Oklahoma. The 2,200-mile walk came to be known as the Trail of Tears, and for good reason. Approximately four thousand Cherokee died of exhaustion, disease, and starvation along the way.

By the end of the decade, roughly 46,000 Native Americans had been driven off their ancestral lands, some twenty-five million acres worth, and were pushed west of the Mississippi River, even as white settlers flooded in, many of whom were already giving thought to what lay to the far West.

In 1863, in response to Navajo uprisings in Arizona Territory, Colonel Kit Carson was given orders to quell the situation. He led his troops in decimating crops, slaughtering livestock, destroying precious water sources, and razing entire villages. And then he got tough.

Nine-thousand Navajo surrendered to Carson and his troops, and for their acquiescence were forced on a torturous three-hundred-mile walk from their homeland in Arizona, called "Dinétah," to Fort Sumter in southeastern New Mexico. On the journey hundreds of Navajo died from afflictions such as exposure, frostbite, starvation, and exhaustion. Others were shot for showing signs of anger or for traveling too slowly. Official records state that 336 Navajo died on the journey, though two thousand remain unaccounted for.

Bodies were left by the roadside, along with those too weak to continue. Nighttime brought its own terrors, as tribes whose lands the Navajo were herded through stole into camp and made off with women and children. Soldiers looked away, finding it easier to not engage this fresh enemy.

They made it to Bosque Redondo, an internment camp they were forced to share with longtime enemies the Mescalero Apache. There the Navajo became a huge labor force, much needed to achieve Major General James Carleton's lofty goals of creating an agricultural Eden in what was intended to be the first Indian reservation west of Indian Territory. From the start the Navajo were treated as little more than slave laborers, endured brutally long hours, and received the barest of sustenance and clothing.

By 1868, with its agricultural schemes and dreams collapsing, Bosque Redondo was declared an abysmal failure—conditions were tight, with ten thousand people crowded into a space intended for half that. Crops died, water supplies were foul and brackish, food was brought in at great expense, the Pecos River flooded, firewood was scarce, and tribes raided incessantly. On June 1, 1868, the Navajo, weakened and spent, reluctantly agreed to a lopsided treaty that nonetheless allowed them to return to their beloved—albeit ruined—homeland, Dinétah.

Colonel John Chivington, US Army hothead and commander of the Third Colorado Cavalry, bellowed orders of attack on November 29, 1864, on the long-peaceful camp of Cheyenne Chief Black Kettle and the two hundred Cheyenne and Arapaho who lived there in southeastern Colorado Territory. Never mind that Black Kettle had long flown the United States flag over his tent, Chivington's men, some seven hundred strong, rode down hard on the unsuspecting camp—a camp two-thirds filled with women and children. When the firing commenced, Black Kettle ran the white flag of truce up the flag pole, to no avail.

Popularly known as the Sand Creek Massacre and the Battle at Sand Creek—though the notion of it being a battle suggests it was two-sided—it is more appropriately called the Chivington Massacre. When the gunsmoke cleared, as many as 163 Cheyenne lay massacred. But Chivington and his men weren't through. They scalped one hundred, looted the camp and bodies, and mutilated as many corpses as they could lay hands on, hacking body parts off men and women and adorning their hats and saddles with them. They cut off ears and fingers for their jewelry, bashed in the heads of women and babies, and the scrotums of men were later made into tobacco pouches.

Colonel Chivington, himself a Methodist preacher and opponent of slavery, and his men escaped unscathed, never having been held accountable for their foul atrocities.

Though Chief Black Kettle's wife was shot nine times at Sand Creek, the distraught chief carried her to nearby Fort Lyon, where she survived her operation. Almost four years to the day later, at the Battle of Washita River, Black Kettle and his wife, still promoting pacifism, were shot in the back and killed by Custer's men while trying to cross the river.

In 1868, with the Treaty of Laramie, the US government officially ceded six thousand square miles of the Black Hills region of Dakota Territory, land sacred to the Sioux. But six years later, in July 1874, under orders from General Philip Sheridan, Lieutenant Colonel George Armstrong Custer led an expedition into the Black Hills. Consisting of one thousand soldiers, nineteen hundred mules and horses, three Gatling guns, sixty-one Indian scouts, plus scientists, journalists, a photographer, and a sixteen-man military band, Custer's mission was ostensibly to scout an ideal spot to locate a fort to help westward-bound emigrants.

Custer was actually under orders given him by General Sheridan to scout for gold in the Black Hills, which he found in promising quantities. The region, Custer reported back, offered "gold in paying quantities," and that a man might "reasonably expect . . . to realize from every panful of earth a handsome return for his labor." This news was met with much excitement, as the US government's postwar coffers were still quite bare, made worse by the widespread financial panic of 1873.

Before it could renegotiate treaties with the Sioux, however, civilian gold seekers, tipped off by Custer's pet journalists, flooded into the Black Hills, prompting numerous treaty violations and renewed attacks by the Lakota Sioux.

The US government, hoping to prevent further bloodshed, offered the Sioux $6 million for the Black Hills, ignoring the fact that as ground sacred to the Sioux, it was not for sale. The government said fine, have it your way, and began withholding guaranteed winter provisions it was lawfully beholden to provide to the Sioux. Faced with bitterly cold weather and encroaching starvation, the Sioux reluctantly surrendered their six-thousand-square-mile home so that they might eat. Long before negotiations were finalized, ten thousand whites had flooded into the Black Hills seeking gold.

In July 1980 the Sioux Nation pursued a lawsuit against the US government all the way to the Supreme Court for violation of the Fort Laramie Treaty of 1868. The court ruled that the Black Hills had indeed been taken illegally from the Sioux. The Sioux won the 1980 lawsuit, a hollow victory, as the government refused to return the land.

Though the court mandated that remuneration of the initial cash payment offered in 1876, plus interest, must be paid, the Sioux refused the money. So it resides in an escrow account, slowly gaining interest, and is rumored to total roughly $800 million today.

As commanding general of the US Army from 1869 to 1883, one of William Tecumseh Sherman's primary goals was to ensure safe settlement of the West and the Plains regions. And his biggest impediments to doing so were the increasingly hostile native tribes, incensed because whites were displacing them from their hunting grounds. Chief among the troublesome tribes was the Sioux. In 1866 Sherman famously wrote to General Ulysses S. Grant: "we must act with vindictive earnestness against the Sioux, even to their extermination, men, women, and children."

Sherman also famously advocated annihilation of bison herds in order to assist in the army's efforts in weakening Indian opposition. In his eyes he was acting as a soldier charged with a duty to perform, and his solutions were considered practical and efficient, if severe. . . .

"So you see, gentlemen, the only way to keep the savages in line is simple." From under dark, beetling brows, General William Tecumseh Sherman eyed the men before him, arrayed in relaxed poses about the long gleaming walnut table. A burly General Grant, seated at the far end of the table, drew on his thick stogie and plumed a broad cloud of blue-gray smoke from between his large jowls. "Are you saying what I think you are, Sherman?"

The general spoke, nodding his head with the words, a measured effort. "Yes, I am. There is only the one course of action left available to us, only the one way we might once and for all defeat the Lakota Sioux—the same way you would any animal: starve them into submission. It can't help but work."

"That's rather callous, don't you think?"

"Callous? When they've been taking every opportunity to flee the reservation, to kill white settlers and soldiers?"

"Ceding land that was already theirs was hardly a generous offering on our part."

"Hardly the point." Sherman's dark eyes squinted even narrower. "Don't you see the need?"

"I see the need to do something to minimize attacks by the savages on poor folks traveling westward, yes. But to starve children? Women? The old?"

"It will only be a ploy, a short-lived attempt to get them to change their ways." Sherman stood and toyed with his own smoldering cigar. "At least that is my fervent hope. What they do with the opportunity is up to them."

Grant snorted a bark of wry laughter. "'Opportunity'? Heck, Sherman, you ought to run for office. Talk like that gets votes."

Another of the men smirked, hid it behind his hand, and looked down at the table when Sherman raked the assemblage with his flinty glare.

"Be that as it may, it is an opportunity for us to get a leg up and over this problem once and for all." The men still looked away, obviously ill at ease with what they were hearing. Sherman leaned heavily over the table, punched down with his knuckles. "I tell you now that if you want to subdue the Indians, you take away their food supply. And that means taking away the buffalo."

"What?"

"You heard me." Sherman turned away, massaging his reddened knuckles, his flushed neck and ears betraying his rage. "Every damned last one of the big shaggies." He turned back, wagged an accusing finger at the room. "Take away that primary means of sustenance and they will have no choice but to comply, to knuckle under, to . . . behave themselves."

"You make them sound like petulant children."

"Hardly children. The Sioux and all the others of their ilk are much more savage. But once they can no longer feast, they will fall into line or fall dead. At this point I don't much care which."

"Seems a drastic way to get what you want."

"If anyone here has a better way of doing it, then by all means let him speak up."

"Once the buffs are gone. How will you feed the remaining Indians?"

Sherman smiled. "That's the beauty of it. Then we'll provide them with just enough to get by on. And if they become unruly once again, why we'll just have to withhold provisions."

"Sounds like prison," said Grant, shrugging into his jacket.

"It can't be helped." Sherman stared at the ceiling.

The big man sighed. "It's a rough scheme, Sherman." He looked up. "But it bears thought." With that he left, trailing a stream of thick smoke behind.

For long moments no one said anything, then Sherman spoke up. "I take it none of you are any more impressed with the plan than he is."

To a man they hesitantly shook their heads, not daring to meet Sherman's hard gaze.

One of the more tragic events in a long history of tragedies stippling US history in the West during the nineteenth century is the sad end of the Nez Perce War of 1877. This trek of desperation was led by Chief Joseph and his band of seven hundred, of which fewer than two hundred were warriors. The tribe traveled more than seventeen hundred miles across five states (Oregon, Washington, Idaho, Wyoming, and Montana) for three and a half months.

They hoped to make it to safety in Canada, where they would be beyond the reach of their tormenting pursuers, the US Cavalry. The army had cornered and engaged them in fights time and again on the journey, during which 120 Nez Perce were killed (fifty-five of whom were children and women). And yet the Nez Perce managed to strike back even as they fled, killing 312 soldiers.

But freedom was not in the cards for the Nez Perce. On October 5, 1877, they were trapped by an early winter storm in a valley in the Bear Paw Mountains of northern Montana. Surrounded by his people, starving, diseased, and freezing to death, Chief Joseph surrendered to General Nelson Miles.

He closed his famous surrender speech by saying, "Hear me, my chiefs! I am tired. My heart is sick and sad. From where the sun now stands, I will fight no more forever."

General Miles promised they would be allowed to return to their homeland. That promise was never kept. Instead the Nez Perce were herded to an Oklahoma reservation, far from their ancestral lands in northeastern Oregon, from where they had earlier been forcibly removed by the US government to make room for white settlers.

In Oklahoma many more of his people died in squalid conditions rampant with disease. Chief Joseph died on September 21, 1904, aged sixty-four, on the Colville Indian Reservation in Washington, never having been allowed to return to his ancestral home.

In 1887 the US government passed the Dawes Act, also known as the General Allotment Act, an effort to assimilate Indians into mainstream American society, to end the ownership of tribal property, and to put an end to Indian government. The "indian land," according to the act, was to be divvied up for use by individuals and not their tribes. By accepting an allotment of land, an individual also agreed to live apart from the tribe and would then be eligible for United States citizenship. The Dawes Act was a continuance of the widespread federal practice of what was popularly and piously referred to as "killing the Indian to save the man."

The obvious subtext was that Indians were regarded as little more than uncivilized savages who, for their own good, should no longer be allowed to be part of their tribes, practice their native forms of religion, or speak their native languages. Rather they should be taught how to be "American" by learning such occupations as farming.

Critics of the plan pointed out its flaws, to little avail. One such outspoken voice, Colorado Senator Henry M. Teller, said in 1881 that the underlying motive of the allotment plan was "to get at the Indian lands and open them up to settlement. The provisions for the apparent benefit of the Indians are but the pretext to get at his lands and occupy them. . . . If this were done in the name of Greed, it would be bad enough; but to do it in the name of Humanity . . . is infinitely worse."

From owning 150 million acres in 1880, native-owned land reduced to seventy-eight million acres by the turn of the century. Common notice boards read: "Indian Land for Sale: Get a home of your own; Easy payments; Perfect title; Possession within thirty days; Fine lands in the West; irrigated, irrigable, grazing, agricultural, dry farming."

On behalf of the Dawes Act, a meeting was held at the Standing Rock Indian Reservation on August 22, 1883. Revered Hunkpapa Lakota Chief Sitting Bull was verbally attacked by Senator John Logan of Illinois:

> *I want to say that further you are not a great chief of this country. That you have no following, no power, no control. You are on an Indian reservation merely at the sufferance of the government. You are fed by the government, clothed by the government, your children are educated by the government, and all you have and are today is because of the government. If it were not for the government, you would be freezing and starving today in the mountains. I merely say these things to notify you that you cannot insult the people of the United States of America or its committees . . . the government feeds and clothes and educates your children now, and desires to teach you to become farmers, and to civilize you, and make you as white men.*

Assimilation, it seems, was the means and the end, a way to eradicate the culture of Native Americans and replace it with something whites found less threatening. The government's steps toward assimilation were broad and unflinching. In the latter decades of the nineteenth century, Indian children ages four and up were removed without permission from their parents' homes on reservations and forced to attend federally run boarding schools so that they might assimilate into white society. They were not allowed to dress as Indians, wear their hair as Indians, or speak in their native languages, and if they did, they received beatings.

Given no alternative, these young, impressionable people gave in and became, for all intents and purposes, whites—though they were never allowed by whites to forget they were most definitely not white. Nor, as they were reminded when they returned to their families, were they quite Indians.

On the cold morning of December 29, 1890, the Lakota Sioux were already reduced to a state of near starvation on a paltry, windblown patch of land at Wounded Knee Creek, on the Lakota Pine Ridge Indian Reservation, South Dakota. A deaf warrior, Black Coyote, was told by US Army troops to give up his rifle, but he refused, saying he paid much for it and should be compensated for its value. A scuffle resulted in a single fired shot.

That act of weary defiance triggered a terrible overreaction among the assembled soldiers. Five hundred US troops opened fire with four Hotchkiss revolving-barrel guns. Most of the Sioux had already been disarmed. The rest were women, children, and the elderly.

The soldiers rampaged for an hour, massacring without discrimination. More than two hundred Lakota Sioux were killed (some historians claim the number is closer to three hundred) and fifty-one wounded, to the army's twenty-five dead and thirty-nine wounded. Many soldiers were shot by friendly fire by their fellows manning the blazing fifty-five-round-per-minute Hotchkiss guns.

In desperation, women and children fled on foot across the snowy wastes. They were hunted down by mounted officers and killed. Others died of hypothermia. Three days after the slaughter, ten surviving Indians were discovered, among them four babies found beneath their mothers' dead bodies.

The commanding officer, Colonel Forsyth, was initially denounced and relieved of his command, though later an Army Court of Inquiry exonerated him. Eventually he was promoted to the rank of major general. Twenty of his soldiers were awarded the Medal of Honor for their participation in the Wounded Knee Massacre, regarded as the last major conflict of the Indian Wars.

Instances such as the above merely scratch the surface of a long and unfortunate history of mistreatment by a powerful force of a smaller and weaker force, a group that deserved far more compassion than it received. As Henry Wadsworth Longfellow wrote of Native Americans years before he penned his famous epic poem *The Song of Hiawatha*, "It appears . . . that they are a race possessing magnanimity, generosity, benevolence, and pure religion without hypocrisy. They have been most barbarously treated by the whites both in word and deed."

Once a renowned Indian fighter, William "Buffalo Bill" Cody over time developed a deep, thoughtful understanding of the Native American plight. He was friend and employer of many Indians and spoke eloquently on behalf of Native American issues, once famously saying, "Every Indian outbreak that I have ever known has resulted from broken promises and broken treaties by the government."

Oglala Lakota Chief Mahpina Luta, more commonly known as Chief Red Cloud, similarly said, "They made us many promises, more than I can remember. But they kept but one; they promised to take our land, and they took it."

He also said, "Look at me: I am poor and naked, but I am the chief of the nation. We do not want riches, but we want to train our children right. Riches will do us no good. We could not take them with us to the other world. We do not want riches. We want peace and love."

CHAPTER 12

AL SWEARENGEN
DEADWOOD'S DEADBEAT

The swarthy-featured man curled a thick finger around his cigar and drew on it deeply, then breathed out. Blue smoke coiled upward like a hypnotized serpent, and a low purr rumbled in his throat as he read the letter.

Dear Mr. Swearengen: I am writing to thank you. Your letter of March the first was most promising and I am in receipt of the one-way ticket you sent post-haste to me in response to my inquiry. As you say, the fact that I was able to send a daguerreotype portrait of myself helped you to make up your mind without having to wait to see me on your next business trip back East. I am indebted to you and thankful for your faith in me, with so little to go on.

As I mentioned in my previous letter, I am a singer and actress by design and study, and an assistant seamstress by occupation at present. Your faith in me has made all the difference and I am confident that you will not be disappointed in my abilities when we finally meet. I expect to board the Westbound train, then, per your instructions make my way to Deadwood by stage. Not having traveled such distances in the past, I can only hazard a guess as to the length of time it should take me to arrive in Deadwood, but you can rest assured I will do everything in my power to ensure I arrive in as quick a fashion as I am able. In the meantime, I am nearly through with wrapping up my affairs here in Boston. I have quit my job (gladly!) as assistant to the seamstress I mentioned, and I have redoubled my practices involving the vocal arts.

I am confident that you will find your time, money, and efforts have not been wasted on me, Mr. Swearengen. I remain faithfully yours. We shall meet soon (not soon enough for this budding young star of the stage!)

Kind Regards,
Miss Tessa Smithroy
Boston, Massachusetts

Al Swearengen, owner of the Gem Variety Theater in Deadwood, South Dakota, set down the letter on his cluttered desk and snorted back a laugh as he prodded the papers on his desktop. After a few moments he found what he was looking for and held up the daguerreotype. His eyebrows rose at the letter, its tone, its hopefulness. Would they never learn? He laughed again and stared at the girl. He remembered her now, the wide mouth, the high forehead, full cheeks. Baby fat, some of the men liked that, but working here would toughen her up, lean her down. Give her that driven edge he preferred, that hungry look that told him and them that he was the boss and that they never would be.

"Can't be too soon," he said, tossing the image on his desk, leaning back in his chair, puffing on his cigar. He mused on the fact that he lost another girl the day before. Like this one, she'd been a plump young thing when she arrived two years earlier. Or was it three? Hardly mattered. She was dead, couldn't handle her liquor, her laudanum. Tried to make off with that big, dim-witted Swede whose claim would never pay off because Al sold him the worthless gravel cutbank himself.

Not for the last time that day, Al Swearengen closed his eyes and sighed. Owning the Gem was a bittersweet deal, to be sure. But with a moneymaking place like this, he had little to complain about.

"Who's that?" Swearengen nodded toward the front of the bar, by the front door.

His barkeep looked up briefly. "Said she was hired by you, come all the way out from the East. Said you would know her, said you sent for her."

"She said all that, did she?"

Bartender shrugged. "She's a chatty thing. Like all the rest of 'em, you know."

"Yeah, I know. I know."

He approached her and pasted on his widest smile.

She still stood by the door, clutching a small handbag to her belly as if it were a baby. Beside her feet sat a heavy-looking carpetbag.

As he drew closer he inspected her face. She must be the one who'd sent the photograph. Not bad, not bad. Aside from the fact that she looked about ready to cry. She was a bit wide in the hips, though some of that had to be that god-awful coat she wore. "Swearengen's the name. And you are?"

Relief crept onto her features. "You're Mr. Swearengen?"

"Yes," he said, still smiling. "You look disappointed."

"Oh, no, no," she said, shaking his proffered hand. "Only I was, or rather I am just a little taken aback. . . ."

"Oh? By what?" still smiling.

"Well, I hate to be rude," she said.

"But . . . ?" still smiling, though barely now.

"I had expected the Gem Variety Theater, that is to say, it somehow seemed different, perhaps."

"Oh, don't let the looks of it fool you. This place is the fanciest in the region. Why, we're practically the only place worth visiting anywhere in these parts."

"But the entertainment . . ."

"Ah yes, you're a singer, correct?"

"Yes, I sing and act. And I have been working hard to learn the rudiments of dancing."

"Now that very fact right there, little lady, does my heart good to hear. You see, as it happens, I have need of a dancer at present. That will no doubt lead to other opportunities for you. But to begin with, I think I'll have Missy here show you around," he nodded to a haggard-looking woman who had just entered carrying a galvanized bucket with wet rags draped along the edge.

"Missy, come over here."

The woman did as she was bade. As she came closer, the new girl's eyes widened and she drew in a sharp breath, realized how rude she'd been, and apologized.

"No need to," he said. "Missy here's a clumsy thing, always walking into posts, doors, falling down and hurting herself. She wasn't much to look at to begin with, and I'm afraid now that's she's taken to the sauce, she's a harder-looking thing than ever. I'm not sure what we'll do with her." He turned to the new girl. "She started out as a singer, too. Ended up a dancer, though. Seems like all the girls do, eventually. Right now though, what I really need is some-one to help Missy deal with the rooms, keep up with the dirty glassware and cutlery, the crockery and so forth. And help cook for the rest of the sows."

There was a long pause, during which Swearengen let his gaze rest on the girl's face, daring her to utter protest. He knew she would. And she did.

"But Mr. Swearengen. I was hired as an entertainer. You promised in your letter that I would be a performer."

"Yes," he said, slowly nodding in agreement. "And a performer you shall be. That's the word for it, all right. And I do have need of someone who can dance, yes. But around here we all pitch in, do what needs to be done. Isn't that right, Missy?"

Not much to his surprise, the new girl stared at him, then thrust out her bottom jaw. "Mr. Swearengen, I very much regret to inform you that I feel your end of this bargain between us was not as I had been led to believe."

"Oh?" he said, looking at the girl, then at Missy, who continued looking down at the floor, the half-filled bucket of brown water and rags swinging pendulously from her bony arm.

"Well, I am distressed, naturally, to hear you say that, girly. But then of course as it was a legitimate business deal, I will have to insist on full compensation for my expenses laid out on your behalf." He leaned forward and said, "In full."

And as he expected, the girl's bold chin wavered, a slight tremble set in, and he knew he had her.

"Mr. Swearengen," she said in a slightly quieter voice. Her eyes looked down briefly, then met his again. "I don't have the funds at present to repay the cost of your ticket."

"Plus my time, effort, the housing, the room we have made in our schedule. . . . Oh, the expenses," he said, raising his hands and letting them drop as if in frustration, shaking his head to add to the effect and to hide his smirk. God, but this was fun.

"Mr. Swearengen. I am a capable seamstress. I can find employment here in Deadwood and repay you with all haste."

He shook his head. "The deal, girly, was for you to work for the Gem Variety Theater, providing entertainment and other duties as required. I assume you recall that from our correspondence?"

She slowly shook her head, made as if to speak, but he stepped in and grabbed her stiff arm, drew her to him, close and tight. She smelled good, like lavender, he thought. "If you do not do as I say, I will have you arrested and

Al Swearengen (believed to be the man in the buggy to the left), proprietor of Deadwood's famed Gem Variety Theater (pictured here in 1878), lied to dewy-eyed young women, luring them to Deadwood with promises of good-paying jobs as legitimate entertainers at the Gem. They didn't know they would soon become diseased, drug-addicted prostitutes with short life expectancies. *Courtesy Deadwood History, Adams Museum Collection, Deadwood, SD.*

thrown in jail. For as long as I like, is that understood little girl? You may then do all the singing you like from your cell. And we all know that caged birds sing a sad, sad song, now don't they?" His voice was like a long, low purr. He knew it and he worked it straight into her ear.

"Have I ever asked you for anything? Hmm? Have I?" The man's thick-fingered hand lashed out as if it were held back by a spring-loaded mechanism. It struck the crying woman's puffed, bruised cheek high, his diamond ring gouged a furrow across her cheek, stopping just beneath her eye.

Her head whipped backward and she lost her balance, fell into a squat chest of drawers that caught her in the lower back. She spun around once and landed on her face on the floor at the man's feet. She lay there, stunned, sucking in stuttering breaths through split lips and a new bloody gap where minutes before there had been a tooth.

"I don't ever ask anything of any of you filthy cows, do I? No, and do you know why? Because you have nothing I want or need, at least nothing that can't be easily replaced. Why in hell don't you just up and die so I can work on getting my money's worth out of some other sow in my stable?"

"But . . . but Al, what did I do? You didn't tell me what I did?"

Swearengen swigged from a nearly empty bottle of Cutter's Rye on the bedside table. The fiery liquid stung his throat, the warmth spread in him. Maybe he should have knocked back a few swallows before letting the woman speak. Lord knows he shouldn't keep on belting them . . . bad for business.

He sighed. "Listen, Tina. . . ."

"I'm Tessa," she said in a small voice, barley a squeaking whisper. He glanced at her, saw her eyelids flutter, her bleeding mouth go slack as she passed out.

He saw red, could only think of the wages this mouthy little hussy lost him the night before. He tamped down the anger, breathed deep once more. Had to hand it to the girl, she was tougher than most. Most of the girls in his employ wouldn't dare talk back to him. Some did, but he let them get away with it—to a point. They were the ones who still had a little something to offer him. The ones who hadn't let the opium or the morphine get to them . . . yet. But it would happen eventually. Always did.

This one, she still had spirit, even though she had no right to.

Three months later, Swearengen stood inside a dingy little room staring down at the dead woman, an empty laudanum bottle on the bed beside her. The drugs had leeched from her anything of promise she once had to offer. Which one was she? Tina? Yes, maybe that was it. Close enough, he thought. Not like it matters now. He looked at her face again, thought he could see what she had been.

A soft knock on the door pulled him back to the present. Here we go, he thought. Time for the waterworks.

Two girls filed in, hesitantly. Others hovered outside the open door, peering in through dark-ringed eyes.

"What was her name?" whispered a new girl.

"Tina," said Swearengen, turning from the room.

Beatrice, the girl with the least to lose, said, "Tessa. Her name was Tessa."

Swearengen stopped in the doorway, felt that fire tighten his neck muscles, bunch his cheeks. Through gritted teeth he said, "Tina. And that's final." He headed downstairs to the bar for a drink. He'd rather listen to the foolish blather of his barkeeps and the miners who did more drinking than digging. At least they weren't women.

As he stomped down the last few steps, he tugged on his braces and finished buttoning his fly. He paused on the last landing, surveyed the smoky, dark room below. What light shafted in through the few front windows floated with dust motes.

His heavy-lidded gaze came to rest on a tall, thin figure in a high-crown fawn hat standing at the bar, one elbow propped on the stained surface, a small coffee cup tweezered between two fingers. The cup was halfway to the man's mouth when he spied Swearengen looking at him.

"Why, good morning to you, Al," said the tall man, smiling.

Swearengen groaned audibly. He continued his way down the steps. "Bullock. I might've known only someone as depressingly happy as you would show up on a morning like this. What's a marshal doing here this time of day? Too early for complaints of bar fights."

The lawman lost his smile. "I've heard tell another of your girls has passed over to the other side, as they say."

"Not that anything that happens here is any of your business, but what's it to you if nature claims back her own now and again, Bullock?"

"I take it from your response that it's true. And I haven't got a thing against nature's ways—if they are caused naturally, that is. What I do have a problem with is the fact that so many of your . . . employees seem to be women of a poorly constitution. They don't start out that way, mind you. But most of 'em end up poorly not long after they arrive, and that's something you can't much argue."

Swearengen rapped knuckles on the bar, stood ten feet down the bar from Bullock. "Pete, give me a cup of coffee. Don't bother freshening the marshal's here. He was just leaving."

"You're right on that score, Swearengen. Tell me, what was her name?"

The proprietor of the Gem Variety Theater sipped his coffee, stared at himself in the mirror-backed bar. "I don't recall."

Al Swearengen was a rascal of the highest order and a man deserving little more than scorn. As seen through the long lens of historical observation, the rapacious rapscallion, the thieving brute, the lying huckster epitomized the worst traits of the frontier opportunist. He chose pimp as one of several means of moneymaking, capitalizing on the misfortunes of others. While prostitution was a perfectly legal way to make money back in the Old West, the manner in which he procured his employees was not only illegal but immoral.

Swearengen knew the real money in such an establishment as the Gem Variety Theater came in the form of whiskey, gambling, and women. And not in that order. So he devised elaborate and alluring fantasies, promising young girls back East that they would become famous performers. They would practice their craft, he told them, on the stage of a famous theater in the heart of one of the most promising and bustling burgs in all of the frontier. And at its prime the Gem truly was an impressive establishment—twice rebuilt following fires, the last time in 1879, it lasted for the next twenty years as a three-story theater, gambling den, bordello, drinking and dining establishment, and more.

But to fill out his "stable of girls," Swearengen intentionally duped dewy-eyed young women, lied to them, lured them to his domain under false pretenses, then made their lives hell. He forced them into indebtedness and servitude, and worst of all, he plied them with addictive drugs that sapped them of their strength, their health, and, when they were little more than diseased wastrels, their lives. If they displeased him, Swearengen and his thugs beat the women, sometimes to death, then covered up the crimes.

But evil, as the old saying goes, will out. And in Swearengen's case, this Deadwood pioneer ended his days himself the victim of a murder. He was found dead, having been clubbed in the head, on a Denver street on November 15, 1904. (A popular but erroneous account of his death has him missing his mark as he tried to hop a freight train.)

Another similarly slimy character who seemed to have studied the Swearengen playbook was Charles "Big Time Charlie" Allen, who breezed into Denver in 1916 and commenced operation of the biggest prostitution ring in the city's history. Big Time Charlie was a larger-than-life character who liked to hear himself talk, and puffed up his past with tales of big strikes in Alaska and battles alongside Pancho Villa way down in old Mexico.

If you were a woman in his employ, however, life was anything but a fun-filled adventure. Charlie got his painted ladies, who numbered in the hundreds, addicted to opium and heroin, then kept them in his employ by taking all their wages and paying them in dope. This tactic made him a millionaire, and the kickbacks and hush money he paid to city officials kept the shady business running for years.

But greed got Charlie in the end. The prostitution biz wasn't enough for Big Time, so he began selling drugs to the citizenry. Raids followed, his various businesses were closed down, and Big Time Charlie Allen headed to Leavenworth for five years to think up new lies and schemes.

In the gold rush days of the Old West, venues of accommodation were often rather funky affairs, more suitable digs for the high numbers of rats that lived in them than the miners themselves. They could be built of brick, timber, or stone, but more often than not they were hastily erected affairs of canvas, sometimes with dirt floors, and occasionally they were caves dug out of crumbling hillsides.

Such temporary abodes also became home to spiders, scorpions, lizards, and snakes, and these uninvited interlopers could be surly at times about who they shared their newfound spot with. Stories abound of miners being bitten by such critters, though there were far more reports of hardworking rock hounds becoming infested with lice, chiggers, and fleas when they bedded down in frontier hotels.

But such critters were hardly the sort to operate out of any malicious intent. Not so with the numerous nefarious hoteliers who set up shop either with the intent to roll their boozy guests or who developed a taste for such lowdown thievery as opportunities presented themselves.

There were numerous ways conniving innkeepers hustled their customers: cramming them into large rooms with nothing but chalk outlines on the floor delineating one's rented sleeping space, and bunk beds many layers tall that allowed for little room between berths. Those men lucky enough to garner the top spot in such flimsily constructed affairs were able to avoid the showers of chaw spittle that rained down on their lower-level fellows. The floors of such places ran thick with brown drool from the tobacco habits of scores of rough, unwashed, drunken men crowded, spitting, and getting little sleep in such tight quarters.

Consider the person of one Clifton Hotchkiss, a man who took to the hotel trade late in life. He'd spent a good deal of his gravy years as a magician's assistant and had little luck as a prospector himself. As proprietor of a boarding house located near Sonora, New Mexico, he was finding that innkeeping was not much more lucrative than grubbing in the desert for sign of gold. But he did have a cat for company. And rumor has it that during his days as a lackey for the circus magician, Hotchkiss learned a thing or two about hypnotic suggestion.

One day while looking into his cat's eyes and relating his various miseries to the only creature in the world who seemed willing to listen, Hotchkiss allegedly became mesmerized by the creature's mysterious, trance-inducing eyes. When he snapped out of his brief reverie, the buddings of a new business came to him.

He figured he could fall back on his old circus skills and induce hypnotic trances in his guests. Only those with the fattest pokes would be the lucky recipients of the squirrelly landlord's odd attentions. And it worked! He was able, over several years, to hypnotize a number of his lodgers and relieve them of their hard-won dust, nuggets, and various other valuables.

Eventually his beloved cat was eaten by a mountain lion, and not long after, Hotchkiss was thrown from a horse. Paralyzed and unable to care for himself, he spent what remained of his days as a patient in a San Francisco hospital.

But he was not the only creative caretaker in the wild and woolly days of the hospitality trade on the frontier. An exemplar of frontier felony, Conrad "Happy" Horlick, much like Hotchkiss, employed the abilities of another creature most ubiquitous on the frontier. His critter-in-crime was a packrat who lived in his establishment. Sensing a fellow thief, Horlick was able to parlay the rat's need for collecting shiny tokens into a profitable sideline, all the while keeping himself a safe distance from the actual act of thievery. Each night the packrat, which Horlick had nicknamed King, made the rounds of the flophouse floor, scavenging items such as rings, pocket watches, knives, coins, small pokes of gold dust, and more. Horlick periodically relieved the rat's nest of the choicest items and over years amassed quite a haul for himself.

CHAPTER 13

PEGLEG SMITH
KING OF ALL LIARS

If ever there was a man most deserving of the appellation "swindler," it was Thomas L. "Pegleg" Smith. Although he wouldn't hit his swindling stride until adulthood, even from his humble beginnings Smith's life is a well-documented and storied series of classic early-West experiences. Born in Crab Orchard, Kentucky, on October 10, 1801, he longed for a life of adventure from an early age. As a teenager Smith ran away from home and hopped a flatboat on the Mississippi River. When the boat reached St. Louis, Missouri, the fabled jumping-off place for all points west, young Smith landed a job as a genuine mountain man, trapping fur in the Rockies alongside such now-famous men as Kit Carson and Jim Bridger.

Years later, while out scouting for Alexander Le Grand's expedition in New Mexico Territory, Smith gained the reason for his colorful nickname. In a skirmish with Indians, Smith was shot below the right knee, necessitating the amputation of that portion of his leg. In some stories he claims to have performed the operation himself with a knife. As he was with fellow trappers, it's unlikely—but highly entertaining.

Tall tales aside, Pegleg Smith was not above breaking laws, moral or man-made, as when in the 1840s, he found a brisk trade in kidnapping Indian children, then selling them to wealthy Mexicans as slaves. Finally, facing increasing danger from Indians who were hunting him, Pegleg joined forces with a couple of his trapping chums, Jim Beckwourth and Bill Williams, and for a decade operated what was considered the largest horse-rustling ring in the entire Southwest. One memorable run had Pegleg leading 150 Ute Indians over the Sierra Nevada, wrangling hundreds of horses they stole from Mexican ranches.

But it is his prospecting ventures in one of several regions, including the Santa Rose Mountains and the Borrego Badlands, where he claimed to have discovered a vast, rich deposit of gold-bearing quartz. . . .

On a warm spring day in the late 1840s, in a craggy wash in the Borrego Desert, Smith wandered alone with his horse and burro, farther and farther

In his 65 years, Thomas "Pegleg" Smith told a lot of windy stories to a lot of gullible people. He also sold them maps and claim shares to his "Lost Pegleg Mine," even though it likely never existed. Each year in April, people gather at the Pegleg Smith Memorial in Borrego Springs, California, to spin tall tales in the Pegleg Smith Liars Contest.   *Photo by Jennifer Smith-Mayo, 2014.*

into the bleak country, yearning for a pull on his canteen but pacing himself, knowing he had at least another hour to go before he could indulge in a sip. He traveled slowly, stumping along on one good leg and one wooden leg, leading the animals and eyeballing an outcropping of quartz for sign of color.

And by gum, wasn't that just what he found himself looking at? More promising quartz he'd never seen. Struck through with the telltale dull coloring of raw gold ore, or he wasn't Pegleg Smith! And all around him, scattered like they'd been tossed by some giant baby, lay curious little black nuggets that for some reason he just couldn't ignore. He'd been stuffing them into his pockets and possibles bag, something in the back of his mind telling him they were more than they appeared to be. But what? High-grade ore, dare he hope?

Then he stopped short and dropped low—the tough old cob of an Indian fighter felt something whistle by, feather soft but too close. He knew just what it was. An arrow, and the only thing that let loose with an arrow at another man was an Indian. All this he deduced in the time it took him to pull in a sharp breath and hold it.

Instead of whipping upright to scout for the offending sender of the arrow, Smith dropped to his knees, his wooden peg leg scraping and clunking the rock he'd been inspecting for sign of gold.

And just when he'd found it, the Indian had found him. Smith clawed at his old cap-and-ball pistol, his preferred weapon of choice and damned dependable in a pinch. He low-crawled a half-dozen feet downslope, in part to check on his horse and burro. Yep, the horse stood quietly, head down, nosing for a snack and coming up empty. And the burro, that ornery beast, stood flicking an ear and looking about ready to doze off and fall over, oblivious to the fact that an Indian attack was in the offing.

Pegleg also low-crawled to keep himself from being punctured and looking like a buckskin-covered pin cushion. When he figured he'd gone far enough, he risked a glance up over the shelf of rock that had partially protected him. His new position had not been suspected, so he was able to see four men—Apache, by the looks of them—loping low and steady away from where the arrow had come. So there were at least four of them.

He leaned back and thought of his canteen longingly. He was panting hard and didn't like the feeling one bit, priding himself as he did on rarely exerting himself in such a manner. But then again, it had been a while since he'd been shot at. There was nothing for it—too many of them. He'd have to wait them out.

After a while of stewing in the heat, he realized he had one piece of luck in his favor. A short scramble down a knobby, twenty-foot declivity stood the horse and burro. If he could make it down to the beasts, he might be able to sneak on out of there and put ground between himself and the Apaches—enough so that he might live to come back to that promising outcropping another day.

This was not the first time he had been attacked by local tribesmen. But as much as it pained him to admit it, it would be the last—at least for a while. He had to get on out of there, get back to civilization, and find out if these peculiar black nuggets were really the high-grade ore he suspected they were. He'd be back, he swore it to himself as he grunted his way downward.

And as he finally made his way, none too quietly, back down the odd escarpment to his waiting beasts, Pegleg Smith kept glancing back at the rocky terrain above and beyond him. He wanted to avoid being sneaked up on by a bloodthirsty Apache. He scrambled down the last bit and hoisted himself into the saddle, awkward as ever, in part due to his wooden pin, in part due to his paunch. Then he rode away at the fastest clip he could muster, glancing back to emblazon in his mind the exact spot of what he was sure was the find of his life. The one he'd been searching for all along. And now, thanks to the dang Apaches, he had to leave it. Not fair.

As he rode he spied arms, heads, then men waving, shouting at him from the rocky ridgeline. He was still close enough to see they were drawing back on their bows. Pegleg urged the horse into an all-out gallop back toward civilization, the burro working its little legs double-time to the horse's, but keeping up, nonetheless.

Getting run off by the Apaches might not be fair, but it sure as hell was fun. And good to be alive! He'd be back . . . back with a vengeance. But just now, he couldn't wait to hit a saloon—no one was going to believe this story.

"The information I'm about to tell you is something we need to keep betwixt you and me, you understand?" The chubby prospector winked but didn't smile.

"I beg your pardon," said the young man to whom the prospector spoke. "I never asked you for any advice."

"Not the point, fella," said the first. "I'm offering it. And what's more, I'm offering something you will never hear again from another of the likes of me."

The man looked the fat man up and down. "I certainly hope not."

"Judge me if you will, but I'm not going to let the matter drop that easy. I'm here to offer you untold wonders that wealth will bring."

"Wealth, you say?"

That seemed to trip some switch, as if the prospector had known just how to make the man's eyebrows arch.

The brief moment of surprise popped like a soap bubble with the slamming on the bar top of an empty beer glass. "Pegleg, knock it off, huh? I warned you yesterday and the day before that."

"Aww, Ned, you know I don't recall such things. After all, I'm a wounded man. And here I've got a business transaction in the offing!"

"No you don't, Pegleg. You have one minute to drag your sorry hide out of my bar."

The chubby prospector glared for long moments at the barkeep, who returned the hard look, his bent nose and bunched cheek muscles adding menace, until Pegleg had to look away. His gaze lightly raked the stunned newcomer he'd been chatting up. Then the prospector slid off the barstool, planted his foot, and winced as he set his other leg down. It was then that the newcomer noticed the man he'd been talking to had a peg leg. He'd thought the bartender was just being cruel. But no, this man was truly missing a limb.

Pegleg leaned briefly on the barstool, then glanced again at the bartender, who shook his head and jerked his chin toward the door. The gimpy prospector stumped his way to the batwings, and just before he shoved through them to the hot afternoon outside, he looked back and said, "See you tomorrow, Ned."

The bartender had resumed wiping the bar top and without looking up said, "Same time, same place, Pegleg."

The newcomer was stunned. "What might I ask was that all about?"

The bartender smiled, finished wiping the length of the bar top, then walked slowly back, folding the rag. "Can I get you another?"

"Sure," nodded the visitor, hoping that a second beer would help the bartender come out with the story.

"That man," said the barkeep once he'd set the freshly filled glass down in front of him, "was Pegleg Smith, the one and only."

"Should I know who he is?"

"Not if you aren't from this town or haven't been taken for a ride by him before."

"How's that?" said the man, sipping the cool beer. It was a welcome sensation on such a hot day in this tiny dust-choked California town.

"You know," said the barkeep, "you should be thanking me." He said it with a grin, but the newcomer felt there was a ring of truth in it. "You see, he was about to put the touch on you."

"The touch?"

"Yep. He owns a mine and he was about to sell you shares in it."

"How is that putting the touch on me? In fact, how do you know that what he was about to offer isn't just what I came out west for? It's why I left my job as a journalist back in Boston! Why, you might have ruined my very first opportunity to get in on the ground floor of something I've been searching for."

"Oh? Tell me, what is that?"

"It's a career in the mining industry."

"And you figure this is the place to do that, eh, friend?"

"Yes, it surely is," he said, sipping the beer.

"Tell me, if it's so easy to strike it rich out here, how come it is that I'm tendin' bar?"

"Well . . . but you own your own establishment, right?"

The barkeep laughed, nodded. "Yeah, it's a real daisy, this place. And tell me this, if Pegleg's mine is so valuable, why does he look like he's been rode hard and put up wet?"

"I don't follow you."

The barkeep sighed. "I'm telling you that while Pegleg Smith might or might not have a claim somewhere, the thing ain't paying much. If it was, he'd not want to fracture it by selling it off piecemeal to every stranger and drifter who's unlucky enough to wander into this two-bit town."

The newcomer sipped his beer. "As bad as all that, eh?"

"As far as I know . . . yep. Heck, he hasn't paid for a beer in months. I feed him one a day, if I'm feeling generous. Other than that, I'll tolerate him, but I'm tired of him peddling his tall tales of fabulous wealth in here. Seen too many innocent, dewy-eyed folks get the touch put on 'em."

The newcomer mulled this over while the barkeep wandered off to the other end of the bar to serve a dusty cowpoke. The man had taken off his tall-crowned hat and set it on the bar top, exchanged a few words with the bartender. It appeared they knew each other. Then they both looked down the bar at him.

He looked down at his beer and felt his cheeks redden. Damn, he hated to be humiliated. Was this what the West was all about? People doing their best to embarrass you? To gouge you? To cheat and steal from you? He thought he'd outrun that back East when he left Boston.

He looked up to see the bartender and the cowboy both smiling and sidling down the long length of the bar toward him.

"Say, tell me this story ain't true and I'll listen to what you have to say."

Pegleg jutted his stubbly chin and scratched a moment, considering the proposition. "Seems like I can't lose with a suggestion such as that, now can I?"

"I reckon not."

"What is it you wanted to know?"

"I heard that at one time you used to steal Indian children, then sell them south of the border. That can't be so, can it?"

To the young man's surprise, the man called Pegleg let out a sharp bark of a laugh, smacked his twill trousers, releasing a cloud of dust that he didn't even seem to notice. His mouth had split into a smile, cracking his round bearded face. "Why, boy, that is about the most funny thing I've heard all week. No, no, all month!" He wagged his shaggy head. "Yep, I do believe you've been talking to folks who are plumb jealous of me, yes, you have, and all my successes in life. You see . . .," he leaned forward then, all trace of mirth vanished. "You are young and not so used to the finicky ways of the world as I am, because I have lived longer than you. I will say that I have also lived more dangerously and more thrillingly than any man you are likely to meet." He leaned back as if he'd just revealed an amazing truth, and nodded as if that was all there was to say on the topic.

The young man sat still a moment, regarding Pegleg. Finally he said, "I do believe I am beginning to understand what it is you are all about, Mr. Smith."

"Oh, and what's that, young man?"

"You are everything people have said, and more. Much more."

"How's that?"

"I was warned if there was a question you weren't inclined to answer that you would talk circles around it until the person asking the question was addled and befuddled."

"And are you befuddled, boy?" Pegleg laughed again, leaned back, quaffed a couple of sips of the warming brew on the bar top beside his elbow, and considered a moment. "I'm not quite sure how to take these bold accusations, young man. On the one hand, you seem to have made up your mind about me, and that without having heard my entire life's story—which I daresay will take considerably more than a glass of beer to get through. It's dry work, I tell you. Dry work."

"What's the other hand?" said the young man.

"Huh? Oh, yes, ah, well, I'm a more complicated character than you will give me credit for, no doubt."

"Well, let's say we start at the beginning, then, Mr. Smith."

"Well now, could be I'd be up for such a session of jawbonin' and chinwaggin', provided the person doing the listening was . . ." He hoisted his glass and the young man saw the reedy old throat work back the last of the beer. "Provided," he said through a thunderous belch that brought a smile to his face and headshakes from a few folks seated nearby. "The man doing the listening was also doing the buying."

The young man smiled and nodded. "I'm buying."

"Good. Then let's get started." Pegleg rapped his knuckles on the bar top and beckoned Ned.

"Where should we start, sir?"

"Why, boy, you have to start where every good story starts . . . at the beginning! I was born at a very young age. . . ."

"How did you come by the name Pegleg, Mr. Smith?"

"Now how do you think I come by it? I can assure you it was honestly."

The bartender snorted. "That'd be about the only thing, eh Pegleg?"

"You hush up, Ned. I want any contributions from you, I'll tap your shoulder. Until then you just keep those opinions to yourself, you hear me? Now, where was I?"

"Your leg . . ." said the young man.

"Oh yes, 'the incident,' as I like to call it. You see, I was guiding for Le Grand, you heard of him? Alexander Le Grand's expedition? Yeah that one.

Oh, they were heady days for a youngish man," he winked. "First expedition to trap down around Santa Fe, and we made the most of it."

"Is that when you were injured?"

"I'm getting to that, I'm getting to that. Hold your peace, will you? My word, these younger generations sure are in a hurry. And if there's one thing I can't abide it's someone in a tizzy to get a story up and over with. Takes the steam out of a thing, if you know what I mean." He stopped and stared at the young man before continuing.

"Well sir, one day I was out rousting up them flat-tails along the Platte River when we come upon a passel of Injuns, I don't recall what stripe they was. Me and St. Vrain, that's who I was trapping with, surely you've heard of Ceran St. Vrain, hell of a man, not much of a gut for blood, but a decent sort, good in a pinch. Though in hindsight, maybe not that day. You see, we spooked one of those rascal savages and he opened fire on me. There I was, one second talking to St. Vrain—might be we were arguing about the best way to scent a beaver set, might be we was jawing about other things, I don't rightly recall—when all of a sudden I see a flash of something, that was the Injun, and smoke belched at me! Next thing I know I'm in a welter of blood and agony, rolling on the ground like a stuck pig, howling and wondering just what happened. Turns out the rascal shot my leg south of my knee and north of my ankle hinge.

"Well sir, I took a good long look at that mess that had been my leg and I said to St. Vrain and the others, I said, 'Boys, you got to cut it off. Else it will set to mortifying and I'll be dead in a day, maybe two.'"

The young man held his pencil poised above the half-filled page in his notebook. "What did you do then, Mr. Smith?"

"What could I do—lordy but this is thirsty-making work." He made a face and stuck out his tongue as if it were somehow offending him.

The young man nodded to the barkeep, who had been slowly moving close and listening in on the mounting story. He fetched a beer.

"I couldn't raise hide nor hair of effort out of those lily-livered so-called friends of mine. Well, ol' Martin Sublette—you recall him, don't you? Well, Marty, he lent a hand. I'll admit he was less of a cringing babe than the rest. So I had them fetch me a butchering knife and I commenced to cut off my leg as neat as I could muster. I passed out twice, they revived me, and I set to work again. Blood was a-squirting everywhere, the bone kept poking at me, slowing my progress, but I got her cut clean through. Then we swaddled it up in fine shape and I set to drinking to take the fiery edge off the situation. Now boy, you look plumb skeptical, but I tell you now that was the truth. But the deal was far from over. The boys finally lent a hand and yarned me overland to our winter hidey-hole along the Green River.

"Once she commenced to heal, she pained me something awful. I had to rub it with bear grease and a hot-tempered liniment just to keep it from waking me in the middle of the night with chills and howls. Finally I felt around there with my fingers and found I'd not gotten all the bones out of there, so Sublette grabbed hold of them with a bullet mold—don't tell me you don't know what that is—and tugged and dragged and nearly upended me, but we got 'em out. Course she commenced to bleed again.

"But my woman, a Flathead, with the finest set of . . . oh you never mind that now, she had her Injun ways and means and herbs and tinctures and she'd go out gathering roots and berries and leaves and grind 'em and heat 'em and mix 'em with this and that—family secrets you know—and soon enough I was on the way to healing once again. Finally, along about springtime, just in time to set to work again, I had carved a decent stomper for myself out of a length of firewood. Strapped it on and I never looked back. Even rigged up a special stirrup for my saddle, I did. Now, is that something that a man could just make up, I ask you? Naw, I'll answer for you, boy, naw, I say!"

"I heard you also, ah . . ."

"Out with it, boy. You won't get anywhere in life if you don't give full vent to your thoughts and opinions. If you can offend me, why I'll eat this here beaver hat." He thumped the battered topper resting like a lopsided old fungus atop his balding head.

"Okay then," the young journalist cleared his throat. Perhaps emboldened by the whiskey and his companion's increasingly chatty behavior, he asked the question he'd been dying to ask for hours. "I've heard you—remember you told me I could say anything to you, now!" He smirked and held up a finger in semi-comedic warning. "It's back to my question of earlier: I heard you stole children from Indians and sold them as slaves to Mexicans. And furthermore . . .," he quickly gulped down the last of the fiery whiskey. "I was also told that you have stolen more horses than any man alive."

"Well now," said Pegleg, puffing up and not looking offended in the least. "As to the latter accusation, I'll gladly admit that there is not, nor has been, nor ever will be a man who has liberated as many horses as the very man you are looking at right this minute, youngster!" He slapped a knobby hand on the bar top and fumbled for his nearly empty glass.

"And as to the former, all I can say is that the morals of the time made me do what I needed to do. Hell, that was the way of the world then. You do what you need to do. Don't make more or less of it than it needs. They were there and I was in need of money and that's the way it was. You got me? Business, it's all business. Like when a hungry wolf takes down a pretty young pronghorn. You don't cry and moan about it and say, 'Oh boy, that critter had such a long and lovely life ahead of it,' now do you? Aw, you don't neither. You say, 'Well at least that wolf had his belly filled and he'll be around for another sunrise.' That's the way of the world."

He slapped his hand on the bar top, thrust out his bottom lip. "Now, back to the matter of horse stealing—that's a serious accusation, mister. But one I am fully willing to admit to, and willing also to defend. You see, come 1840 or so, which is roundabout the time all this fancified horse thievery is said to have taken place, the hind end of the beaver-fur market dropped out from under all us so-called mountain men. We preferred to call ourselves mountainous men, by the way. So what was a man to do when the one thing he'd been good at, the one thing he'd been counting on doing for purposes of putting food in the mouths of his bairns and womenfolk, just dried up?"

The young reporter shook his head, knowing he was about to hear another prime justification of the swindling lifestyle. And also knowing that Smith knew that he knew.

"Why, a man had to do something to make a living. Man has to have a rhythm going in life, you know what I'm on about, pup?"

The young man looked at him, not at all sure what it was he was 'on about,' but nodded anyway.

Pegleg sighed and shook his head. "You don't have a notion at all as to what I'm yammering about. Why, I'm talking about this here," he grunted as he bent low and rapped knuckles on his wooden leg.

"I am afraid I will admit I don't understand what you're, as you say, on about." The young man hated to admit it, as he knew doing so would open him up to all manner of chatter for hours to come, but blast it, Pegleg Smith was so unnervingly engaging.

"I knew as much. When I talk about a rhythm, I mean with an ax as much as with anything in life. You take a man swinging an ax, see?" He paused, an expectant look on his lined, hairy face. "I was standing atop a long log one day, see? Swinging for all I was worth, doing what men with axes do to long logs—making them into smaller logs!" His laughter bubbled out of him, interrupted by a coughing spasm he quelled with a sip from his beer stein.

"But my rhythm was waylaid, see, by a rogue Indian, Paiute, I believe he was. He come out of nowhere, savaged me without even touching me! No sir, didn't use arrows nor spears, just his very appearance was enough to do it. Do what, you ask? Why, he threw off my rhythm! Lopped my own leg off quick as you can say 'Granny's got a secret'!"

This time Pegleg didn't laugh, just stared at the young man.

Finally, the young man spoke. "I had been under the impression that you lost it in a fight with Indians, yes, but they were Apache. And you had been shot by them, with a gun, I believe you said."

"I might have said that, yep. Then again, I might not have. Could be you're misremembering what I said."

And that is very close to how Thomas L. "Pegleg" Smith finished out his long, adventure-filled life—astride various bar stools in California, spinning outlandish windies and selling maps and shares to the Lost Pegleg Mine to fellow prospectors, or whoever was gullible enough to bite. He ended his days in 1866 in a hospital bed in San Francisco, stretching the truth like taffy to his end.

But his life and stories, real, imagined, or more likely a combination of both, have helped establish his reputation as a teller of tall tales, a master of hoax, and a swindler of the highest order. And it's a sure bet he wouldn't want it any other way.

Most people agree that Pegleg's stories of lost gold are more hoax than hard evidence. But there are a good many who feel certain the old fibber was nonetheless onto something with those little black nuggets he found somewhere in the Borrego Desert of Southern California in the 1840s.

It is curious that, in recent decades, a number of people who swear his stories were true, claim to have found significant and promising quartz deposits rich in gold ore . . . in the general vicinity of where Pegleg vowed his lost mine resided.

Still others claim that the Lost Pegleg Mine continues to remain lost because it never existed in the first place, unless you consider where it came from—Pegleg Smith's own mind.

Nowadays a whole lot of people gather every year on the first Saturday in April at the Pegleg Smith Memorial in Borrego Springs, California, to participate in the Pegleg Smith Liars Contest. Participants compete to see who can spin the tallest, most outrageous story involving lost gold, naturally.

CHAPTER 14

SHERIFF HENRY PLUMMER AND HIS GANG OF INNOCENTS

KILLERS AND THIEVES

A man set on filching from another would be hard-pressed to find a more forgiving or ideal setting than the old mine camps of the West. Often established hundreds of miles from civilization, law and order were in short supply (along with most everything else, from flour to liquor to women). These towns—their very appearance often stretched the definition of that word—were nonetheless peopled primarily with men hard at work pulling gold from the ground.

In a thousand mine camps throughout the West, hothouses of possibility all, outlawry thrived. Crimes ranged from the theft of a can of milk to wagon-loads of bullion rerouted into the pockets of masked road agents. One version of this last scenario is famous throughout the West for the unparalleled bold actions taken by both sides. The accused, a group of thieves living a lie among people who trusted them, and the accusers, a citizen-formed Committee of Vigilance like no other. And the cause of it all? A swindler by the name of Henry Plummer who flourished in the midst of it—for a short time, anyway. And he went about his swindling with a cunning not seen in the remote camps.

Plummer was a consumptive young man who headed west in 1852 from his family home in Addison, Maine. In a somewhat spotty career on the frontier, records show he killed four men—all allegedly in self-defense. One has to wonder what Plummer was doing each time to instigate such enmity. Was he an abrasive soul? Not according to the numerous people who signed petitions supporting his claim of self-defense each time it was said he should suffer for his killings.

Plummer had spent time in San Quentin Prison, less than six months of a ten-year sentence, for second-degree murder. He was given an early pass because his weak constitution led the prison physician to determine Plummer,

Henry Plummer was sheriff of Bannack, Montana, when he was hung on January 10, 1864, for being the ringleader of the very band of road agents he claimed he was tracking. The gang, calling itself "The Innocents," is said to have had roughly 100 members who stole hundreds of thousands of dollars, drygulching their friends and neighbors, holding up stagecoaches, and murdering 100 citizens in 1863-64. They were finally stopped by a group of frustrated citizens, the "Montana Vigilantes," who lynched nearly two dozen of the Innocents and ran others out of town. The Story of the Outlaw *by Emerson Hough, New York, The Outing Publishing Company, 1907.*

as a "lunger," a common term for someone suffering from tuberculosis, was "in imminent danger of death." Plummer also left behind a murder, several shootings, and hasty retreats from various towns he'd visited in his wide-ranging travels to the Nevada, Washington, and Idaho Territories.

Plummer and a friend, Jack Cleveland, made their way to Bannack, Montana, in the middle of the winter of 1863, when the town was still a snow-covered mudhole but offered the promise of rich diggings. The two men had been up by Fort Benton, both courting one Electra Bryan, the sister-in-law of the agent at the Indian Agency. She agreed to marry Plummer. They weren't in Bannack a month when Cleveland, in a jealous rage, provoked a gunfight. Plummer shot Cleveland dead. His claims of self-defense were backed up by the handful of people who witnessed the shooting.

But that wasn't good enough for Plummer, who secretly worried that while Cleveland lay dying he may have mumbled something incriminating to Bannack sheriff Hank Crawford. So Plummer decided to kill Crawford to prevent him from catching Plummer in a nefarious scheme he'd been cooking up, something to which only Cleveland had been privy. This created a tense situation that reached its zenith one day in early spring when Crawford and Plummer exchanged gunfire across the muddy street of Bannack.

This time, though, it was Plummer's turn to feel the sting of another man's bullet. The sheriff managed to shoot Plummer in the arm, but fearing the newcomer's obvious vindictive nature, Crawford skedaddled in the night, leaving behind the town and his post as sheriff.

As the hard winter broke into a muddy spring, miners straggled into town in droves. Among them were known nefarious sorts, outlaws such as Boone Helm, a beast infamous for slicing men apart with little provocation.

By May Plummer had ingratiated himself enough into the lives of the townsfolk that he was elected sheriff of Bannack. It's rumored that his physical appearance was pleasing to not a few ladies of the small town. A description of this mine-camp Romeo can be found in the clerk's admittance book at San Quentin, when he was booked there years before: "Henry Plummer: Maine; murder of second degree; age, 27; occupation, clerk; 5 foot, 8½ inches; light complexion; gray eyes; light brown hair."

Once installed as sheriff, Plummer began appointing deputies, including some of the aforementioned hard cases. These known vultures descended on gold-rich towns, picked free what they wanted before moving on, leaving a trail of crimes and killings in their stead. Among them were men named Ray, Stinson, and Gallagher. Curiously, Plummer also hired one J. W. Dillingham, a straight-shooter whose past was not pocked with illicit incident.

Alas, poor honest Dillingham was soon shot by three men—Deputy Stinson plus two others with the names Forbes and Lyons. The three were detained and brought before a miner's court—an impromptu court of law in which the townsfolk ruled the case. Forbes pleaded his own case and, as a man with a gift for verbal persuasion, he was set free. The other two, Lyons and Stinson, were due to be hanged. But some in the crowd cried foul and arguments ensued. Soon enough the two men were also released and ordered out of town.

In August of 1863, Plummer, already sheriff of Bannack, was appointed deputy US marshal for the territory of Idaho east of the mountains. And all the while he and his growing gang of road agents had been preying on traveling miners, wagons, and stagecoaches hauling gold and other valuables. They had secret meetings at which they were admitted only after uttering their shocking password: "I am innocent." Ha! They also wore kerchiefs knotted in a certain way so they might tell one another apart in the daylight hours.

As winter rolled in, it was customary for miners who had spent the long, backbreaking hours of spring, summer, and fall to head southward, back to what was called the "States," where for many, families and homes awaited them. And of course, they took their hard-earned gold with them. These lone travelers were of particular interest to the road agents.

Knowing the increased dangers of traveling with gold on their persons, many of these miners chose to tell no one their plans and often struck out alone at night with nothing but the moon's stark glow to guide them. And they were never heard from again—they would end up murdered, their pokes taken, their bodies dumped.

Such disappearances happened with increasing frequency over the next few months, but they raised only a low level of concern among the townsfolk. Then on December 17, saloonkeeper William Palmer brought the frozen corpse of a young German errand boy, Nicholas Tbalt, into town in the back of his buckboard. The youth's body sported a puckered and frozen bullet hole over his left eye, and rope burns were visible around his neck. His hands, frozen into claws, were grimed with leaves and soil, show-ing he'd been dragged, strangling before he died, scratching at the earth in desperation.

The sight of the well-liked young man laid out dead lit a fire under the townsfolk. Two dozen posse men hotfooted with Palmer to the spot where he'd found Nicholas Tbalt's body. They rode to a nearby shack, the same house at which Palmer had asked for help in loading the young man's body into his wagon. At the time the occupants had declined to help. Now, however, the men in the shack, on facing so many angry men, backpedaled. One accused another, George Ives, one of Plummer's deputies, of the crime.

Ives was brought to Bannack and, with the help of trained lawyer Wilbur Fisk Sanders, who had come to town months before, a proper trial was held. A twenty-four-man jury listened to back-and-forth rhetoric for three days before convicting Ives of the murder. He was hanged on December 21, 1863. After the trial Sanders and a handful of other men took matters a step further in an effort to end the disappearances, thefts, and murders that had descended on the little towns of Alder Gulch, Bannack, and Virginia City.

Within days members of this Vigilance Committee, calling themselves the Montana Vigilantes, set out to track down those men in the cabin who'd been with Ives when he was taken into custody. They felt sure those rascals still had useful information. On the trail they met a man named Red Yeager, who claimed the men they were looking for could be found at Deer Lodge. The vigilantes traveled on and realized once they got there that they'd been had by Red. They backtracked and caught up with Yeager. His stories didn't add up, so they applied vigilante tactics on him.

He cracked under whatever pressure they put on him and made a list of all the members of the Gang of Innocents—including himself. And topping his list was Sheriff Henry Plummer.

Where was Plummer this entire time? He was acting as sheriff, riding with his deputies to find the road agents who'd been terrorizing the good people of his towns. But his lame efforts drew to a close on the cold morning of January 10, 1864, when a hard knocking sound echoed through Plummer's little house.

"Why, yes, the sheriff's here. He's resting on the sofa in the front room."

Sheriff Henry Plummer listened to a man's low voice respond, then step inside. His sister-in-law shut the door and said, "Right this way. . . ."

Plummer sat up, stretching and sighing. He was sheriff, after all. Some-one probably needed something from him. That was the only drawback to this job—people were so damned needy. He looked up and saw members of the Vigilance Committee gathered outside, some stepping in. They stared down at him, hard looks on their faces.

"Well, gents, what brings you here? I'm afraid you caught me snoozing. Had a long night last night, making sure the road agents keep their distance—"

"Your talk is wasted on us, Plummer." The men continued to stare at him, then the one in the lead slowly shook his head. "It's over. It's all out in the open now."

Plummer stood quickly, swallowed, and told his sister-in-law to leave them be. Then the man in the lead said, "Let's go." He nudged Plummer toward the door. "And don't try anything foolish. I've a revolver here and plenty of men outside."

They stepped out, down the steps, and Henry saw a cluster of men surrounding his two deputies, Ned Ray and Buck Stinson. Ned's face was red and his eyes were glassy, as if he'd been crying, and Buck's jaw was set tight in defiance. Plummer knew the look. Their eyes met, then Plummer looked away. Buck Stinson shook his head.

The group walked down the snowy street through town. The closer they drew, the more people were gathered on the boardwalks and standing beside the lane. Most were talking among themselves, staring at them and shaking their heads in disbelief. As they drew closer to the lot at the end of the street, full understanding hit Plummer like a fist, and he stiffened and stopped walking.

"Now wait a minute! This thing you think you're going to do—it isn't right. I tell you this isn't right! I'm your sheriff. I was chosen by the people to uphold the law here, and what you're doing is against the law—"

Shouts of "Liar!" "Murderer!" and "Thieves!" rose all about them and they were urged forward. Plummer spun and tried to bolt, but there were too many men around him. He stiffened once more and shouted, "No, no no—this isn't right. I beg mercy of you! I am an innocent man! Innocent, I tell you! I've not done what you say!"

The men shoved him forward and Buck Stinson said, "That's enough, Henry! Die like a man, dammit."

The sheriff continued sobbing but let himself be pushed along, the stark new lumber of the gallows looming taller with each step. The gallows he had ordered to be built just days before.

Dutch John Wagner swallowed and straightened his bent back—long, hard days stooped over, chipping at rock, had made him feel twice his age in a matter of months. But that was the price you paid for the chance to strike it rich. Only it hadn't happened that way. He'd been at it for nearly six months and all he had to show for it was a sore back and worn-out tools and boots. And then Plummer and his gang had come calling.

Dutch John hadn't wanted to get involved with what he'd heard was going on, but then Greaser Joe Pizanthia, another rock hound on a nearby claim, had visited him late one night and told him that if he joined Plummer's gang—they called themselves the Innocents—he'd be set for life. Sure they'd be road agents, said Greaser Joe, but wouldn't he rather be a well-off road agent than a poor and crippled gold digger? Besides, Joe had said, as sheriff, Plummer was all but untouchable. It was a foolproof scheme.

It so happened that was either the best or the worst day Greaser Joe could have asked him to join the outlaw faction, as Dutch John had just that day nearly been killed by a cave-in on his claim. He hadn't had a proper meal in a week. The clincher, he knew, was exactly what Joe had said: Henry Plummer was also the recently elected sheriff of Bannack, and nearby Virginia City as well. His reach was long and his word was law.

But on that cold morning, in the small hours of January 11, 1864, Dutch John found himself outside the shack of his friend, Greaser Joe Pizanthia. He knocked lightly on the wood door and heard the throaty clicks of Joe's shotgun. "Joe, it's me, Dutch John!" he hissed. "Don't shoot me, for God's sake, Joe!"

The door opened a crack and Dutch John felt the cabin's heat waft over him.

"Get in here, then." Greaser Joe ushered his friend into his one-room shack and peered into the snow-bright night. He shut the door and turned on his friend. "What are you doing here? You'll draw attention to us and we don't need that right now."

"It's too late," said Dutch John.

"What do you mean?"

"You ain't heard then. . . ."

"Heard what?"

"They got Ned Ray and Buck Stinson. And Plummer."

That got Greaser's attention. He spun on Dutch John. "It ain't so! Not Plummer! And Ned and Buck too?"

Dutch John nodded but said nothing. They were quiet a few moments, then Greaser Joe said, "I ain't goin', I tell ya. I own these diggings and I ain't goin'." Greaser Joe folded his arms.

Dutch John Wagner recognized the action as Greaser's final say on the matter. But he had to keep trying to convince his friend anyway. "But they know what we done!"

Greaser Joe turned away from him, just like a kid, to face the cabin's little woodstove.

Dutch John sighed and clunked to the door. He turned in the doorway. "They wrote their warning on your cabin wall too, Joe. They'll kill you."

Instead of Joe continuing to ignore him, Dutch John was surprised to see Joe turn to him. "I saw it earlier. Just what does that mean, anyway? '3-7-77'?"

The two men went outside and regarded the large, scrawled numbers on the cabin's siding.

"I heard it's the dimensions of a grave. You know, three feet wide, seven feet long, and seventy-seven inches deep. But all it really means is 'Get gone or get hung.'"

Greaser Joe folded his arms again. "Let them come, then. I got nothing to hide."

Dutch John snorted. "Is everyone in your family as crazy as you? 'Cause you're as guilty as Plummer and Ned Ray and Buck Stinson, and they're deader'n hell right now."

The next morning, before he had time to finish packing his one satchel, Dutch John heard boots crunching the snow outside, then a hard rapping on the door. Greaser Joe, he thought. Has to be. He's seen reason and he wants to travel together away from this forsaken place. He opened the door wide and there stood a man he recognized, though the name was not coming to him.

The man held a cocked rifle and sported a pistol in a holster on his waist. Someone from town? A saloon, maybe? In the early light, over the man's shoulder, he saw a dozen more lined up at the edge of his trail, their breath pluming into the lightening sky. Far behind them were more men, most on horseback, some leading the other men's horses.

He backed up to the far wall of the cabin and said, "But the warning. I'm heading out. I'll leave right now. I swear it. Let me go, just let me go."

"You had your chance, John Wagner. Now it's up to the Vigilance Committee."

"No, no! I don't want to die. I killed nobody. . . ."

Three more men pushed by the first toting the rifle. They burst into the little cabin, its door slamming inward and spasming against the wall. All four men muckled onto Dutch John, dragged him down the path to the pole barn. He fought them, bucking and growling, thrashing in desperation. Dutch John saw the rope with the loop waiting for him and he knew then that he should have left in the night instead of trying to warn Greaser Joe. That man was no friend, it turned out. And now all was lost. Dutch John Wagner's last thought was of the pretty woman in the picture in the satchel he'd left on his bunk. The pretty young thing back East.

She would never know, never know. . . .

A group of Vigilantes two dozen strong marched across the rough, rutted ground, muddied and caked with brown snow, toward Greaser Joe Pizanthia's cabin. When they were within twenty yards, one of them shouted, "Greaser Joe? Greaser Joe Pizanthia . . . come out empty handed and you'll get a trial."

"Like hell I will!"

Shotgun blasts boomed and chased the cornered miner's words straight at the mass of men. One pitched over and lay still, another dropped to his knees, moaning. The mass of men erupted in noise, volleying vile threats at the cabin.

Through the gap where the leather strap hinges had sagged against the doorframe, Pizanthia saw the group of men part, and between this group and the cluster of horses and riders far behind sat a Howitzer cannon, its mud-caked wheels pivoting as it was spun around to face the cabin. He gritted his teeth and ran to the side wall. Through a crack he saw more men, and the same through the other wall. The cabin was built into the hill—there was no escape. He raised his shotgun and cocked both barrels, but before he could pull the triggers he heard a whooshing sound and the cabin shook as if it was blasted with nitro.

Pizanthia came around as four of the Vigilantes dragged him down the muddy path toward the rank old tree that had been in his way since he started digging a year before. He knew he should have cut it down for firewood. He also knew what they were going to do with him. Dutch John had been right.

Joe lashed out with a leg, caught one man on the side of the head and at the same time turned to bite the arm closest to his face. He'd just sunk in his teeth when a fist slammed his face. He stayed conscious but stunned, just aware enough to notice the ragged, frayed hempen rope the Vigilantes had slung up and over the tangle of branches barely eight feet off the ground.

Upward of a dozen men clamped his flailing arms and legs to his side and as he shouted, another hand clamped over his mouth. They slipped the noose, a flimsy, poorly knotted affair, over his head and snugged it tight just under his right ear. He gritted his teeth as they all backed away and, without hesitation, let him drop. Flashes of heat ran up the back of his head and the thin rope felt like forge-fired wire. He gasped, hot breath gushing from his mouth. He bit at the air, popping his teeth like a riled bear, but no sounds passed his trembling lips.

Joe smelled sweat and bitter copper in his nose.

As his vision blurred he heard cracking and snapping sounds and could just see the two dozen men standing all around him, unloading their guns into him. He felt the bullets like stings. At first they blazed and bloomed deep inside him, sudden agonizing fists. Soon, though, he felt them less and less. And then they didn't hurt at all. Nothing could hurt him now.

After the Vigilance Committee hanged Greaser Joe Pizanthia, they pumped more than one hundred rounds into him while he kicked and struggled, then they set his shack alight. He had, after all, shot at them and killed one of them when they arrived. As a parting gesture the Vigilance Committee cut him down and tossed his body on the fire.

The Vigilantes were brooking no excuses and taking no prisoners, at least not for long. Three days after they hanged Dutch John and Greaser Joe, the breaking dawn found them already en route to Virginia City, their forces bolstered by dozens of armed miners who were tired of living in fear of the road agents. They arrested six men, among them Frank Parish, George Lane, Jack Gallagher, Haze Lyons, and Boone Helm. The sixth was let go due to lack of evidence.

After the Vigilantes' customary hasty trial, the remaining five were marched, hands tied behind their backs, up the street, where they were prodded along, then herded into a half-built structure. Inside, they were strung up and a small crowd watched their legs kick, spasm, and tremble. Long minutes passed before the bodies of the five men hung unmoving, slowly spinning on their ropes.

On the same day, another faction of the Vigilantes headed to Hellgate. There they hanged eight men, among them Cy Skinner. And a few days later a suspected road agent, Bill Hunter, had his neck stretched somewhere along the Gallatin River. His death brought the total of known Vigilante victims to twenty-two.

Filled to the brim with months of blatant thievery caused by rampant road agents pillaging gold from freight wagons and stage coaches, the citizens of Virginia City, Montana, did the only thing they felt they could do—they took the law into their own hands by forming the Committee of Vigilance. And in less than three months, from December 21, 1863, through February 4, 1864, they hanged no fewer than twenty-two men. These men were suspected (that's the key word here) of being the road agents causing their towns' woes. For good measure, some were shot before they were hanged.

The story of Henry Plummer and his alleged misdeeds is still one of the long-bandied and much-debated stories of the Old West. Was he or wasn't he the ringleader of the gang of thieves who swindled their fellow townsmen out of their hard-earned gold? If he was that bad man, as had been popularly believed for more than a century, then he ranks as one of the scurviest swindlers to walk bowlegged down the penny-pinching pike.

If he wasn't . . . well, revisionists have devoted much ink to the idea that a number of the men who were hanged for the crimes were, if not entirely innocent, certainly not deserving of having their necks stretched. That they did not receive a fair trial is an unfortunate misstep, to be sure. But the jury—despite the lack of one—is still out on that score, as irrefutable evidence has yet to be established.

For the sake of argument, let's say that the revisionists are correct and Plummer himself was innocent of the charges piled atop his moldering corpse. That doesn't mean there wasn't a murderous, deceiving gang whose members called themselves the "Innocents." A gang rumored to be responsible for dry-gulching and murdering 102 miners.

CHAPTER 15

LAND WARMONGERS OF JOHNSON COUNTY
DEATH OF A CHAMPION

In 1872 a number of large ranchers in Wyoming formed the Wyoming Stock Growers Association. In its early years it was strictly a social group that convened for functions at the Cheyenne Club. But this was no hayseed affair—members of the WSGA were among the richest residents of Wyoming Territory. And then, as now, wealth equated with power.

Under the guise of protectionism, of keeping safe their investments, these wealthy, powerful men spent years riding roughshod over anyone they deemed a threat to their livelihood, especially after the disastrous winter of 1886–87, also known as the Great Die-Up, when tens of thousands of head of cattle and other livestock froze to death all over the Upper West.

The members of WSGA carried their unrepentant zeal to such a degree that they instigated what has come to be called the Johnson County War, a protracted mess in which they cheated small ranchers out of their property any way they could.

On the morning of April 5, 1892, in what less than a century later would resemble a scene in dozens of Hollywood Westerns, fifty-two heavily armed men disembarked from a private, special train just north of the bustling cattle burg of Cheyenne, Wyoming. They mounted up on healthy, well-rested steeds led there specifically for them, to carry them northward to the Johnson County seat of Buffalo. Grim-faced to a man, these fifty-two had no interest in taking in the scenery. Of them, twenty-three were not cattlemen nor cattlemen's top hands. They were hired guns, raw killers who were good at their chosen profession.

They were all there to deal in the harshest terms with the seventy men whose names appeared on the "kill list" tucked in the breast pocket of Frank

Canton, one of the men leading the grisly expedition. Until recently he had been the sheriff of Johnson County, Wyoming. He'd left that office for this more fruitful employment at the urging of Frank Wolcott, a big-money rancher of the North Platte region and mover and shaker within the big rancher's Wyoming Stock Growers Association. Wolcott was also the man who'd drawn up the kill list of the men he wanted shot, hanged, stabbed, clubbed—he didn't much care which as long as they ended up dead and no longer a burr under his wide saddle.

This brutal force felt secure in the knowledge that their impending heinous deeds, if not sanctioned by the law, at least would be cloaked in the obscuring smoke and thunder of Wolcott and his cronies' clout and cash. They also had the power of the press on their side, however yellow the various Cheyenne papers were. By printing falsehoods that claimed Buffalo was awash in "range pirates" and "the most lawless town in the country," the papers painted a grim picture. They depicted every small-time operator as a ruthless cattle thief bent on destroying the livelihoods the cattle barons had worked so hard and long to build.

History shows that nothing could be further from the truth. By the mid-1880s the cattle barons, sitting fat and happy, saw little reason to slow their range-devouring ways. They wanted a lock on the market, especially after the early 1880s when beef prices soared. They overpopulated the rangelands with cattle, greed overriding reason, telling themselves that more was better. This resulted in an inevitable glut of beef, which naturally affected the wallets of the barons. Then a drought in the summer of 1886 was followed by a drastic winter that became known as the Great Die-Up, when tens of thousands of cattle and other livestock across the upper West froze to death. Feeling the resultant pinch, the greedy barons couldn't stand—or afford—the idea of further alteration to their income.

Concurrent with the earlier rise in beef prices, a number of newcomers were attracted to the region. These smaller ranchers, called "mavericks," began establishing their own modest spreads, running cattle on the same land—open range that belonged to no one and to everyone. But the barons didn't see it that way. They reasoned that since they were there first, why should they share their own (overcrowded) range, land that they felt they all but owned? The appearance of yet more ranchers, even small upstarts, was not to be tolerated.

To keep the entire range to themselves, self-important cattle barons of the Wyoming Stock Growers Association ambushed, shot, and lynched small ranchers of Johnson County, Wyoming. Rancher Nate Champion (above) dared to fight back. He held off a gang of hired killers for hours before making a break for it—and dying in a fusillade of lead. Champion wrote diary entries during the siege, and they make for riveting reading.

Courtesy Hoofprints of the Past Museum, Kaycee, Wyoming.

The number of cattle the small-time operators turned loose on open range was miniscule compared with the massive numbers the barons ran.

So why make a fuss over it? Did the barons really feel threatened by the small-time operators? Many of these newcomers were known to the barons, having worked for them as cowboys. Others were newly arrived settlers looking to build up herds and ranches of their own. As was allowed by law, they established homesteads to which they had legal claim, and in doing so they settled on some of the choicest locations on that range.

Toss into this boiling stew the long-running practice of mavericking, or marking unbranded calves for one's own. The legal procedure allowed anyone with a registered brand to obtain legal ownership over any unbranded young stock, no matter whose cattle had birthed them.

So what did the big cattlemen of Wyoming do about this perceived threat? They began a long and brutal public smear campaign, claiming in simple but emphatic terms that the small ranchers were little more than opportunistic rustlers intent on stealing every critter on the range, branded or no. As the barons had the press in their back pockets, their smear campaigns were most effective. It wasn't long before the press cooked up far-fetched, sensational stories about a lawless element running amok in Johnson County, where cattle rustlers were ruining the very lives of the kindly cattle barons.

In addition, since the WSGA also had the governor of Wyoming—and even the president of the United States—in their other back pockets, the cattle barons began introducing and implementing new laws regarding mavericks and roundups, laws that overwhelmingly favored the good old boys.

As expected, the small ranchers protested, claiming the barons were greedy and sought the entire range for themselves. With all their purchased public and political support, the Wyoming Stock Growers Association felt as though they had the perceived culprits sighted in and just had to pull the trigger. So they settled on that timeless solution—violence—to rid themselves of their nuisances. And then the reign of killing began.

On July 20, 1889, the cattlemen lynched a woman named Ella Watson. Known as "Cattle Kate," she along with her fiancé, Jim Averell, a local merchant in Rawlins, were also small holders, working homesteads to build up their own herds of cattle. Their land happened to control a mile of valuable frontage on Horse Creek. One of the biggest cattlemen, Albert John Bothwell, tried several times to purchase their land from them, but they declined. These and other tensions between Watson, Averell, and the WSGA ranchers escalated, culminating in accusations by the WSGA that Watson and Averell had rustled cattle, specifically from Bothwell, rebranding them as their own. Bothwell dispatched a handful of his own men to arrest the lovers and bring them to Rawlins. But they never intended to bring them to town. Instead they strung them up from a roadside tree.

The barons' claims, that the pair were rustlers, couldn't be proven. But a glimmer of hope glowed from the savage incident. The event was seen by four witnesses. However, before anything of consequence could come up in court, one witness was poisoned, two more disappeared, and another was paid off and fled the country.

More determined now than ever to rid themselves of this annoying menace to their nefarious livelihoods and rampant greed, the cattlemen hired stock detectives, a misleading appellation given to private gunmen who operated in a gray area of the law, which allowed them to "investigate" as long as they were hired by a legitimate rancher. In this case, it was the collective known as Wyoming Stock Growers Association. The directive given the stock detectives was simple: Get rid of the small ranchers any way necessary.

These early detectives in the employ of the WSGA came in the form of rough characters disguised as quasi-lawmen. The first, Frank M. Canton, had barely escaped Texas as an outlaw and was known to them as the recent sheriff of Johnson County. His two cohorts, Joe Elliott and Tom Smith, also had checkered Texas pasts. Not long after, on June 4, 1891, certain of these stock detectives paid a visit to local horse rancher Tom Waggonner and dragged him off at gunpoint while his wife and children looked on. A few miles down the road, they strung him up until he stopped thrashing and swung dead. As the hired killers worked their way down the kill list, they came to Nate Champion.

Of all the small-time operators in the Powder River region at the time, Champion rose to prominence head and shoulders above the others. It was not because he sought a leadership position among his fellows, but because he could not allow such blatant oppression to exist. And so it was in 1891 that Nate Champion rose to local prominence and an unofficial position as voice for the downtrodden ranchers.

Originally from Texas, Champion arrived in the Powder River region as a young man and quickly became known as a popular and dependable roundup foreman for a number of the big ranchers. All went well until Champion, an ambitious young man, saw a legal opportunity to expand his own fortunes, to build a life for himself. He dared to dream and so in his spare time began mavericking unbranded calves as he found them.

The barons retaliated by blacklisting him, preventing him from making a living doing what he did best—cowboying. They hoped this would convince him to skedaddle back to Texas. But it only made their problem worse—Champion was not a man to be pushed around.

Sadly, neither were the barons. They decided Champion would be the ideal man to make an example of. And on November 1, 1891, they made their play—but they didn't reckon on Champion besting them.

Nate Champion and a friend were holed up in what was known locally as the Hall Cabin, hard by the Middle Fork of the Powder River, in the heart of Wyoming's infamous Hole-in-the-Wall country. . . .

"Thought I heard something. You expecting anybody, Nate?" The man leaned back in his chair and reached to part the grimy oilcloth covering one of the cabin's two small windows.

The man to whom he spoke, Nate Champion, though on the small side, was wiry of frame and keen of mind. He looked up from his breakfast plate of bacon and beans, tin spoon dripping bean juice halfway to his mouth. His eyebrows arched and his keen dark eyes looked first from his friend, then to the door. He heard nothing and resumed eating. "I expect," he said, chewing, "you're hearing the cattle." He smiled. "Or maybe it's men sent by Bothwell and his boys. You know how much they like me."

"Yeah, that's who it is, Nate!" His friend jumped to his feet, knocking his chair backward to the floor. "But it's no social call—they ain't slowing, Nate!" Even as he said it, he backed to the wall, and looked to Champion, unsure what to do.

Before Nate could push back from the table, the cabin door burst inward with a crack and shuddered on its pin hinges. Two men filled the little doorway, three more crowded close behind, all bristling with drawn firearms, their faces covered.

"Give it up, Champion!"

Still seated, Champion stared at the men a moment, then slowly raised his arms, yawning, stretching, and reached to his bunk, tight behind him in the close confines of the cabin. He grasped his revolver snugged under his pillow and in one swift motion ratcheted back on the hammer and brought it to bear on the uninvited guests.

The intruders opened fire and Nate Champion returned it. Neither side expected any outcome in such close quarters other than death; grievous wounds at best.

Smoke and thunderous claps of weapons in a small, enclosed space soon deafened and half-blinded those inside, their shouts and agonized groans drowned by the gun roar. There was no way the intruders could miss. No way at such close range—mere feet—and with their prey seated and caught unaware. And yet, miss they did.

Despite the number of shots they unleashed into the small space, Champion emerged with nothing more than powder burns on his face—proving how close they had stood to him—and a distinct ringing in his ears.

Champion's shots, however, found fleshy purchase in one man's arm, and in the gut of another. That shot would prove fatal. Even through the haze of the smoke-filled room, Champion was able to identify one of his attackers, Joe Elliott—stock detective in the employ of WSGA.

Tenacious bulldog that he was, Nate Champion went to the law, fully confident that he was once again in the right. And while the reluctant wheels of Wyoming justice ground painfully forward, the hubs of which were greased by the WSGA, Champion went to the press. He began with the *Buffalo Bulletin*, because it was one paper he felt reasonably sure had not yet sided with the cattle barons.

That he and his friend lived through the attack was little short of a miracle to Champion. That his goon squad failed was a source of boiling rage to Bothwell, who bellowed at anyone within earshot when he heard of the outcome of the botched mission. The next time Champion was set upon, Bothwell demanded a more satisfying outcome.

But long before that happened, more surprising developments in the cattle war would arise. . . .

The attack had taken place on November 1, 1891, and in the month that followed, every resident of Johnson County howled in fury, pointing their fingers. In the ensuing investigations that took place in both public forums and in private sleuthing, a member of the group of men sent to silence Champion was coerced into giving up the names of the others in the ill-intentioned little group. Those names were spoken before two other ranchers from the Powder River region. One is believed to be Orley "Ranger" Jones and the second, John A. Tisdale.

Charges of attempted murder were brought against Joe Elliott while the public's outrage called for similar treatment of the employers of the killing squad. But in early December 1891, before any further action could take place, the two men, Jones and Tisdale, were themselves victims of the killing squad.

Orley was dry-gulched and shot three times, it is believed by Frank Canton. Three days later John A. Tisdale, though fearful for his life, nonetheless vowed not to be cowed by the cattlemen and their killers. He donned his best suit, loaded up his shotgun, and drove his buckboard to Buffalo for vital supplies, including Christmas gifts for his wife and children. On his way home, where he'd told friends he was fearful for his life, Tisdale was shot in the back and left to die, sprawled in his wagon and bleeding out in what is now known as Tisdale Gulch. It is believed he, too, was a Canton victim.

Public outcry reached a fever pitch and demands were renewed to charge those who had hired the killers. Sadly, most folks knew who they were—the wealthy cattlemen who, it seems, would stop at nothing to quash even the mildest opposition to their ever-expanding empires and wallets.

Johnson County authorities worked overtime to assemble a tight case against their one ace in the hole, WSGA stock detective Joe Elliott, fingered by Nate Champion. Johnson County attorneys suspected if they could convict him, and threaten him with a long jail term, he might come clean with the names of his employers. The case went to preliminary hearing on February 8, 1892, with Nate Champion as the plaintiff's key witness. His testimony was effective enough that a trial date was set on the charge of attempted murder. A conviction seemed imminent.

And then all hell broke loose: The ranchers decided to send their hired men north to Johnson County to deal with the problem before it grew worse.

And so, on that early April morning in 1892, fifty-two heavily armed men, an assassination squad, disembarked from a private train north of Cheyenne, then mounted up and rode at a steady pace toward Buffalo, the Johnson County seat, where they were to receive their orders. Their leader, Frank Canton, whose most recent position had been sheriff of Johnson County, had in his possession a list of seventy names, men designated to die by the squad's hand.

The mass of killers were met by a man in covert employ as a spy. He related welcome news: Rustlers, he said, were holed up at the KC Ranch, barely north of where the killing squad now stood, their horses blowing in the chill early April air. They kicked forward with haste and purpose, toward a cabin with a handful of men whose names were on their list, chief among them, Nate Champion.

The cattlemen and their hirelings knew that if Champion were to take the stand in the actual trial, Elliott would crack like a dry twig. As he was in their employ as range detective, the unthinkable would surely happen—the barons themselves would be implicated in murder. And jail time—or worse—simply could not be allowed. Champion must die.

When they received the news that he was holed up but a few miles distant, the killing crew of fifty-two, led by a smiling Canton, milled about for long minutes on their horses. Some of the men were unconvinced that killing Champion was the right course of action. Word would surely get back to the law and higher ups that some of them were behind it. How could it not?

"What in the hell is wrong with you, Wink?" The surly fat rancher sat his horse loosely, his jowls working a quid of tobacco as though it were a mouthful of fine steak. He loosed a long brown stream and fixed his oldest friend with a quizzical look. Many of the others did the same.

"Aw hell, we're probably in the right. But I will register my voice right now as stating that this thing could just as easily blow up in our faces. You all hear me?" Wink received a number of nods, and before anyone else could comment, Canton broke in. "Let's put it to a vote."

Murmurs of approval hastened him onward. "Who's in agreement that Champion should be stopped, at all costs, right now at the KC Ranch?"

A majority of hands shot up. Canton began counting them, but the fat rancher spit again. "Oh for heaven's sake, that's the lot of them. Let's get going, Frank!"

The former lawman nodded and raised an arm. "Men, to the KC Ranch." And they rode, these hired killers, ranchers, assorted ranch hands, and even two newspaper reporters, all purportedly on a mission to run aground cattle rustlers.

There were four men in the cabin that night of April 8, 1892. Two of them were old friends and had hunkered down there for the time being, using the cabin as a base for their forays to their traplines. A third man, Nick Ray, was also in temporary residence, and the fourth was Nate Champion.

Nate thought he'd heard clipped shouts of the two men—maybe it had been the two trappers—some while after they left the cabin. They'd only gone to the Powder to fetch water. . . .

His friend and fellow cowboy, Nick Ray, rolled a quirley, thumbed alight a lucifer, and set fire to the cigarette as he leaned against the open door's frame.

The first shot, sudden, clean, and cold, tightened Nate Champion's gut. It came quick, sliced through the morning air and delivered a ragged, smoking hole in Nick's chest and a larger, fist-size mess to the left of his spine in the back, where it exited. A second shot caught him once more before he spun, twisting in place, his feet seeming to have forgotten what to do next. His teeth had clamped down on the smoking quirley and his lips stretched hard against them; his eyes wide in surprise sought Champion's for the last brief moment they would ever have to focus on anything again. Then Nick Ray convulsed once, dropped toward the floor, slamming into a chair and the table, upending a tin cup of coffee and a half-empty corked bottle of whiskey on his way down.

Champion saw it all as if time had slowed. Already he was on his feet, thumbing one of his braces up over a shoulder of his longhandles, the other hand clawing at the Colt revolver that had been his truest and most constant companion these past long months since the nightmare with the big ranchers had begun.

He dashed to the open door, felt the sizzle of air as a bullet missed its mark and buried itself in the planking of the room's back wall.

One hard-rammed boot kicked the door closed. Champion waited a moment for the bullets to stop whanging into this last thing to move. He had no idea how many men there were, but they weren't far off for the bullets to do that much damage that close in.

Champion leaned against the table leg, one hand on Ray's chest. The man was alive, but in a bad way. From Nate's experiences with such wounds, Nick was going to slip free of life in a short while unless Nate could get him help. But even as he began speaking low, encouraging words to his friend, Nate knew it was hopeless. And from the look Nick gave him, behind his filming eyes, the shot man knew the score.

"Nick," said Champion, leaning close and hearing the thready breathing of the wounded man. "We'll get you to a doc, no worries there." He forced a smile, though his mouth, like the rest of him, shook with the sudden raw horror of the moment. He groaned in anger with the realization that they were likely pinned down six ways from Sunday. That's what he'd do if he wanted someone bad enough.

Champion bit back a harsh swallow of bile, gritted his teeth. He'd foolishly let his guard down, knowing full well the barons would be desperate to kill him to keep him from testifying. And now here it was, he was sure of it. Those two men who'd stayed the night in the cabin with him and Nick were just innocent trappers. Had they been killed too?

But he didn't have much more time to consider his situation because that's when the real shooting began. An unrelenting fusillade of bullets rained down onto the cabin, drove at its walls like angry bees, thudded from all angles, and filled the air with the raw, violent sounds of intended death. His. He would let them think he had been hit, then when they came to investigate—not all of them would, surely, but a few might—that's when he would let them have it. He checked his ammunition, noted he had less than he'd like. . . .

Champion had fleeting thoughts that someone over the vast open miles of range land might hear the unusual amount of gunfire. Little did he know that someone had indeed heard. Two someones, in fact. Jack Flagg and his stepson, Alonzo Taylor, who were passing by, took notice of the sounds and the layout of the siege. They rode hell-for-leather to Buffalo, straight to the law, Johnson County's sheriff, William "Red" Angus, who bellowed for posse men.

It didn't take long for him to raise a group two hundred strong—locals knew the score in that besieged town. Knew that it was most likely Champion who was pinned down. And if it wasn't him, it would soon be, or worse, one of them. These small holders, hardworking folks all, mounted up and headed to KC Ranch, raising dust and loading their revolvers as they galloped.

Hours passed since the siege began. Hours in which there had been long lulls of silence. Shouts from the attackers helped Champion get a bead on them, helped him figure out who among them he might know. Champion used the time to his best advantage, alternately low-crawling from one side of the cabin to another, peering through the shot-up wood for any sign indicating the attackers were moving in on him.

Several times he had squeezed careful shots, gauging distance or just plain taking advantage of a too-good-to-miss shot, and had scored hard return fire, evidenced by the shrieks of the men who'd felt his rifle's sting. He'd fired nearly two dozen times and felt sure he'd hit a half-dozen men. Whether any died, he had little way of knowing. Nor did he care. A wounded man was less likely to charge the cabin.

As the morning aged, Champion also did his best to tend to Nick. It had been obvious from the first that the man would likely die of his wounds. It seemed that the man no longer heard him, but Nate kept up his low patter, mostly for himself, to somehow reassure himself all would end better than he suspected. It was a fruitless course of thinking, and he was not a man prone to flights of fancy, but it helped pass the time and keep him from dwelling on the inevitable.

He also recalled the notebook and pencil in his pocket and commenced to detail the events of the day in hopes his notes would help defeat the besieging bastards, the WSGA, should he not survive. He wrote down the names of the men he was certain he'd recognized in fleeting glimpses when he spied them through cracks and bullet holes in the walls.

Without warning a new round of shots volleyed at the cabin. At him, the only occupant left alive. As he low-walked past, he stole a quick glance at Nick Ray. The man's glassed eyes and slack mouth told Nate his friend was dead.

Random shots stippled the day's near-silence. Save for the soughing wind and the stomping of hurried boots across gravel—always it seemed, coming to him from beyond the wall he was not peeking through—there was precious little other sound. And with full darkness would come his only chance at escape—the cover of dark or not at all. It was going to be risky, but no less risky than sitting still in this little shack while they jammed it full of lead pills and then set it alight.

Nate scooched lower and dragged himself backward along the floor. Wouldn't be long now, he thought as he squinted to see through a sliver of late-day light needling between rough wallboards. There were two of the rascals—looked like Mike Shonsey and another man. Nate gritted his teeth, rose up fast on his right knee, and stuffed the rifle snout through the low right corner of the long-since shot-out window.

He knew there was precious little time to sight, but he made himself take the time. He would have a couple of seconds at best before they saw him in the window. He sighted, squeezed, and in the span of time it takes to snap a finger—between squeezed trigger and stifled shriek—Nate watched one man convulse, fling his arms upward, and whip backward, his long gun clattering off a rock.

Shouts and a volley of shots laced the air, pounded the poor cabin's puckered boards. Nate flattened himself to the floor as splintered wood and icicles of glass rained in. He saw a bullet plow up a furrow along the underside of the table, smelled raw smoke from gunfire, and shook his face quickly to dispel the muddiness of his hearing from the latest fusillade. He heard shouting, angry barks of men. A grim smile pulled his mouth tight. They were angry with him—all because he called them on their thieving, killing ways. Now that was truly something.

He retreated to the one corner he knew might provide a few more minutes of safety, such as it was, and thumbed in his last four shells. Then he pulled out his journal. He licked the nub of pencil and set down the rest of the names of the men he believed he'd seen stalking the perimeter of the yard around the cabin. Out of habit he glanced to each side, moving his head back and forth, one eye squinted, trying to see what he might through the gaps in the boards. He turned his attention back to the journal and wrote hurriedly:

> *Well, they have just got through shelling the house like hail. I heard them splitting wood. I guess they are going to fire the house tonight. I think I will make a break when night comes, if alive. Shooting again. I think they will fire the house this time. It's not night yet. The house is all fire. Goodbye, boys, if I never see you again.*
> *—Nathan D. Champion*

He looked through the gap again, and that's when he saw it—the unmistakable wavering raw light of living torches. His eyes widened. They were pushing a burning wagon toward the cabin, damn them!

It shouldn't shock him—he'd known all along this was his likely end. And they were going to do it before full dark too. Smart of them—it's what he would do were he them. *But then again, Nate*, he told himself. *You could never be like them.*

He stuffed the journal back into his coat pocket and looked about the room. There was nothing else here he'd need. Where I'm going there's no need for much of anything, he thought. And even less need for such thinking, he told himself as he pulled in a deep draught of air. It was bitter and warm and not likely to get much better any time soon.

"Oh," said Nate Champion as he retreated back to the corner and got up on one knee. He levered in a shell, patted his pocket where the journal resided, and said, "Oh, God, please be with me." And then he low-walked across the room to the door. Outside it was near dark, good as it was going to get.

Smoke crept in through the gappy, shot-to-pieces little cabin, and the pungent sting of burning wood began its slow, winning war with the dry old shack.

A single torch whipped at the window, hit the frame, and still managed to flop inside, rattling against the upended table and landing, flaming bright, despite its quick journey, on the floor close to Nick Ray's lifeless form.

"Sorry, old friend," said Nate and reached for the door handle, while shoving away the crates and firewood he'd jammed against it earlier. They'd know he might leave through the door. Heck, they'd be watching all the windows too. Was there no other way to get out? No. The door it would be, then.

With a grunt and a muttered oath for his life, Nate Champion edged the door open just enough to snake through. He peered out. No one in sight, not that he could see far in the smoky gloom.

Emboldened, he made for it, not daring to waste what little time this play might have brought him. He ran as fast as he could, keeping low and not daring to look too far left or right.

He made it ten, twelve feet from the door when the first gunshot caught him in the backside, then another in his left leg, low down. He spun, shouting, "No!" and even before he slammed to the ground, he knew he would not make it, knew they'd been lying in wait for him to do just this. But he'd had no choice.

All this he thought as he fell, spinning to the hard-packed dusty earth, rocks gouging him, bullets driving into his guts, his chest, his arms, so many, as if it would never end. As if it would never end. . . .

The killers stared down at the dead man, shoeless and shot to pieces. Sticking out of his coat pocket was a book of some sort. Canton bent, retrieved the bloodied little book, and thumbed it through.

"Kept a diary," he said out loud. Then, as he came to his own name written among the hurried entries, he scratched it out. Amazingly, he tossed the book back onto Champion's body.

Before the killers left, they pinned a sign on Champion's shirt front that read: "Rustlers Beware."

Hours later the Invaders, as the killing force was called, making their way north, learned that a large group of hostile citizens and lawmen had heard of the events at the KC cabin. The Invaders rode hard for the TA Ranch, where they soon found themselves pinned down by that force, made up of local law, small ranchers, and citizens from Buffalo, numbering in the hundreds.

For three days the enraged force, tipped off to the savage attack at the KC cabin by Jack Flagg and his stepson, Alonzo Taylor, rained lead on the dug-in Invaders. The killers were getting desperate, running out of ammunition, low on food, and unsure what they were going to do next. The irate citizenry were ready to fire the barn and house when once again money and power won out.

The US Cavalry from nearby Fort McKinney, on orders of Wyoming Governor Amos Barber, senators, and ultimately President Benjamin Harrison, rode in. The contingent, it seems, was dispatched just in time, taking the besieged group of hired killers, the Invaders, into custody and to jail in Cheyenne. If their attackers, the small ranchers, few honest lawmen, and citizens of Buffalo had any illusions that those captured killers would soon be brought to swift justice, they were to be disappointed.

The men were so well connected that judicial and political strings were pulled. The governor, a puppet for the WSGA ranchers, refused to allow the Invaders to be questioned by investigating officers, and did everything he could to prevent the prosecution of the hired gunmen.

With the truth obfuscated, the mess dragged on for eight months until the trial, where a suitable jury could not be seated. And so, the charges against the hired killers and the men who hired them were dropped, and they were never charged for their crimes.

They had invaded Johnson County, had caused untold levels of strife and damage, and got away with it. The bloated cattle barons continued to ply their vile trade, though they did keep a lid on their hired killings. But their shameful acts, now recalled as the Johnson County War, were anything but admirable.

Champion was slandered, misrepresented, tormented, hounded to ground, set upon by lecherous slinking dogs, and finally murdered, but history has nonetheless shown that Champion and his comrades were on the side of right while the big cattlemen were little more than that which they purported to abhor—killers and thieves.

In an interesting side note, shortly after the killings at the KC cabin, the coroner ventured out there and loaded up the bodies of Champion and Ray. He found Champion's body had twenty-eight bullet wounds. Sadly, on his way back to Buffalo, the coroner himself died—of apoplexy.

CHAPTER 16

DR. SAMUEL BENNETT
KING OF THE THIMBLE RIGGERS
(AND OTHER
SLEIGHT-OF-HAND MEN)

Born in New Hampshire on the first day of the year of 1791, Samuel Bennett was not cut out to be a lifelong New Englander. By adulthood, Bennett had tried on a number of occupations as he traveled westward, including shopkeeper, saloon owner, and fur trader. And the entire time he carried with him a simple setup of three sewing thimbles and a tiny ball of paper, basic items he had used from an early age as a source of amusement. Before long, however, his skill with them allowed him to make money—as a thimblerigger.

Unlike many other folks who played at this variation on the more common shell game (three walnut shells and a dried pea), Bennett developed such a high degree of skill, most notably in palming the ball of paper, then placing it under whichever thimble he wished, that he ensured he would never lose. And it is said that he never did.

Much of Bennett's success lay in his passive approach to the game. He would sit quietly whisking the thimbles and ball around in a crazy-eight pattern. Eventually this would attract the attention of curious passersby, and though they would ask for further demonstration of this skill, he would quietly try to abstain. Only with seeming great reluctance would he launch a demonstration.

Despite his obvious skill, and the fact that he likely cheated, people would become mesmerized by his adroitness. As if they could not help themselves, they would lay their money down and point to the thimble they felt sure hid the ball of paper. And when they invariably guessed incorrectly, the strangers would feel as if they instigated the entire affair, so they had little reason to complain when he took their money.

For years, Bennett worked his craft up and down the Mississippi River aboard riverboats—a likely place for swindlers to congregate since games of chance were what drew high-roller gamblers aboard in the first place. The wealthy would take trips onboard the huge steamers just to gamble, and they liked nothing better than to indulge in quick games of chance such as the thimbles. But when they tangled with Dr. Bennett, they lost their wad.

Until his death in Shreveport, Louisiana, on September 21, 1853, Dr. Samuel Bennett continued to ply his trade as a cunning master con man, known as "the Napoleon of the Thimble Riggers," despite the fact that he was the reason a handful of states made thimblerigging illegal by the early 1840s.

"Is it not true, good sir," the man in the blue velvet dinner jacket made a point of slowly looking to his right, a calculated casual glance, so that all at the large round table, and not just his comely companion, might see. "I say, isn't it true, Dr., ah, Bennett, that you are also known as the King of the Thimble Riggers?"

The object of his attention was a somewhat portly older gentleman with neatly oiled hair, plain but trim moustaches, and kindly, but weary eyes. It appeared the young man's revelation was something the older gent wished to have kept silent.

A titter bubbled up from the speaker's lady friend, and another joined in, somewhat coyly. And a couple of the men paused their after-dinner cigars, eyebrows raised and eyes fixed on the blushing older man.

Could it be possible that this was the legendary "King of the Thimble Riggers," the man whose skill was such that the states of Georgia, Tennessee, Alabama, and Mississippi all banned the practice of offering games of chance with thimbles? Could it be this man was in their presence? That is what the men around the table and a good many nearby spectators all were thinking.

"Oh, dear me," said the old dapper man. He lifted a glass of water to his lips, in a none-too-steady hand, not a few spectators noted, and sipped. "That, well, that was a long time ago. I'm nearly seventy now and . . . well . . ." He offered a limp gesture. "I'm traveling on this fine craft for no other purpose than to visit kin downriver."

"Then your thimblerigging days are behind you?"

"I am afraid so, young man." He stood, "Now, if you'll excuse me." He smiled, nodded to the ladies.

Dr. Samuel Bennett, "King of the Thimble Riggers," made his mark as a con man cruising Mississippi riverboats plying his sleight-of-hand tricks, involving three thimbles and a ball of paper. Similar tricks, such as the shell game (above), involved three walnut shells, a dried pea, and a pair of adroit hands. Colorful practitioners Lucky Bill Thornton and Umbrella Jim Miner warned gullible galoots they were about to take their money—and they did, every time. What are the odds?   Marion Daily Mirror, *October 13, 1911.*

The young man's female companion whispered, "What's a thimblerigger?"

He sighed. "You know, the shell game? Walnut and peas?"

Still she seemed confused.

The young man sighed again and spoke to Dr. Bennett's retreating form. "Hold on there, old-timer. I wonder if you wouldn't dazzle us a little with your skills—purely for fun, you understand."

The old man half-turned, smiled, and slowly shook his head. "No, no, I am afraid those days are long past, as I said."

"But if I could procure a trio of thimbles, I'd be honored to buy your drinks for the evening, purely for the sake of entertainment." The young man leaned forward. "I'm fascinated, you see, by the dexterous abilities of men," he nodded to the ladies at the table—"and women of your . . . former occupation. Such legerdemain!"

The beseeching young man looked about the table, nodding vehemently, his high color rising on his otherwise fair, youthful face. His enthusiasm roused the others to cheer and clap, to shout, "Please, sir!" and nod at the blushing Dr. Bennett.

He reluctantly smiled, then nodded. "All right, all right, then. I shall try. But I must warn you, as I used to say, 'Sometimes I am severe, sometimes not so sly.' I suspect the latter is the case nowadays."

Within moments, it seemed, a cabin boy appeared with three somewhat matching thimbles, presumably retrieved from the basket of a shipboard seamstress.

Dr. Bennett, still looking about the group with a hint of trepidation, nonetheless took the thimbles, arranged them before him on the gaming table's baize surface. He requested and was given a scrap of paper, stripped off a ragged piece, and rolled it into a pea-size ball.

All the while, his little but growing crowd watched with much interest, cigars pluming, glasses quietly filling, as the dapper old man worked the thimbles, increasingly faster, but by no means impressively.

He looked up after a few moments, as if he had just been awakened. "Oh, yes. So, young man, what can I show you?"

The velvet-wearing man smiled. "Perhaps you could let me guess which thimble the paper pea is under?"

"Of course, of course. But be kind," Bennett smiled broadly. "I am not so sly nowadays."

"Posh. Now," the young man leaned forward. "You mix them up and I will give it my best guess!"

Bennett nodded, his hands sped up, twice he knocked over a thimble in his efforts and had to begin again, his cheeks flushing deeper each time. After a number of rotations and seeming obfuscations, the young man guessed correctly. This happened several times in a row. Then when it looked as if the King of the Thimble Riggers might bow out and fold up the game, with a sly smile the young man offered a suggestion.

"I would like to place a bet, Dr. Bennett. I posit that the very reason you are not playing, shall we say, up to snuff, is because there is no edge, no risk, no potential for reward."

To the considerable surprise of the small gathering, Bennett nodded in agreement. "I do believe you may be right. I admit you have gotten my interest in the thimbles aroused, at least momentarily. And I should like to get a good leg up and over it before I hang it up for good. But only a few dollars, mind you."

"Good, then. Only a few. Ha! Glad I prodded," said the young man. "Now, what say we open the ball with . . ." He rubbed his hands together, a diamond ring on his little finger of his left hand catching the attention of all gathered. "$20?"

Bennett looked mildly alarmed. "Hmm, you have a keen eye. And as has been evidenced thus far, mine is far from keen these days. What say we go your $20 to my $10?"

"Fair enough for me," said the young man.

And so they went at it anew, the good doctor's efforts redoubled with the cash laid down. The young man won two games, then with a cheer around the table, the doctor won. Relief was writ large upon his face. Others demanded a turn, the doctor reluctantly agreed, he lost more rounds, the little paper pea seeming easier to find with each turn. Occasionally he gained an edge and won. Just enough to keep him from backing down.

And as for his part, the young man could not help himself. He laid out more money, others upped the betting. Dr. Bennett appeared to have a comeback, his pink hands blurred, seeming to regain their old memories of play.

The crowd grew, pressed in closer. More strangers demanded to play, and Dr. Bennett, looking like a reborn man, could do nothing to dissuade them, seeming with each passing minute as if he loathed to turn them away. He won and won, lost here and there, but many a person—for the ladies opened their own purses too—pointed with brash confidence at the thimble they knew beyond all doubt to contain the paper pea . . . only to find they had lost.

Soon hundreds of dollars had amassed in a stack in front of the doctor. A tall, thin man, who up until then had remained silent, smoothed his gray silk waistcoat with one jewel-ringed hand. He cleared his throat, gently and slowly rubbed his hands together, and pointed at Bennett.

"I have been watching you, good sir. And wonderful amusement aside, I now know, beyond a doubt, your secret—indeed the very secret—to this game." He raised a hand with a flourish and slapped down a healthy wad of cash. "And I should very much like to wager that amount—some $250— against the same of yours. I daresay you have that much before you. Therefore, double to nothing."

The doctor, who for the previous thirty minutes had bloomed into the paragon of confidence, appeared to have sudden misgivings. He nibbled a lip, then nodded, a cautious smile spreading on his face. A cheer went up from the crowd. He counted out $250 of his own money and laid it out beside the other wad.

"Best of three?" he said to the bold newcomer.

To the surprise of all, the gray-suited man shook his head. "One go is all I need."

Bennett offered a slight nod, a small smile playing his lips. "Very well. Shall we?"

The stranger nodded once, his eyes narrowed, focused on the doctor's hands. Bennett set them up, paused, lifted the left thimble, nothing. The right, nothing. The center, revealing the paper pea. He nodded to the man, who indicated he'd seen where the pea resided. Then Bennett's hands began their dizzying, mesmerizing, darting, circling, figure-eight pattern. Once, twice, three, four circuits. Then . . . he paused, palms up, revealing the three thimbles.

Whispers here and there were shushed. The thin gentleman ran his tongue tip along his bottom lip. Someone giggled. He flinched, then pointed at the thimble to the left, a sly smile raising one corner of his mouth.

Dr. Bennett's own smile drooped. He reached for the thimble, paused, his hand well away from it, as if it were throwing heat. Then he sighed and with a finger, tipped over the thimble, revealing . . . nothing beneath. The crowd cheered, and he tipped the other two, the pea sitting patiently beneath the middle thimble.

The wealthy gent in the gray silk suit stood unblinking, the crowd jostling him, a few men close by patting his shoulder. He slowly shook his head, then locked eyes with Dr. Bennett, and a weary smile spread on his face and he nodded. "Well done, sir. Now if you'll excuse me, I shall retire to the bar and lick my wounds." He offered a slight bow and made his way through the chatty crowd.

"Well, Dr. Bennett." The young man in the blue velvet jacket clicked the cabin door closed behind him. "It worked," he said in a quiet voice. His high color and smile contrasted with the quiet level to which he was trying to keep his voice.

"Of course it worked," said Bennett. "Who do you think I am, anyway?" He stared at the young man, then winked.

"King of the Thimble Riggers, yes sir."

The old man just shook his head, his smile fading.

"Doctor, there is one thing I'm curious about. You really played up that bit about being retired. Almost to the point of exhaustion, I'd say."

"That was necessary, as we'd discussed. If the rest of them had any inkling I'd never given up my trade, why . . . let's just say we'd have wasted our ticket money."

"Well, sir. I would like to thank you once again. It's been an honor working with you." The young man laid a hand on the doorknob, nodded, and turned to go.

"Not so fast, kid."

The young man held his spot and sighed.

"I'm waiting."

"But . . ."

"Don't play dumb on me, kid. I'm no dummy and I don't choose dummies to work with."

"I guess I should take that as a compliment," said the young man.

Bennett shrugged, his stony stare fixed on the younger man's face. He held out a hand, the palms and long fingers pink and clean.

The kid sighed again, pulled on a smile, and slipped a wad of bills from his coat pocket. "By my count here's five, ten, ten, and ten more makes thirty-five." He laid the cash in the rigger's outstretched palm, which stayed outstretched.

"Your count, kid, needs work."

"Huh?"

"You want to play it like that, eh? Okay. Thirty-five starts the ball, yes, but it was a three-to-one split, as I recall. Now I'm not so old as to be forgetful about such things. The day that happens, ol' Dr. Samuel Bennett will hang up his thimbles for good. Where's the rest?" While he spoke his voice rose from a soft, tremulous, soothing old man's voice to a hard-edged blunt thing, decades younger sounding than moments before.

"Oh, the split, yes." The kid swallowed, lost some of his high coloring. "I'd forgotten about that."

"Mmm-hmm." Still the big hand hovered palm up in the air.

The kid peeled off a significantly larger number of bills, laying them on the others in the doctor's hand. He slowed, looked at the old man, who inclined his head and nearly imperceptibly nodded at the money. The kid laid down two, three more bills.

Bennett smiled, nodded, and tweezering the money with his fingers, he stuffed it into an inner breast pocket. "Been good doing business with you, kid." Bennett offered the youth a two-fingered salute off an imaginary hat brim. "Hope you learned a little something."

The young man offered his hand quickly, shook with Bennett, then turned to the door, opened it, and stepped out of Dr. Bennett's cabin. "I did," he said as he closed the door. "I hope you did too."

Dr. Samuel Bennett, King of the Thimble Riggers, stared at the closed door with narrowed eyes. "Now what could that mean?" he said. He patted his coat pocket, his jaw canted to one side. The breast pocket was empty. But Bennett smiled, holding the rest of the young man's substantial wad of cash in his other hand. "Ol' Dr. Bennett, indeed."

KEEP YER EYE ON THE PEA

James "Umbrella Jim" Miner, the "Poet Gambler," always began his shell game under an umbrella, rain or shine, indoors or out, and always warned his potential victims in rhyming couplets on the Mississippi riverboats that he was about to take their money. And he did. With three walnut shells, a dried pea, and a little sleight of hand.

In the gambling saloon aboard the Riverboat *Delphine*, the fat man gulped the last few swallows of his drink and turned his attention to the mild commotion at the far end of the room. "What's going on out there?" he said aloud, half to the bartender.

"I expect it's Umbrella Jim. He always gets people all worked up." The bartender smiled and nodded toward the crowd.

"Who's Umbrella Jim?" The fat man asked.

"You don't know that, then mister, you'd do well to go and see. It ain't likely you'll forget any time soon."

"Hmmph." But the fat man pushed off his bar stool and padded down the length of the long, narrow barroom. It was barely midday and to either side the gaming tables were only half-filled. From the far corner behind him, he heard the tinkling keys of the piano, the player warming up for another long run at the ivories. As he walked through the already-heavy gauze of cigar smoke, he heard the random clink of chips on chips on baize-topped tables.

He made his way out onto the deck, craning his neck to see above the crowd. And there was an umbrella, all right. And standing under it was a thin, small man, head bent to his task, all eyes on him.

The fat man moved closer, edging his girth through the crowd to the front. He smirked. Now he saw what the commotion was all about. It was a sleight-of-hand man. Every person in the growing crowd stared not at the man under the umbrella but at his hands as he quickly shuffled three walnut shells atop a small folding table before him. He paused, looked up, and feigned surprise at the gathering.

"Well, well, good day to you, ladies and gentlemen. I am Umbrella Jim Miner," he bowed and held up his hands and said:

A little fun, just now and then,
is relished by the best of men.

If you have the nerve, you may have plenty;
five draws you ten, and ten draws you twenty.
Attention give, I'll show to you
how "Umbrella" hides the peek-a-boo.
If right, you win; if not, you lose.
The game itself is lots of fun,
Jim's chances, though, are two to one.
And I tell you, your chance is slim
to win a prize from Umbrella Jim.
And that, ladies and gents, is why they call me the "Poet Gambler," and
you have been warned. . . .

He winked and once more set to work on the shells, lifting one to reveal the pea beneath. He nodded, catching the attention of several folks, among them the scowling fat man. They locked gazes for a moment, then Umbrella Jim said, "Keep your eye on the pea, my good man."

He shuffled the shells once more, rotating them in quick order, though not so fast that the fat man couldn't detect under which shell the pea still hid. Abruptly, Umbrella Jim stopped, lifted his hands free, palms facing the crowd. Then he turned his gaze on the fat man. "Care to wager, sir? You look like a fellow with keen eyesight. Perhaps you know under which shell the pea sits, waiting to be uncovered?"

The fat man smiled. "Of course I know. And just to prove it," he reached into a vest pocket and pulled out several coins, "here's $10."

"Very good sir, and if you should win, then I will double that. But if I should win, I keep your ten."

The fat man nodded, not even trying to hide his smirk. He pointed at the shell on the left. Umbrella Jim's face was the very picture of worry and woe. Until he lifted the shell, revealing nothing. Then he tipped over the shell on the right, also empty beneath. The shell in the middle remained, and he quickly upended it, revealing the pea, of course.

"Care to go again?" Umbrella Jim looked at the fat man.

"That's impossible," said the fat man. "I know for a fact where that pea was and it wasn't under the middle shell!"

"That's why they call it a con game," said a tall, well-dressed man beside him.

If Umbrella Jim heard him, he didn't let on. "Anyone else care to make a friendly wager?"

Someone else was about to speak, but the fat man spoke up, then set down his money, another $10.

"Ah, just enough to cover your losses, eh?" Umbrella Jim began working the shells again. And again, he won.

They repeated this procedure several times, and with each round the fat man's face reddened and his jaw muscles bunched tighter. This was impossible, and yet as close as he watched the man's hands, there was no way he could detect how this Umbrella Jim character was cheating him. And yet he had to be. . . .

Another round, then the fat man shook his head. "I'll be jiggered if I can tell how you did it, but I know . . ." He held up a meaty finger half-pointing at the thin man beneath the umbrella. "I just know that you cheated. I just know it."

Umbrella Jim's eyebrows knitted together. "Sir, I am offended you would think that I did anything untoward. I am merely adept at rearranging the shells. That's the beginning and end of it." He leaned forward and said, "I tell you what. I'll gladly give you the opportunity to reverse your recent losses." He winked and smiled.

The fat man's face purpled and he made a strangled grunting sound, then spun and parted the tittering crowd. It was time for a drink. He patted his vest pocket as he strode back toward the bar, but stopped short in the middle of the long room. The pocket was empty. He had bet, and lost, all that cash. All gone. From behind him, he heard the annoying shell-game artist's rhyme. . . .

FEELIN' LUCKY?

William B. "Lucky Bill" Thornton came into the world in the 1820s in Chenango County, New York, and though not much is known of his life over the coming couple of decades, there is plenty of information about his exploits as a forty-niner heading to California's goldfields.

En route with a wagon train, he ran a shell game and managed to clean out the wallets of a number of his fellow travelers. This did not endear him to the pioneers, but he managed to make it to Sacramento relatively unmolested and with a lot more money in his pockets than when he began the trip. Within two months in Sacramento, he made a further $24,000 and decided he did not need to mine for gold when mining the miners was working out to be so lucrative.

Unfortunately for Thornton, he was, as so many of his customers, an unrepentant gambler himself. His game of choice, faro, with its notoriously long odds and house-favored play, managed to empty Lucky Bill's wallet time and again. And each time, he worked his rigged shell game harder than ever just to keep himself in faro money.

By 1853 he managed to stay away from the gaming tables long enough to build up a stake that he used to buy a ranch in Carson Valley, Nevada. Here he and his family settled in, and Lucky Bill buckled down and operated a sawmill and toll road. By all accounts he was a respectable gent, though he did continue to gamble when and where the opportunity presented itself.

Thornton's story took a sad turn on June 18, 1858, when he and a handful of others were arrested, convicted by a vigilante court, and hanged for the murder of a Frenchman. It seems Lucky Bill's luck had finally run out.

CHAPTER 17

LOU BLONGER
MR. FIX-IT (AND MORE
INCURABLE CON MEN)

If Soapy Smith is Denver's most notorious and well-known swindling son, and Doc Baggs was its genteel grifter, and Canada Bill Jones the town's resident card sharp, then Lou Blonger and his brother, Sam, ten years his senior, were the long-term, long-lived patriarchs of that city's con scene. Makes you wonder . . . why was Denver such a hotbed of deceit and trickery?

At that time, in the latter half of the nineteenth century, Denver was a geographic nexus of mining activity, surrounded as it was by innumerable gold camps, small and large. They ranged from single men working placer outfits to crews of partners working diggings to large-scale mining operations employing hundreds of men working around the clock to extract those all-important precious metals.

And with all that newfound wealth circulating, it was only natural that a locus fulfilling real needs—food, supplies, tools, assaying services, banks—should bloom into something more widespread. Numerous establishments stepped up, offering all manner of non-necessities, such distractions as gambling, prostitution, alcohol, opium in the Chinese quarter, dance halls, fine- (and not so) dining establishments, fancy hotels, and more.

As the months turned into years, it became apparent that Denver was not destined to become a played-out mine camp. The Mile-High City would instead grow, become home to a burgeoning government center, to families with children, and to numerous businesses large and small—a good many of which were still aimed at making a fast buck.

And in the midst of all this growth, one man, more so than all the other notable Denver swindlers, flourished. Louis Herbert Blonger was a gifted grifter who plied his trade in Denver for forty years. He became head of what was called his "Million-Dollar Bunco Ring" and worked every available angle. Like a chef seasoning a stewpot, Lou Blonger organized and shaped the town's

As a young man, Lou "The Fixer" Blonger, with his brother, Sam, was a lawman in Albuquerque, befriending the likes of Doc Holliday, Wyatt Earp, and Bat Masterson. But it was as a Denver crime boss that he made his mark—and fortune—setting up fake gaming houses and running a massive gang of con men. In 1922, an upstart DA finally infiltrated his gang and the next year sent Blonger to prison (mugshot above). *Colorado State Penitentiary, 1923.*

fortunes, from government to private sector, as much as any of Denver's upstanding founding fathers. At the peak of his formidable game, Blonger's organization employed five hundred men, every one a con artist engaged in varying levels of chicanery throughout the city. A number of them were politicians, lawyers, journalists, and policemen.

A high percentage of those in Blonger's network were contract workers who split their take right down the middle with the boss man, a reasonable cut given that Blonger provided a level of protection from the law they would otherwise be unable to afford. Rumors circulated about the level of Blonger's power—one stated that he had a direct and dedicated telephone line straight to the police chief's desk top. Given that for a stretch of twenty years, no one in Blonger's employ was sent to prison, there may well be truth to the rumor.

A chunky little man with an unattractive appearance, Blonger made up for it with a keen intellect and an uncanny knack for sniffing out opportunity where others only saw complications that required too much effort. But that played right into Blonger's hands, as organization was his strong suit. But

Blonger never sacrificed his long-term security for short-term gain, the primary reason for his longevity as king of Denver's con games.

He also kept a tight lead on his minions, ordering beatings for anyone in his employ who didn't measure up. On occasion he came across as a softy, as illustrated by the tongue-lashing he gave a grifter in his employ who was caught and arrested by an out-of-town Colorado lawman. The grifter had tried to swindle the lawman in a hotel lobby and was caught.

Blonger, as unspoken boss of the town, was called to the scene. He showed up and berated the thief right in front of the police: "You were recommended to me as a first-class bunco artist, and the first thing you do, you damned bastard, is pick up a deputy sheriff. What the hell are you tackling the law for, anyway? Don't you have sense enough to let Colorado people alone in Denver? I paid your transportation to Denver and put you to work. Now you walk back, and start now."

While Blonger concentrated his efforts on greasing palms and keeping the machine of his empire well-oiled and running smoothly, he employed a foreman of sorts to make sure the daily take wasn't short, and that everyone grifted accordingly. That right-hand man was Adolph W. Duff, aka Kid Duffy, a rascal of the lowest order who, nonetheless, was able to keep the lowlifes in their place and earning without skimming more than their share. Duffy was so successful he was able to manage the minions even when Blonger's vast network spider-webbed out well beyond Denver to Florida, Louisiana, and Texas.

Blonger's longtime rivalry with Denver's other big swindling fish, Soapy Smith, came to a head one day in 1895. Soap and his brother, Bascomb, liquored up and frustrated with their own gang's eroding powers, bulled through a number of establishments along the Larimer Street saloon district. Soapy was on the warpath for Blonger and anyone else he perceived as a threat.

The men left behind a trail of wreckage, thrashed a saloonkeeper, and came seconds from receiving a shotgun blast by Lou Blonger himself, who'd crouched behind the bar when the Smith brothers stormed into his establishment. The police intervened just in time, and shortly thereafter Soapy and gang vacated Denver for good, leaving the town wide open to Blonger's operation.

Long before the Blonger brothers arrived in Denver, they had already led lives brimming with adventure and excitement. Lou had been in the Civil War, wounded as a fifteen-year-old fifer, before striking west from the family homestead in Wisconsin (where they'd moved from Vermont when Blonger was a lad of five).

From there he met up with Sam, who had spent years traversing the West as a guide, a miner, and a lawman. The two brothers threw in together and became saloonkeepers and lawmen, and they invested in mining ventures. For several years they were well-regarded lawmen, notably in Albuquerque, New Mexico. While there they helped Wyatt Earp and his fellow vendetta riders who were on the lam from the law in Tombstone after tracking down and killing men responsible for Earp's brother's death. All the while, the Blonger brothers kept up a lifelong interest in gambling, specifically in rigging games, a mercenary and satisfying method of padding their wallets.

So when they arrived in Denver in 1888, they did so with thick wallets and a passel of life experience. Their first order of business was to open a modest-size saloon, offering libation, all manner of gambling tables, and a number of women to ensure patrons' glasses stayed filled, among other duties.

From this lone initial venture, the Blonger boys parlayed their growing fortunes into a number of saloons that eventually gave way to the crown jewel of them all, the Elite Saloon, the fanciest such establishment in all of Denver. With mahogany fixtures, frescoed ceilings, marble floors, a cafe—and offering patrons a shot at every popular vice of the time—the Blongers struck gold with the Elite.

Despite his considerable wealth and power, Lou, the savvier of the two brothers, nonetheless suffered periodic business-related setbacks through the years. The most devastating came in 1897 with the foreclosure of the Elite. Such a blow would defeat lesser men, but not so with Lou Blonger. The setback only seemed to make him more determined and resilient.

Every time his bank accounts dipped into the red, he put more pressure on his network of con men and turned up a fresh crop of rubes. As famed swindler and showman P. T. Barnum is reputed to have said, "There's a sucker born every minute." There couldn't be enough of them to satisfy Blonger's rapacious desires. Frequent newspaper reports told of a handful of his organization's victims. One such was the sad story of Harry B. Waldorf, who killed himself while visiting Denver after he'd been duped by Blonger's men out of $400, then forced to sign checks his account could not cover. Waldorf had been distressed over the thought that his predicament would bring disgrace to his family. The article pointed the finger squarely at Blonger.

Through the years the Blonger organization increased its influence on city politics and was eventually able to rig entire elections. One of his men voted for four candidates more than a dozen times each, all in the same election. Multiply such efforts by a couple of hundred employees and you have a recipe for a cooked election.

Blonger also used extensive lists of citizens, living and deceased, to rack up votes for whichever candidates he deemed worthy of holding office. It was not uncommon to see Denver policemen ushering people to polling places. As long as a vote was cast, it mattered little to anyone in Blonger's employ whether they were willing, qualified, or had already voted. Blonger's compensation was the knowledge that city hall remained in his back pocket, useful to a man who might require a favor at any time.

Blonger's prime years as a Denver crime boss were punctuated with episode after episode of blatant graft and corruption. From pick-pocketing summer tourists on a Denver street to shaking down city hall officials, crimes occurred with fast-paced regularity—and brought in big bucks. Enough cash rolled in that Lou was able to spend winters in Florida, soaking in the heat, while his minions performed admirably in his stead.

Over time, however, Lou Blonger's meticulously crafted empire began to crack under the weight of its own bloated corruption. Still, Lou was able to maintain his grip on the city's throat—at least until 1920, when idealistic District Attorney Colonel Philip Van Cise assumed his new post.

Blonger should have known change was in the air when he tried to bribe Van Cise with campaign funds and votes while the man ran for the job. Van Cise refused Blonger's assistance, which he knew would lead to one very bad thing—a professional life stunted and filled with degrading bowing and scraping to the crime boss. When Blonger approached Van Cise with his proposition, Van Cise, a straight arrow, warned Blonger that he intended to pursue and prosecute him and his grimy pals to the fullest extent of the law. That was all the fair warning he would give. It was up to Blonger to heed it.

But of course he didn't. Why would he, especially when he held city hall in a grip of fear? But Blonger hadn't counted on the old truism, "You reap what you sow." He had spent much of his life in Denver swindling money from people, many of whom were affluent enough to take the sting and lick their wounds, chastened and perhaps wiser. But a good many more of Blonger's victims were poor saps whose lives were made all the poorer after a run-in with his men.

It is true that Blonger and his henchmen never forced anyone to take the bets offered, never forced them to buy into a deal that seemed too good to be true. But once someone did, there was no quarter given. Take George Kanavuts, a Greek immigrant with a poor grasp of English. He was sucked in for much of his savings, $25,000, through a fixed stock-market scam run by Blonger's men. He complained to the police but was rebuffed because the police were on Blonger's payroll. Instead of giving up, Kanavuts turned to District Attorney Van Cise, and his case added welcome fuel to Van Cise's steadily growing bonfire.

Van Cise built up his case against Blonger and his boys in a methodical, studied manner. Since he was well aware that much of Denver's police force was beholden to Blonger in one way or another, Van Cise sought private donations to help fund a covert investigation of the criminal's empire. It took him a year, but he built a bullet-proof case against Blonger that included rummaging through the con man's trash, locating spies on street corners, and planting a Dictaphone, as hidden surveillance, in Blonger's office. Back in his own office, Van Cise fed false information to a corrupt police officer he had planted there—an ingenious way to directly mislead Blonger's gang.

Finally, by the summer of 1922, Van Cise used that corrupt policeman to leak something as seemingly mundane as his own vacation plans. The subtext of the news, however, was that Van Cise intended to lessen the heat on the gang while he was away. Soon, Blonger's con men roved Denver openly, bilking and fleecing and filching to their heart's content.

What they didn't know was that Van Cise was still on the case, ready to spring his biggest trap yet. And he used the fortuitous appearance of a Texas rancher named J. Frank Norfleet, who had been fleeced twice by gangsters affiliated in a roundabout way to the Blonger crowd. Norfleet, in Denver seeking information that might lead him to his own quarry, was only too happy to help DA Van Cise expose the nest of swindlers.

Van Cise planted this easy, out-of-town mark in the lobby of the now-famous Brown Palace Hotel and waited. And he didn't have to wait long. Norfleet, disguised and going by the name "Mullican," was soon buttonholed by a pair of Blonger's men, who commenced to embroil him in a phony stock scam.

Norfleet's involvement was enough to lure a number of Blonger's cronies out of the woodwork and the trap was tripped early the following day.

The first two people arrested at sunrise were Lou Blonger himself, and his right-hand man, Kid Duffy. Their offices were cleaned out and boxes of incriminating evidence were unearthed and hauled off—a boon to Van Cise's office. The rest of the day was a busy one for the DA's handpicked task force, which included a small selection of trustworthy Denver policemen, as well as a number of Colorado Rangers. By the end of that first day, they had rounded up thirty-two more gang members, and they treed more the following day. In an effort to tip off as few of Blonger's still-at-large cronies as possible, Van Cise imprisoned the gang in a church basement and not at the city jail.

Blonger spent the months leading up to the trial working his minions from every angle, threatening to kill men who might turn state's evidence, splashing out with lavish payoffs to bribe others to stay away. His logic was simple and sound: If DA Van Cise couldn't get anyone to testify, he couldn't land that all-important conviction. But it didn't work that way. Blonger's long and wormy reputation caught up with him. Victims came to Denver from all over the United States—one man even made the trip from England. They rejected Blonger's blood money, his threats and bribes, and his foot stamping. And they testified.

Blonger even tried to implicate Van Cise himself in a scam by importing a fetching lady from New York City to entrap the DA in a compromising position in a hotel room. Van Cise refused to rise to the bait. And the woman, who'd been set up in plush digs and paid $2,000, took the money and skipped town.

The trial proved to be a huge affair that garnered national press coverage. It involved tight prosecution and defense teams, heated debates, and fistfights in the courtroom. Van Cise himself engaged in fisticuffs from the bench, and after being barred from court, merely orchestrated his case from the more-useful location of his office.

Backed into a corner, Lou Blonger, the old grifter, resorted to the only thing that had ever worked for him. He did his unlevel best to buy off the jury. All he needed was one juror in his pocket to disrupt the unanimous vote required. Blonger's luck, it seemed, was about to change. Of the twelve jurors approached, he managed to buy off three. But a fourth, an Irishman named

Herman Okuly, took the money he was given—$500—and turned it over to the judge, then told the DA's office about the bribe. Oddly enough, he was allowed to remain a member of the jury.

In court, Van Cise revealed how, between the years of 1919 and 1921, the Blonger organization made several million dollars through scams large and small. His case was helped mightily by Blonger's bookmaker, fourth-in-command Len Reamey, who spilled a whole lot of beans on the stand. He explained the intricate details behind the organization's systematic bilking of hundreds of victims.

The testimony portion of the trial lasted seven weeks, during which Blonger's attorneys shocked the assemblage by refusing to present a single witness. They also offered a proposition to the prosecution—send the case straight to the jury without either side offering a closing argument. Though this was unheard of, Blonger's attorneys were gambling on the fact that, as far as they knew, they had three jurors in their pocket. The prosecution, confident in its case, agreed to the odd terms and the case was handed to the jury.

For five long days the twelve men deliberated. Time and again, when a vote was held, they came up with nine for conviction, three for acquittal—the same three who had been paid off. The fourth, Okuly the Irishman, finally admitted his attempted bribe to the other jurors and told them: "The difference between me and you three . . . is that I got my $500 but turned it over to the judge, and you've still got yours."

That meant that nine of the jurors, Okuly included, were honest, and three were bent by bribe. The nine worked day after day on wearing down the three corrupted jurors. And one by one, they turned. The last, a man named Andrew Frank, took the most convincing. And even back in the courtroom, when each jury member was polled, Frank dragged his feet until finally the judge nailed him down to a commitment of guilty.

As with all the victims whose pathetic stories bubbled to the surface, Lou Blonger himself begged DA Van Cise at the eleventh hour to abstain from sending him to prison. Have a heart, have leniency, he said. I'm old and unwell. To which Van Cise, ever the straight arrow, offered his now famous reply:

What leniency have you shown to others? What God have you
worshipped except the Almighty Dollar? When you stole Preacher

Menagh's trust funds, did you hesitate? When, overwhelmed with shame, he committed suicide, did you give any aid to his family? When you took the life earnings of old man Donovan of New Orleans, and reduced him from comfort to penury, what did you do to ease the last months of his life? You have been a criminal from the time of your youth. You have been the fixer of the town. You have prostituted justice. You have bribed judges and jurors, state, city, and police officials. You have ruined hundreds of men. With that record, tell me why a death sentence is not your due?

And with that, the seventy-four-year-old Lou "The Fixer" Blonger, already in fragile health, arrived at the Colorado State Penitentiary on October 18, 1923. He served just six months of his seven-year sentence for conspiracy and fraud, dying of organ failure on April 20, 1924.

INCURABLE CON MAN

Big Ed Burns's life story reads like a bad joke. Surely no one could get himself arrested as many times as he! Yet throughout his roughly seventy-six years, Edward "Big Ed" Burns was a train wreck of a man, arrested and incarcerated numerous times on all manner of charges, in states north to south, east to west. At times he was in the chips, boss of his own roving gang of con artists, at other times he was penniless and alone.

From humble beginnings in 1842 in Buffalo, New York, Big Ed, so called because of his robust physique, made his way to Chicago in 1861. There he found work as a stonemason—and moonlighted as a bunco artist. Soon he dispensed with the stonemasonry altogether, finding the work of fleecing people with loaded dice much more rewarding.

Adventure called and he heeded, becoming a mate on a private yacht on Lake Michigan. Then, in 1866 he choked a man to death and served a nine-year sentence in Joliet Prison in Illinois. Freshly released, he was shot in the back by a former victim but lived to tell the tale. He rose to a position of prominence in a bunco ring on Chicago's South Side.

Over time his gang grew bigger and more powerful, strong-arming voters, shaking down shop owners, and, presumably, kicking dogs for sport. Burns was shot again, this time in the leg, then came a series of arrests for buncoing, vagrancy, and robbery. He worked his way back onto the water and sold illegal booze from a boat on Lake Michigan. The law closed in, but he jumped overboard and the press stuck him with the name "Elephantine Edward of the Floating Palace." He was arrested soon after on a different charge but was extradited to Detroit on a string of pick-pocketing charges.

It seems he'd run out his welcome in the Midwest. He decamped to Leadville, Colorado, where he fronted his own gang of thugs, thieving at will. Chased by irate citizens who wanted nothing more than to stretch his neck, the gang hit the railways and roved all over the West, from Colorado to Kansas to New Mexico, and then made their way down to Arizona.

Now known as the Burns Gang, Big Ed and crew plied their bunco crafts in Benson, Tucson, and Tombstone, where they earned the enmity of Wyatt and Virgil Earp, the law at that time in Tombstone. Eventually he overstayed his Arizona welcome and made his way to Denver, working for a time in Soapy Smith's gang.

At the dawn of the twentieth century, Big Ed still popped up all over the US map, usually traced through the police blotter of local newspapers, from California to Florida to Washington State and over to Illinois, where he'd begun his bunco career decades before. The last mention of him in newsprint appears to be in 1918. Big Ed Burns, roughly seventy-six years old, was in prison in Indiana, a broken-down old scam artist who just couldn't keep his hands out of other people's pockets.

THE CONFIDENCE MAN

Sharp-dressed, dapper William Thompson was also a con artist of the very first order. Indeed, his exploits and deceptions are the basis for the popular phrase "confidence man," from which "con artist" derives. And though he plied his sleazy trade in New York City, Thompson's sheer bravado—shall we say confidence—inspired a generation of slick characters who roved the West, liking nothing better than skinning suckers.

The genius in Thompson's tricks lies in their simplicity. Dressed impeccably, Thompson would approach a stranger, concoct a false acquaintance with him, claiming to know him through so-and-so, engaging him in erudite, friendly conversation, then worm his way around to ask a question, usually involving pocket watches: "Pardon me for asking, but I wonder if you would have the confidence to trust me with your watch, just until tomorrow?"

The unusual request, oddly enough, often yielded Thompson a fine watch, merely on loan, of course. But what the falsely confident mark failed to realize until much too late was that William Thompson had no intention of returning with the watch. Unfortunately for Thompson, though fortunately for the public at large, the chatty dandy was recognized by a former victim one day on the street.

Thompson's capture and final con were reported in the July 8, 1849, issue of the *New-York Herald*, the paper that also referred to him for the first time as the "Confidence Man":

Arrest of the Confidence Man.

For the last few months a man has been traveling about the city, known as the "Confidence Man," that is, he would go up to a perfect stranger in the street, and being a man of genteel appearance, would easily command an interview. Upon this interview he would say after some little conversation, "have you confidence in me to trust me with your watch until to-morrow;" the stranger at this novel request, supposing him to be some old acquaintance not at that moment recollected, allows him to take the watch, thus placing "confidence" in the honesty of the stranger, who walks off laughing and the other supposing it to be a joke allows him so to do. In this way many have been duped, and the last that we recollect was a Mr. Thomas McDonald, of No. 276 Madison street, who, on the 12th of May last, was met by this "Confidence Man" in William Street, who, in the manner as above described, took from him a gold lever watch valued at $110; and yesterday, singularly enough, Mr. McDonald was passing along Liberty street, when who should he meet but the "Confidence Man" who had stolen his watch. Officer Swayse, of the Third Ward, being near at hand, took the accused into custody on the charge made by Mr. McDonald. The accused at first refused to go with the officer; but after finding the officer determined to take him, he walked along for a short distance, when he showed desperate fight, and it was not until the officer had tied his hands together that he was able to convey him to the police office. On the prisoner being taken before Justice McGrath, he was recognized as an old offender by the name of Wm.

Thompson, and is said to be a graduate of the college at Sing Sing. The magistrate committed him to prison for a further hearing. It will be well for all those persons who have been defrauded by the "Confidence Man" to call at the police court Tombs and take a view of him.

CHAPTER 18

LAND HO!

OREGON'S LAND FRAUD AND THE FALSE PROMISE OF MOWRY CITY, NEW MEXICO

XTRA! EXTRA! READ ALL ABOUT IT—POLITICIANS CAUGHT IN SCAN-DAL! Oddly enough, that's not a reference to modern headlines but those that were all too common a century ago. In fact, just after the dawn of the twentieth century, newspapers all over the United States thrummed with shocking headlines claiming well-heeled politicos had been swindling the US public for years. In 1905 nearly all of Oregon's US congressional delegation was indicted for illegally obtaining US government land grants, then selling them to the highest bidders—in this case big lumber companies looking for sources of cheap tracts of land rich in harvestable timber. Much money was made, few heads rolled. . . .

Realizing it had an obligation to help populate with settlers its vast westward holdings, the US Congress devised and passed the Oregon and California Railroad Act in July 1866. Suddenly up for grabs were 3,700,000 acres of prime land specifically for the building of a rail line stretching from San Francisco northward to Portland, Oregon. With most of the land in Oregon, that state would be responsible for doling out the land grants in huge 12,800-acre tracts, one tract for each mile of completed railroad track.

Three years later, in 1869, in a further effort to attract more settlers to the region, Congress altered the terms of the initial grants. This time the tracts were not only reduced in number to 160 acres, but also came down drastically in price to the ultra-affordable price of $2.50 per acre. This alteration began to show the initial desired effect of increased settlement.

In what appeared to be healthy competition, two companies adopted the title of "Oregon Central Railroad," each operating just across the Willamette River from the other, on the east and west sides. From this odd start, the lines merged in time and became the more appropriate Oregon and California Railroad.

Stephen A. Douglas Puter was one of a number of men, including senators and congressmen, indicted for participating in the Oregon Land Fraud Scandal, in which tens of thousands of acres of federal land were fraudulently sold at cut-rate prices to big timber concerns. While in prison (above), Puter wrote his tell-all, *Looters of the Public Domain*, in which he named names.   Looters of the Public Domain *by S.A.D. Puter. Portland Printing House Publishers, 1908.*

Over the next few years, the rail line expanded and the wisdom of the Congressional intention was apparent—towns along the line grew, developing commerce and providing upriver access to the far ends of the river valleys previously unreachable by steamship.

The rail line also provided ample ingress to vast tracts of land rich in timber but difficult to farm, settle, or use in ways potential settlers might profit from. It was remote, thickly forested land, so rugged and raw that settlement was all but inconceivable. But that untouched timber sent speculators into paroxysms of gleeful apoplexy.

It was true the railroads were stuck with this land, but those speculators (who also happened to be the railroad's executives) began to ponder the possibilities . . . what if the railroads devised a way to sell vast chunks of this land—tracts no one was settling on anyway—to the very people who could make use of it? And what if, in the process, the railroad executives happened to turn a tidy profit?

Alas, the massive land grant seemed locked up tight by bureaucratic restrictions. Still, what if there were a way to sidestep the stipulations of the government land grant that prevented the railroad from selling the land at a higher rate? One can only imagine Southern Pacific Railroad's president, Edward Harriman, stroking his chin while a sly smile slowly worked its way on his face and a lightbulb popped into view over his head. . . .

"Stephen, good to see you again. I'm glad you could come down." Harriman rose from behind his desk and shook hands with the man who'd just been escorted into his office.

Stephen A. Douglas Puter was a shady character of his acquaintance who Harriman knew would, for a fee, be willing to do his bidding. And what was that bidding?

"I want you and your men to head down to the waterfront. You know the places, Stephen. The saloons, that's where you'll find the most likely candidates."

"What is it you'd like me to do with them, Mr. Harriman?" But Puter was familiar enough with the situation that a knowing grin worked its way onto his face.

"They need to make their way to the land office."

"And once there?" Puter canted his head, enjoying the way this proposition was unfolding.

"Once there, Mr. Puter, those men will have an undeniable urge to become settlers." He raised a finger in emphasis. "Short lived, mind you. But settlers nonetheless. You see, they'll sign up for sections, each receiving the minimum 160-acre parcel."

"I had no idea you were so concerned about populating that land."

But Harriman ignored the man's sarcastic jab and continued. "They'll transfer title to you and your crew, as representatives of the railroad."

"And that," said Puter, nodding, "is where the 'short lived' part comes in."

Harriman nodded. "Those small parcels will be bundled with others, then those bundles will be sold at auction to whoever bids the highest amount."

Harriman's railroad would stand to make a huge amount of money from the sale of these timber-rich parcels, lots that together totaled much of three million acres of land owned by the government, and therefore owned by the public. His railroad had only been given a grant to run their rail line through it. They did not own the land and so it was not Harriman's land to sell. But sell it he did.

Once bidding kicked off, the land, now bundled in significantly larger chunks, sold for up to $40 per acre—a far cry from $2.50 per acre. And for years the O&C Railroad proceeded to sell this land that was not really theirs to sell, profiting handsomely in the process.

It wasn't until 1904, when a bookkeeper for a lumber company grew suspicious and tipped off a reporter, that an investigation by the *Oregonian* newspaper revealed the long-embedded land scheme by what had become known as the Southern Pacific Railroad (the larger entity that bought the O&C in 1887). The investigative piece revealed that more than 75 percent of the land sold under the guise of the Oregon and California Railroad Act of 1866 was in violation of federal law.

In hindsight, it is likely that in all that time someone must have become aware of the widespread wrongdoing and would have grown suspicious when vast tracts of land were logged by massive timber outfits. As it happened, plenty of people were well aware of the situation, but it was easier and far more lucrative to accept bribes and look the other way.

The *Oregonian*'s investigation kicked off a massive federal investigation, beginning in 1904, that resulted initially in one thousand indictments. By 1910 this figure simmered to a cozy one hundred indictments, then reduced further to thirty-five indictments of the most culpable persons.

Chief among them were US Senator John H. Mitchell, two US representatives, Congressmen John N. Williamson and Binger Hermann, and US Attorney John Hicklin Hall. Of Oregon's US Congressional delegation, only

Senator Charles William Fulton was found to have been unaware of the fraud and thus was uninvolved.

These guilty men and numerous others knew full well what had been occurring. They not only looked the other way, they actively solicited hush funds and helped usher the transfer of land grants to timber concerns.

Oregon's Governor Oswald West, appalled at the situation that had developed right under his nose, was famously quoted as saying, "These looters of the public domain—working with crooked federal and state officials—through rascality and fraud, gained title to thousands of acres of valuable, publicly-owned timber lands, and at minimum prices."

And what of the various scoundrels who took the US for a ride, who bilked no fewer than each member of the US public of millions gained from illicit timber profits? The US District Attorney Francis J. Heney went for their throats. Senator Mitchell was charged by Heney with using his privileged position of power to help his law firm's clients with acquiring fraudulent land claims. Even his business partner and secretary testified against him. A jury pointed the finger of guilt and Mitchell forked over a $1,000 fine, then shuffled off to the slammer for six months. Before his appeal circled back to the courts, he up and died from a botched tooth extraction.

Congressman Binger Hermann, who also happened to be former commissioner of the General Land Office in Washington, DC, got off easy. His first trial, in which he was accused of destroying public documents, found him not guilty. His second trial was postponed for several years, then ended in a hung jury. And Congressman Williamson was similarly somewhat lucky. He was convicted of perjury, but on appeal the verdict was overturned due to jury tampering and witness intimidation.

Lest anyone think US District Attorney Heney was a pushover, he went for US Attorney John Hicklin Hall, who had been the original investigating attorney who ended up canned by US President Theodore Roosevelt for his lack of ambition in investigating the case. Convinced that Hall had been swayed by the promise of padding his own nest, financially and politically, using information obtained in his investigation, Heney prosecuted Hall, and the jury agreed, convicting him in 1908. President Taft later pardoned the ruined Hall.

In 1905 Stephen Puter, puppet for Southern Pacific Railroad president Harriman, was indicted. Several years earlier, Harriman and Puter had words that resulted in Puter's dismissal. So when it became apparent he was going down with the ship, he fled from Oregon and ended up in Boston, braced by a pair of US Secret Service men. He escaped and went on the lam—it would be months before he was finally captured—armed, cornered, and desperate—in Alameda, California.

Finally in custody, Puter was transported north to Oregon, where he sat in a cell in Multnomah County jail for two years. Much bold accusation came from Puter as he gladly turned on Harriman. He testified against his former employer in court, then while in jail he co-wrote the tell-all confessional, *Looters of the Public Domain: Embracing a Complete Exposure of the Fraudulent Systems of Acquiring Titles to the Public Lands of the United States*, peeling the lid off every little detail, nuance, and backroom meeting surrounding the scheme. Despite the fact that he referred to himself as "King of the Oregon Land Fraud Ring," what he wrote raised eyebrows and helped confirm what Attorney General Heney had been working on digging up.

Puter wrote: "Thousands upon thousands of acres, which included the very cream of timber claims in Oregon and Washington, were secured by Eastern lumber men and capitalists . . . and nearly all of the claims, to my certain knowledge, were fraudulently obtained."

Puter continued to be the nexus of the nefarious activities when, after eighteen months into his sentence, President Theodore Roosevelt pardoned him, on Heney's recommendation, on December 31, 1907. He was freed not because he deserved it, but because he agreed to name names—to turn state's evidence. He testified and ended up helping indict a bevy of Oregon's big wheels, private and public, including Senator John Mitchell, Congressman John Williamson, and Congressman Binger Hermann, a full three-fourths of Oregon's congressional delegates, as well as US attorney John Hicklin Hall. He also admitted on the stand to having bribed a grand jury.

After all that, and after experiencing such a close shave and having received no less than a presidential pardon, you would think that Puter would lie low, perhaps explore quiet and legal means of earning a living. Once again, however, we see that once a swindler, always a swindler: Scarcely a decade later Puter again found himself afoul of the law. And this time he dragged his sons and son-in-law with him. In 1916 he was indicted for "Illegal Use of the Mails and Fraud." Some folks never learn.

MOWRY LAND SCANDAL

On private land along a forgettable stretch of Perrin Road, along the Mimbres River northwest of Deming, New Mexico, you'll see . . . nothing. Well, apart from cacti dotting a gritty and rolling landscape, you'll see no sign of the less-than-thriving burg formed by fraudsters and intended as the capital city of Arizona Territory. Never mind that it's now in New Mexico, never was considered as a capital of anything, but rather as a symbol of swindle, and was situated poorly enough that it existed less than twenty years, during which it contained a hotel, a couple of shops, and more saloons than residents.

The people who moved there needed the fleeting escape those saloons represented. They were distraught at being hoodwinked into sinking their savings into Mowry City, into believing this place was a veritable Eden on earth, the locus of the next big thing. When the truth hit them like a long-dead fish to the face, they likely felt they had little recourse but to drown their disappointments in booze. The land was populated with buzzing rattlesnakes and angry Apaches, neither of which were in any hurry to be displaced. It's no wonder the town was a short-lived, abysmal failure. So why did anyone think it would be a good idea to establish a town there? And not just any town: Mowry City was to be nothing less than the capital city of the Arizona Territory.

It's how Mowry City came into being that is the interesting part of the story. . . .

The silence stretched on for many minutes, maybe much of an hour, before Sylvester Mowry nibbled his bottom lip one last time and cleared his throat. He leaned forward from his cramped spot in the stagecoach. "You'll pardon me, sir, I trust, if I say you look like a man who could use a conversation."

The man to whom he spoke, Robert P. Kelley, a slender fellow with dark hair, fixed his piercing gaze on the newcomer. Then he looked back out the window.

"I . . . I do beg your pardon, but please forgive my intrusion." He leaned back, as if both embarrassed and resigned to his own boring fate—at least for the duration of the seemingly never-ending ride.

"No, no," Kelley found himself saying. Quite before he knew what he was doing, he smiled. "It is I who should apologize. This confounded ride has left me sullen and moody." He proffered a hand and the men shook. "I am Robert P. Kelley. I hail from Mesilla. And you are?"

The man seated across from him brightened. "I am Sylvester Mowry."

Kelley's eyes widened. "I know of you, sir. You are an advocate for recognition of Arizona as a separate territory, am I not right?"

"Why, yes, yes, I am pleased you know that. For it means all my proselytizing has not been in vain." He smiled at this surprising meeting. The floodgates of conversation opened and Mowry found himself relieved.

"If I may be so bold, Mr. Mowry. Might I inquire as to the purpose of your trek on this god-awful stagecoach?"

Mowry nodded. "As it happens, I am venturing far from my chosen home, all the way to Missouri to seek backers . . . for my mine." He looked left and right then, as if what he had said was information that should not be overheard. For a few brief moments, the creaking wheels, the choking dust, the slapping of the wholly ineffective window coverings, and the driver's barely audible tuneless singing were all to be heard and felt.

Kelley bunched his brow. "Ah, so it a business venture you're embarking on as well then?"

"Yes," Mowry said finally. After all, he thought. Am I not seeking investors for my mine, large and small, singly and in a group? Is it not conceivable I might find one on this very stagecoach? "Yes indeed," he said, and leaned forward. "I'm happy to tell you about it, if you've no objection."

Kelley smiled wide and leaned back in his seat. "Mr. Mowry, I am a captive audience. Perhaps I might even be of assistance. You see, I am a businessman as well. A speculator, you might say."

"Excellent, Kelley! Say, perhaps our meeting was fortuitous, after all?"

"Time will tell, my good man. Time will tell. Now, what about this mine of yours? I'm all ears."

The two travelers were of a shared mind that the region known as Arizona should be given its own status as a separate and unique territory. Kelley listened politely as Mowry prattled on about the possibilities of his mine, about the possibilities for territorial recognition for Arizona, and on and on.

All of it interested Kelley, and none of it surprised him, for he, too, was a man of vision. At least he liked to think of himself as such. But the one thing he was most interested in was Mowry himself. The man was well known in the region and that alone could be useful. *Yes, useful, indeed*, thought Kelley as he smiled and nodded.

Unfortunately for Mowry, the all-too-friendly and eager-to-listen man he met on that stagecoach was less interested in his mine—they were a dime a dozen—and far more interested in capitalizing on Mowry's renown as a man who had already gained much attention banging the Arizona drum. And on that fateful 1858 stagecoach trip, a plan began to foment in the oily mind of Robert P. Kelley. And soon after he returned to Mesilla following his business trip north, he visited with two like-minded acquaintances, Lewis S. Owings and Samuel J. Jones.

"A freshly minted territory must have a capital city, no?" The blank stares he received from them were less than flattering. He gave it another go. "I propose we do what some other forward-thinking soul will surely do before long. We are as industrious as the next, are we not?" He plowed ahead. "I further propose that we take full advantage of an already established name in order to hasten interest in our venture. This will give us a leg up over competition."

"Do you think others are having the same thought?" Jones said, worry creasing his brow.

"It is quite possible, but I should think that by using the name Mowry City, we will beat them at their own game. You see, Sylvester Mowry, as we all are well aware, is well connected and well regarded, especially back East. We all three of us are businessmen, our interests in Mesilla are vast. But I believe we are agreed that none of this will amount to a hill of beans if we aren't able to broaden our scope. The one thing we need out here is settlers. Settlers who will build and buy and, over time, help make us rich."

"How do you propose we get them here?" said Jones.

"We need more people in the region, in short. We need new money, fresh investment. And the best way to do that is to settle an entirely new town," said Kelley with a smile. "And then attract people to it, fill it with people whose very presence will require all manner of new goods, services, and such."

"Such as what?" said Owings.

"Such as hotels, mercantiles, saloons, gambling houses, millineries, you name it and they'll need it."

Owings clapped his soft hands together, rubbing them briskly. "How do we begin?"

"Good man," said Kelley. "And I anticipated that very question. What I propose is that we publish a pamphlet."

"Indicating our intentions?"

"Further than that—our pamphlet will tell the world how glorious the City of Mowry already is. We'll call it something along the lines of 'Report of the Mowry City Association, Territory of Arizona, 1859.'"

In fact, Kelley had already mapped out a plan that included the printing of the phony report as well as a newspaper of the place, both depicting the wonders of Mowry City and the region. And he conveniently had a printer in mind—his brother-in-law, a printer by the name of D. W. Hughes, in Missouri—far enough away that suspicions would not be aroused.

The pamphlet was printed and widely distributed, and it proved to be a stunning collection of lies. Among the many alleged virtues purported to exist in Mowry City, according to the pamphlet and newspaper, were a perfect climate, a peaceful way of life, a forgiving terrain rich with promise of gold and all manner of minerals, and the materials even hinted at the promise of agricultural pursuits.

The truth, however, was nearly as far from such balderdash as was possible. The location at which the hoodwinkers sited their "city" was already inhabited—by Apache Indians none too pleased to see the increasing incursions of whites, men who acted as if they had some right to be there. In addition to the resident band of hostile Apaches, Mowry City was in a hot, unforgiving place more suited to rattlesnakes and cactus—of which there was an ample supply—than peaceful tree-lined streets suitable for happy families.

But the site was also home of the Mimbres River Station, on the Butterfield Trail Overland Mail stagecoach route. The town received a needed early boost in 1860, when a deposit of placer, or surface gold, was found nearby at Pinos Altos. But the gold soon ran out and Mowry City had to rely on its own rough charms to survive. It seems those rough charms were enough—for a time, anyway.

Despite the fact that it was a depressing, wind-blown locale more suited to snakes than humans, and owing largely to Kelley's abilities to tell tall tales, Mowry City attracted people from the East looking for a new life and a new location in which to pursue it.

The reactions of future hopeful residents of Mowry City, once they reached the promised land, have been lost to time, though in a reminiscence by S. M. Ashenfelter published in the *Silver City Independent*, there is mention of a thriving Mowry City in 1871 as having a "considerable population" and being home to two stores offering general merchandise, a hotel, a flouring mill, and a blacksmith shop.

But in the 1860s, Loreta Janeta Valezquez recorded her candid impressions of Mowry City in her now-famous book of 1876, *The Woman in Battle: a narrative of the exploits, adventures, and travels of Madame Loreta Janeta Valezquez, otherwise known as Lieutenant Harry T. Buford, Confederate States Army*:

> Striking south-westward from Fort McRae we came to Rio de los
> Mimbres, near the head of which is Mowry City, founded by Lieutenant
> Mowry, who could not have had any very clear ideas as to what he was
> about when he attempted to make a settlement in such a place. Mowry
> City has a hotel, one or two stores, and more drinking-saloons than do
> it any good. That it will ever be much of a place I do not believe. There is
> not water enough in the river the greater part of the time to float two logs
> together, and in very dry weather one can step across it without wetting
> the feet. A sudden shower will, however, convert this puny creek in a short
> time into a raging river, which carries everything before it, and then it
> will subside as suddenly as it arose.

The 1861 Bascom Affair, which triggered the twenty-five-year-long Apache Wars, took the wind out of any further promotional plans Kelley may have had for Mowry City, and the settlement began its slow decline. By the 1870s the railroad came through, eliminating the need for stagecoach service and bypassing the town. This effectively drove the last nail into the warped-board coffin of Mowry City.

The few residents eventually drifted away or died of depression or snake-bite. What of Robert P. Kelley and his conniving cohorts? They never lived in Mowry City, so the loss was no great hardship to them. They were also never reprimanded for perpetrating what is considered as possibly the first (but certainly not the last) land swindle in the American Southwest.

As to the man who lent his name to the proceedings, Sylvester Mowry, a successful miner and author of several books, it's unclear if he was aware of the extent of the promoters' fabrications intended to lure settlers to Arizona. Given his lifelong zeal to see Arizona recognized as its own territory, it is conceivable he would have approved any scheme promising to usher in settlers to his beloved land.

CHAPTER 19

MARY GLEIM
MISSOULA'S WICKED WOMAN
(AND A PAIR OF GAMBLIN' GALS)

Mary Gleim was once known as Missoula's most maleficent madam (my, that's a whole lot of *Ms*). In addition to taking part in the number-one trade for women in the Old West, prostitution, Mary Gleim was also one nasty piece of work. She was a convicted murderer, a glutton, an alcoholic, a thug, a bully, an abuser, a serial cheat, a blackmailer, a paranoid ranter, and so much more.

Born in 1849 to Irish parents, Mary was treated to a top education in England and was by all accounts a sharp cookie. Unfortunately, her demeanor was so caustic she made enemies easily. She married John Gleim from St. Louis, Missouri, and with hubby in tow, descended on Missoula in 1888.

Mary was a handful, literally and figuratively. Weighing in at close to three hundred pounds, the brutish fireplug of a woman soon became widely known in Missoula, as much for her formidable presence as for her drunken rages in which she physically assaulted numerous people. Victims of her wrath through the years included a number of her prostitutes, business rivals, probably her husband, a handful of Irish priests, and even her own attorneys—who were kept busy on a constant basis with her howling shenanigans.

Mary Gleim chose Montana as a place to set up shop largely because there was an already-established robust black-market trade with Canada, the very sort of business venture that most interested her. Soon Mary began dealing in smuggled merchandise that included opium, lace, diamonds, prostitutes, and Chinese laborers. Business was brisk, and by May of 1889 she had bought her first house of ill repute, which she called a boardinghouse for women.

Within a year she bought eight commercial buildings fronting the main route in Missoula's red-light district. It also wasn't long before she began appearing before the local magistrate on a variety of charges stemming from her drunken rages. Within a few short years, she became known as the

A number of tough women top the list of the Old West's most famous—and notorious—professional gamblers, including such benign bettors as Lottie Deno, Kitty LeRoy, and Poker Alice Ivers. The latter, in her prime, was considered by many as the greatest gambler the West had ever seen. Women also often fared well as dealers for the house on such popular games as faro, in part because they often revealed charms that male dealers were unable to offer lovestruck gambling cowboys.... *Courtesy Library of Congress, 1911.*

Madame of Missoula because she had virtually cornered the market on that town's thriving bordello business. But the acquisition of her various and widespread real estate holdings did not come without a cost—frequently to the contractors employed to work on the buildings.

She was routinely hauled to civil court because she hadn't paid for work she had hired. She also had a habit of evicting and foreclosing on tenants who were unable to pay or were late with their payments. There was no wiggle room in a business deal with Mary Gleim. In 1893 alone, she was sued for nonpayment of back wages ten times, once by her lawyers. She inevitably lost the cases and paid the full restitution plus court fees.

In 1892 she engaged in one of her most famous attacks. In a drunken rage she attacked two priests, telling them they were not fit to wear their clerical robes, which she then proceeded to tear off them. She then smashed furniture and grew even angrier, howling in rage, when they remained passive and didn't defend themselves. She stormed out of the rectory, then with her wrath still in full bloom, she savaged the driver of the carriage she had kept waiting. Not surprisingly, she was hauled into court on three assault charges.

Two weeks later she was back in court, having smashed a bottle of beer over a man's head. In court on that charge, she railed and ranted, and her red-faced efforts resulted in two counts of contempt of court.

If she was cold in her business dealings, she was downright brutish in her dealings with her many prostitutes. She routinely beat them, cheated them out of their pay, and forced them to live in unacceptable conditions. Perhaps she was afraid she wouldn't have enough money to pay her lawyers for her constantly renewed court dates.

Her biggest incident to date came in autumn 1894 when she was convicted of the attempted murder of her biggest red-light district business rival, one Mr. C. P. "Bobby" Burns. She had a long history with Burns and was the person behind an incident in which he was whipped, then dragged by a team of horses.

Early in the morning of February 12, 1894, Bobby Burns's home in the heart of the red-light district was reduced to rubble by an immense explosion. Beyond all belief, Burns emerged alive, if battered, from the wreckage. Everyone in town knew just who was behind the savage attack.

Within a couple of weeks, several people were arrested, one of whom was later proven to be the man hired to enable the explosion. The case didn't go to trial until August, but by then the prosecutorial team had amassed sufficient evidence that they formally accused Mary Gleim of being the mastermind behind the bombing, even though she had conveniently been in San Francisco on business matters.

She was arrested and, because no one would act as bondsman on her behalf, she was forced to spend the time until the trial in jail. She was allowed into lockup with copious amounts of booze, most unfortunate for a woman in an adjoining cell. Once inebriated, Gleim proceeded to excoriate the hapless convict all night long, haranguing her with vile oaths and threats.

A series of postponements played out, then the trial finally began on September 8, 1894. It came out over the next few days that Mary had been quite vocal all over town about how badly she wanted Bobby Burns dead. She had even talked openly of poisoning his sugar bowl. Finally, on September 14, she was found guilty of attempted murder and the next day was sentenced to fourteen years of hard labor.

Instead of venting her rage in her usual custom, the bloated madam said nothing. But she must have known something no one else did, for by October of the next year, she was back in Missoula awaiting the commencement of a new trial. In the interim, she was allowed out on bail and promptly got up to her old shenanigans once more.

She brutally savaged one of her working girls, French Emma, bludgeoning her so badly the girl nearly died. When Emma appeared in court two weeks later, her eyes were still nearly swollen shut, her face was a bruised and battered mess, and as the *Missoulian* newspaper of February 28, 1896, put it, she looked like "a piece of high decorative art. Her eyes black and swollen . . . a deep brown-colored oil painting covering the side of her nose. One of her hands . . . lacerated, said to have been done by Mrs. Gleim's teeth."

Gleim was found guilty of assault and ordered to pay a $250 fine on top of her attorney's $300 in fees.

And Gleim's good luck just kept raining down—within the month word came out that Bobby Burns, the sole material witness available to testify at Gleim's new trial (the others had killed themselves, left town, or otherwise disappeared), had a fatal heart attack. By the end of May 1896, Mary Gleim once again was free. But it wasn't long before she found herself back in front of the bench, defending her foul personage on a series of cases ranging from verbal assaults to third-degree battery.

In 1905 Gleim, now sixty, showed up again in court as a codefendant, charged with assault with intent to kill. It seems that Mother Gleim, as the press playfully called her, along with two hired goons, entered the home of one C. A.

Clayton and "with bludgeon, loaded weapons, or instrument did cruelly and maliciously, wantonly, and unlawfully assault [him] by violent hitting, hammering, and striking him over the shoulders, in the face, [and] on the head and neck."

Finally, the city of Missoula breathed a sigh of relief when on February 22, 1914, Mary Gleeson Gleim expired, no doubt in a fit of fiery anger, of influenza, at the age of sixty-nine. At the time of her death, despite recent losses totaling $135,000 in a failed brick-making venture, she was still worth nearly $150,000. With no will in place and no children of her own, a niece and nephew inherited her estate.

As annoyingly belligerent in death as she was in life, Mary Gleim was able to once more buck the status quo. Her headstone in the Missoula Cemetery faces the opposite direction as all the rest. The popular story is that she had requested it to be so, in order that she may wave to all the railroad workers who were her loyal customers. The more likely story, however, is that the stone her heirs had commissioned was too large for the space, so it was of necessity turned lengthwise.

SNARLIN' KITTY LEROY

Kitty LeRoy was a notorious woman of the Old West whose life story is as spicy and tragic as her demeanor was fickle and prickly. Just enough is known of Kitty's early life that she remains an alluring enigma. Born in Michigan in 1850, she began dancing for money by age ten, and within a few years began earning a living in dance halls. Somewhere along the line she also learned how to wield a mean pair of shooting irons. That skill would stand her in good stead—for a time, anyway.

Even more useful to young Kitty was the cultivation of her budding seductive powers over the opposite sex. Perhaps she overdid it, for by age fifteen young Kitty was a married woman. True or not, the story of how she decided to marry the man is amusing and somewhat in keeping with what little else is known about the young firebrand. She made it known she would marry whatever man in town would allow her to shoot an apple off his head. The winner was the only man foolish enough to let her try. She pierced the apple and not his forehead, so they married.

Alas, as with everything in her whirlwind life, wedlock didn't last. She would not, could not, keep herself tied to just one man. Kitty LeRoy lit out on her own and ended up in Dallas, Texas, working as a dancer, looking for ways to make more and easier money. She always earned enough to keep her in the comfortable life she was beginning to appreciate.

By the time she turned twenty, Kitty got hitched for a second time and, for a while she and her husband seemed happy. Perhaps at his insistence, she switched her occupation from dancer to faro dealer. She also took to blending gypsy-like fashions and male clothing into an eccentric style of dress the opposite gender found enchanting. Cowboys, miners, and dandies alike lined up for a chance to buck the tiger at Kitty's faro table. Her skills as a gambler blossomed, and her penchant for overarming herself also became apparent. She would often wear a brace of pistols and an assortment of derringers and knives beneath her skirts.

Having bucked and bilked Dallas for all they could, Kitty and her second husband decamped to California, where they intended to run their own gambling establishment. While there, Kitty got up to her old tricks and ran off with a new suitor. They were ill-matched, though, and during an argument one night, the spitting little hellfire attacked her new beau, scratching, punching, kicking, and biting him.

Too much a gentleman, he refused to raise a hand to a woman. This only served to fuel Kitty's hot temper further and she dashed from the room, returning momentarily dressed as a man, demanding he fight back. Still, he rebuffed her. So Kitty LeRoy pulled a six-gun free of her holster and when he refused to draw his, she shot him. He dropped, bleeding and no doubt confused beyond measure by this vicious little hellcat with whom he was in love. Kitty sent for a man of the cloth, who married them while the groom lay dying. The new husband continued writhing in his agonies for a few more days, then expired.

Freshly widowed, and realizing the only real money to be made resided in gold-rich mine camps, she headed to the hot town of Deadwood, South Dakota. She caught a ride on a wagon train, traveling with Wild Bill Hickok and Calamity Jane. Once Kitty arrived, she found work readily as a prostitute, an occupation with which she had some familiarity. In time she realized her dream and christened her own establishment—the Mint Gambling Saloon. She also took on a fourth husband.

This one, a somewhat successful prospector of German origin, intrigued her for a time . . . until his savings dwindled. As she had with past paramours, she became surly and instigated arguments with the hapless digger. It all came to a head one night when she conked him on the bean with a bottle and told him to hit the road.

All this while she built up the Mint's business, providing soiled doves as well as booze and gambling to her eager clientele. By this time she was a well-known character in Deadwood, fawned over by the men—even as she filched gold from their pokes through her faro games—and dallying freely with a number of them. Kitty remained armed to the teeth, carrying a number of weapons at any one time, including a Bowie knife down her back and a pair of revolvers in her skirt pockets.

She had turned the heads of many miners, then just as quickly earned their enmity as she skinned them for all their dust. Her highest haul for one evening's play was $8,000. She was accused of shooting and/or stabbing anyone she caught cheating at one of her games, though her own were likely rigged.

In due course, Kitty LeRoy married a fifth and last time, to a prospector by the name of Samuel R. Curley. If Kitty's previous marriages had been spark-filled, tempestuous affairs, this one was downright explosive. Curley was not the sort of husband to sit idly by while his voluptuous young bride carried on with a handful of other men, among them her recent ex-husband. It is also believed she carried on with Wild Bill Hickok and notorious gunman Sam Bass.

All of Kitty's shenanigans came to a head on December 7, 1877, when hubby five tracked her down to the Lone Star Saloon. He found out what room she was in, stormed up the stairs, cornered her, and they voiced a loud argument. Shortly thereafter, folks downstairs heard a gunshot, quickly followed by another.

Though in Deadwood the sound of gunfire was a daily occurrence, the fact that these shots came from Kitty's room and not the bar heightened the overall sense of alarm. The ragtag band of saloon patrons stormed up the stairs—and when the gunsmoke cleared, the scene was a grim one.

There lay Kitty LeRoy, on her back, looking as if she were asleep, save for the smoking bullet hole in her chest. Beside her lay her husband, Sam Curley, dead of a messy self-inflicted shot to the head.

The tempestuous lovebirds were buried in separate coffins, but side by side, in the same grave at Ingleside Cemetery in Deadwood. Some time later their bodies were reinterred to the Mount Moriah Cemetery overlooking Deadwood.

LUCKY LOTTIE DENO

One of the Old West's most famous gamblers went by a number of names, mostly because she didn't want her family back East to know she was a gambler. She had told them in letters that she was the wife of a wealthy Texas cattleman.

The name she is most known by, Lottie Deno, is but a bastardization of a common phrase coined by a cowboy who claimed she'd made a whole "Lotta Dinero" off him. She was an Old West woman of mystery, known variously as Faro Nell, Maud the Mystic, and Queen of the Pasteboards, though her given name was Carlotta J. Thompkins. And she was one heck of a gambler.

But dallying with cards was more than a pastime. To Lottie, gambling was life itself. And it was an addiction she would discover early on in her life in Kentucky, where she was born on April 21, 1844, into a well-off and prim Episcopalian family.

In addition to her unusually keen abilities as a gambler, she cut a comely figure—she was a handsome redheaded woman, described by someone who knew her as "a fine looker . . . in manners a typical Southern Lady. She had nothing to do with common prostitutes . . . she was not a 'gold digger.'"

She was also accompanied for many years of her life by her black nursemaid, Mary Poindexter. Poindexter, it was said, was so devoted to Lottie that once on a walk together along the Mississippi River's bank, she spied a coiled rattlesnake ahead of Lottie on the trail and threw herself upon it rather than let Lottie get bitten. Mary's wound resulted in a painful, protracted sickness and an amputated finger. This imposing character could always be found sitting just behind young Lottie at the dealer's table, keeping a sharp eye out for cheats.

On one occasion, as Lottie worked a riverboat on the Mississippi, she was accused of cheating by a soldier for the Union Army. In all likelihood he had witnessed a swindling slip in her formidable gambling skills, but his mistake was in lunging for her. He never got much of a chance to prove his claim because big Mary muckled onto the youth and overboard he went.

Lottie had cultivated an air of respectability about herself, going so far as to forbid cursing, smoking, and drinking at her games table. And by the time she made it to San Antonio, she was a widely known and well-liked dealer. All this despite the fact that she had an annoying habit of peeling all of a man's money right out of his pockets.

Lottie was at home in San Antonio, as that town was a gambler's 'round-the-clock playground. She found steady work as a dealer at a respectable establishment called Frank Thurmond's University Club and was quite an attraction to all those lonesome cowpokes. They gladly left off their bad habits for a chance to sit in on a few hands with the lovely Lottie Deno. Soon enough she had earned the nickname "Angel of San Antonio."

Lottie, however friendly to the gamblers, was all business, earning a percentage of each night's take. She had also fallen in love with the owner, Frank Thurmond, a no-nonsense fellow, part Cherokee, and friend to Doc Holliday. He was forced to defend himself one night over a poker game and ended up killing a man with his Bowie knife, which he wore down his back on a leather thong. Frank left town as threats to his life rained in.

Soon after, Lottie followed and caught up with Frank in Fort Griffin, working at a gambling den called the Bee Hive. She quickly became top faro dealer in the place and her considerable gambling skills helped her one evening win all of infamous gunman-gambler Doc Holliday's cash, $3,000, in a hot game of faro. This led, in part, to a two-pistol stand-off between Lottie and none other than close confidante of Doc Holliday, Big Nose Kate Elder. The incident has been documented enough that the basic facts ring true. As Kate regarded her partnership with Holliday as a love match, she became convinced that Lottie was horning in on her man.

It is said that Holliday was fond of Lottie, though to what extent we are unaware. The two women squared off right there in the saloon, possibly with drawn six-guns. Ever quick on the draw himself, Doc leapt between the two wildcats and managed to subdue them before rising tempers led to gunplay.

Faro is an addictive card game not known for its equitable outcome for players, and the house rarely fared poorly. Good faro dealers were worth their wage in a gambling establishment, and women who happened to also run a game could usually count on raking in big-ticket takes at the end of a night's play. That's because the players, often ranch hands and miners looking for a bit of excitement of an evening, were also more often than not love-starved and always eager for the chance to wile away a few hours—and a goodly portion of their hard-earned money—in the company of a lady, even if they knew full well her game was likely rigged.

Lottie was just such a woman, a serious and accomplished gambler, though the jury's out as to whether Lottie truly was a swindler, as well. Odds are the truth lies somewhere in the gray area between all of those designations. Though it might be a stretch to paint Deno with the swindler brush, it's doubtful she could have attained the level of earnings she did, at such a consistent level and for such a sustained period, without working every possible angle for her own benefit.

Given that her game of choice as a dealer was faro, the most-rigged card game of the nineteenth and early twentieth centuries in the United States, and given that crooked faro equipment could be found in nearly every gambling establishment in the nation, it's no wonder Deno came out a winner so often and for so long. Especially when she did all she could to play up her winsome ways, wield her pious demeanor, and flash her coquettish smile. And it worked like a charm.

Lottie was, as are all professional gamblers, always on the scout for a way to pad her nest, as illustrated in a now-famous incident from her days at Fort Griffin. She was dealing faro one evening when two rowdies accused each other of ill use at a card game.

With the first sign of tension, the various games about the room stalled, chips and cards in midplay, cigars smoking silently as heads turned to see what the trouble might be. Only the dealers used the interruption as opportunity, eyeing the unguarded cards of their fellow players.

Smokey Joe was the first to stand, sending his thin wooden chair slamming backward to the floor, sparks fairly shooting from his eyes and venom slicking his sneering lips. "Get up, cheat!" he snarled to his opponent, a swarthy gent named Monte Bill.

Bill was slower to his feet, but for a reason—though his eyes were locked on Smokey Joe's, and showing no less hatred, his right palm already slid upward across the smooth leather of his holster. By the time he stood, his revolver was seated in his hand, his thumb cranking back on the hammer.

But if he thought he had the drop on his opponent, he was mistaken, for Smokey Joe was no dullard and had done the same as Monte Bill. They stared at each other across the card-strewn table. Scarcely a heartbeat passed when each man squeezed trigger and sound, smoke, and ragged flashes filled the room.

Each of the two hotheads dropped where they stood, Monte Bill making more of a mess of the task than Smokey Joe, slamming the table edge and sending cards, chips, an empty bottle, two glasses, and coins scattering.

Afraid of more gunplay, everyone in the place bolted for the door, running low, hands covering their hatless heads. Not long after, the sheriff, Bill Cruger, pushed in fast through the front door. Scanning the room he saw two dead men, blue smoke from their close-in exchange of gunplay thinning and rising to the high ceiling. The only other soul in the room was the handsome young redheaded woman, Lottie Deno, the popular faro dealer, still sitting at her table.

"Miss," he said, bending low and examining the dead men. "I cannot for the life of me understand why on earth you did not leave when the shooting began."

She offered a slight smile, her head canted to one side, her eyes on her hands as they arranged cards atop her table. "But then you have never been a desperate woman," she said in a low, almost-whisper of a voice.

But according to a handful of folks who were there that night, in staying put, Lottie had acted true to her inner dealer. When play resumed some time later, the money that had been on her faro table had somehow disappeared in all the hubbub. No one dared question the demure Southern lady. But a good many gamblers suspected her purse contained more cash than it had before the shooting.

Frank and Lottie spent five years in Fort Griffin, then decamped to New Mexico, marrying there. And trouble followed as Frank once more settled a scrape with his knife, again killing his combatant. Though it was ruled self-defense, the Thurmonds decided enough was enough and left the gambling life behind. They made a home in Deming, New Mexico, where Frank invested in mining ventures and real estate, and in time became a vice president of the Deming National Bank.

Lottie, too, quit professional gambling, save for one incident in 1892 when she hosted a charity poker game that netted Deming's St. Luke's Episcopal Church, a church of which she was a founding member, $40,000.

Lottie remained steadfast and true to her husband, Frank, for forty years, until his death in 1908. She lived many more years alone before cashing in her chips in 1934. Decades after her death, she was the inspiration for the character of Miss Kitty on the long-running television show *Gunsmoke*.

CHAPTER 20

RUSTLERS GALORE!
DUTCH HENRY BORN AND
BLACK JACK NELSON

When is a thief a swindler? Are all swindlers thieves? Is the converse true? Admittedly there is a difference between the two, though with many shades of gray between. Considering the skulduggery of organized and premeditated wholesale theft of big critters from people who not only owned them but relied upon said critters daily, it's a safe call to say that rustlers were a swindling bunch.

Perhaps not all cattle and horse thieves were swindlers, but there were a select few who were so good at thieving, and seemed to do it with such a high degree of panache and a relish for the pursuit, that they are very much like the riverboat gamblers and con artists on street corners who, one surmises, would do so even if they had alternative means of support.

The Old West's most notorious rustler, Dutch Henry Born, who came into the world on July 2, 1849, to German immigrants in Manitowoc, Wisconsin, didn't set out to be a rustler. But he tasted the sweetness of easily picked fruit and discovered it was a flavor he liked very much.

His first known livestock heist took place in the late 1860s. He'd found work as a buffalo hunter in Arkansas and eventually was able to save enough of his earnings to buy a wagon, hire a helper, and make serious money. But his plans were foiled by a Cheyenne attack, which left him and his partner alive but wounded and horseless.

They finally made their way, slowly and painfully—in the melee with the Indians, Henry suffered an arrow through the foot—to Fort Smith, where, hoping to salvage some scrap of his investment, he asked the commander if he might borrow a brace of mules to retrieve his hides. The commander had grown increasingly annoyed with hiders and threatened Born with arrest.

The story goes that Dutch Henry hadn't really considered breaking the law in any serious way until that very night when he swore revenge on the

Horse and cattle thievery was rampant throughout the Old West, as indicated by the popular 1917 novel, *The Rustler of Wind River* (above), by George W. Ogden. No one was more proficient at real-life rustling than Dutch Henry Born, whose gang at one time consisted of three hundred thieves and covered a vast region from the Texas Panhandle to New Mexico, and up to Colorado and Kansas.   The Rustler of Wind River *by G. W. Ogden. Illustration by Frank E. Schoonover. Published by A. L. Burt Company, 1917.*

uppity post commander. He made off with twenty government mules and the commander's prize horse. Sadly for Henry, he was soon captured and sentenced to prison for a lengthy stretch. But you can't keep a bad man down, especially one with an axe to grind. Irrepressible as ever, Henry made an escape barely three months into his sentence. That first jailbreak set a precedent that he would uphold time and again throughout his long career as a thief.

Henry found the rewards of cattle and horse theft much to his liking, and more importantly, he found he was rather good at it. He drifted back and forth over the line of the law for the next few years, finding work as buffalo hunter and freighter. Then, in 1874 he made his way down to the Texas Panhandle and became embroiled in the Second Battle of Adobe Walls, a lopsided siege by Comanche Chief Quanah Parker's men in a brutal effort to wipe out the whites in the compound. Interestingly, another notable in that fight was Bat Masterson, who would, years later, transport Born back to Dodge City on a warrant for larceny.

After that he signed on as a civilian scout for the US Army—specifically for Custer's Seventh Cavalry—but he didn't mix well with a certain self-righteous boy general. Born left his position, claiming that Custer was intolerably mean to his own men.

In time, Dutch Henry Born became the open-range equivalent of a big-city crime boss. At his prime he oversaw a vast network of operatives—as many as three hundred men, according to legendary Pinkerton Detective Charles Siringo. The gang cast a wide net, rustling livestock in a large region stretching from the Texas Panhandle over to New Mexico and up to Colorado and Kansas. Though he specialized in Indian pony and mule theft, Born and his men were certainly not averse to relocating cattle should their net happen to pull them in as well.

While some reports paint Born as the Robin Hood type, roving the vast stretches of the cattle-rearing West, righting affronts to downtrodden small holders by big ranchers, such syrupy accounts conveniently fail to recall the thefts of horses and cattle by him from the very small holders he was said to be helping. They also fail to mention the many deaths attributed to the man. Born's is not unlike the Jesse James story, bestowing on the cold, killing thief the mantle of wise benefactor to his "people."

Born was out to make himself money, and damn the peons who got in his way. That said, Dutch Henry was no run-of-the-mill, murderous brute. Rather he was a clever, bold man not prone to shirking a fight. He was also a fortunate man who slipped out of a number of close shaves and dicey predicaments through the years.

One such incident would bring Born the closest he ever came to losing his life. In 1866 his gang's encampment was discovered by a lone cowboy. The startled man stole toward Dodge City and alerted the law. Born and his men were well-known in the area, having looted cattle and horses from most of the surrounding ranches. Each town responded immediately with a posse, and by the time the riders converged from two directions on the rustlers, the outlaws had begun to scatter.

A dozen members of his gang were shot, captured, and hanged, including Dutch Henry's right-hand man, Chubby Jones. Dutch Henry escaped, though not without serious injury. Some accounts have him on the receiving end of six or seven gunshot wounds. But escape he did, managing to make it to Texas, where he holed up and healed up, vowing revenge on those who tried, but failed, to lay him low.

Numerous stories circulated throughout the West about Dutch Henry's inborn salesmanship. It was said that he once stole a sheriff's horse, then sold the same animal back to the lawman. But as slippery and as ruthless a thief as he was, Born could also be a savvy neighbor.

Not long after rancher Charles Goodnight established his famed JA Ranch below the Salt Fork of the Red River in Texas, he set up a meeting with Dutch Henry and his men at their camp near Fort Elliott, Texas, on Commission Creek. Goodnight proposed that he wouldn't hinder Born or his men if they, in turn, would agree to refrain from raiding in Goodnight's vast range. They shook on it, drank to it, and each remained true to his word.

In 1878 Born was once more arrested for attempted mule theft, this time in Trinidad, Colorado. While there awaiting trial, a reporter for the local newspaper offered this quick description of Born: "... a rather genteel-looking man for a horse thief, road agent, and murderer." It was also while in Trinidad that he met up with his old Adobe Walls fighting compatriot, Bat Masterson, now the law in Dodge City, Kansas. . . .

"I tell you, Masterson, I am as innocent of these charges as a newborn babe is of taking sweets from a grocer."

"Oh, you say that now, and I expected to hear no less from you, Dutch Henry, but make no mistake, you are a rascal and a rogue with a propensity for thievery." Bat Masterson hooked a forefinger around a slowly smoking stogie and leisurely puffed out a blue cloud. "What I want to know is how you made it through all those years of thievery when just about everyone else who ever made off with another man's mount was made to dance at the end of a rope."

The man in the cell leaned back on the cot, stretched his long legs, folded his hands over his belly, and sighed. "What makes you think I could answer that?"

Masterson glanced through the bars at Henry Born, a man he was convinced would end up in history's ledger as the single greatest horse thief in all the West, maybe beyond. He had to admit the man didn't really look like a thief, not that there really was a defining look to such men. But if there was he would guess it would have to be low-built, swarthy, wide of shoulder, narrow of wit, and of dark humor, not clever enough to evade the hangman in the end.

Not at all like Henry Born. The man fairly brimmed dandy. He was on the tall side, with a quick smile and a kindly way about him. No wonder, thought Masterson, that he'd heard the ladies liked Henry Born.

"Masterson, why are you so all-fired eager to drag me to Dodge City?" Born jumped to his feet and grabbed the bars. "Seems to me the rubes in this town could deal with me as well or better than the rubes back in your town."

Masterson puffed the cigar, blew a thoughtful cloud of smoke at the jail-house ceiling. "Talk like that will only get you in hotter water faster—here and in Dodge. And you know full well why I'm going to bring you all the way back to Dodge City—you're a thief and a fugitive from justice, Mr. Born."

"Ah yes, that's right. I'd almost forgotten about that. So much has been blamed on me that I find it difficult to commit it all to memory, the farce from the fact." The famous horse thief leaned close to the bars. "Did you know, Mr. Lawman, that it was said I worked with Custer?"

Now it was Masterson's turn for surprise. "I thought that was true."

"Oh, it was, it was. I scouted for a time—a short time, mind you—" At this he offered a wry smile. "For the Seventh Cavalry. Trouble was, I just couldn't take that man. Not in any shape or form. He thought so highly of himself, yet he treated his men with no respect. That's a fact."

Masterson shook his head slowly, as if he'd just caught a starving puppy wrestling with a flank of beef. "You're talking of a well-regarded man, Mr. Born. And in a most heinous fashion. Might be you'll want to curb that tendency in the future."

"Why, Mr. Lawman, are you a friend of the deceased?"

"No, I didn't say that."

"Well then, neither did I say anything that wasn't the truth. You see, truth is Custer was the meanest man I ever knew. And that's my opinion."

"Fair enough. I'd say you made a wise decision to get on out of the Seventh when you did."

"Yep, that's a fact. Those boys didn't deserve to die that way. Not at the hands of savages."

"Savages, eh? Is that why you've stolen so many horses from Indians?"

The man in the cell smiled but said nothing.

Masterson continued. "And plenty more, I'll wager, from whites."

"Now that's not true. Yes sir, I can say with all honesty that I never stole a horse from a white man."

"Now you're parsing words and splitting hairs. I know for a fact you've stolen plenty of mules from the US Army."

"Whites, for the most part, I'll reckon. Least that's the way I heard it." Born took a turn around the small cell, sat down heavily with a sigh. "What I'd give to stretch my legs up and down the main street of this dusty little devil of a town."

"Not a snowball's chance in hell, Born. The only place you're going is to sleep, and I recommend you make a good night of it because tomorrow we light out for Dodge."

The horse thief stretched out on the cot and closed his eyes. "Might be you're right, Lawman. But that doesn't mean I'm staying there for long."

Masterson did haul Born back to Dodge City to face charges of larceny and as a fugitive from justice. Once back in Dodge City, however, Born was acquitted of the charges because no witnesses could be rounded up.

Instead he was found not to have finished a prison term in Arkansas, and his exchange with the judge in the courtroom shows what a character Born really was. When Born was arrested for stealing mules, and then confronted with the fact that he was also wanted for escaping from prison, he reacted in mock astonishment. "Why, sir, I never did such a thing!"

The judge canted his head, a curious look on his face, "Oh? Then how do you explain the fact that you are here and not there, inside those walls serving your sentence as a prisoner?"

Born shuffled his feet, raised his manacled hands and scratched a whiskered cheek, a look of genuine puzzlement writ large on his face. "I only took that guard at his word. You see, he gave me permission to go look for a shovel. Well," Born raised his hands, then let them drop, "I went and went some more, on and on, all over the country, and I still couldn't find a shovel." He shrugged his shoulders and looked at the judge as if he had just about reached his wit's end in his quest for a shovel.

"Well, Mister Born, be that as it may, and while I would very much like to accept your version of the story as the truth, I am compelled by law and logic to uphold the earlier verdict and remand you into the custody of the penitentiary at Arkansas you left in such an untimely manner, where you will serve the remainder of your sentence. After that, sir, I hope you will repent and refrain from your nefarious ways."

The notorious thief nodded and said, "I think you are doing what you must do, Judge."

"Now, about this latest charge of horse thievery." The judge once again sighed long and loud, rustled a sheaf of papers before him on the bench. "We have waited in vain for the witnesses for the prosecution to turn up in this court. But it would appear that the Indians are all where they are supposed to be—on the reservation. And the US Army soldiers who would have spoken against Mister Born are nowhere to be found. Why is that, prosecutors?"

A weary man in a rumpled gray suit pushed to his feet. "Your honor, those soldiers were sent for, but they had been transferred to other regions, as is the army's wont."

"Then you are telling me you have no witnesses?"

The prosecutor gnawed the inside of his cheek, then finally closed his eyes and nodded. "Yes, your honor."

Once more the judge let loose with a long, low sigh. "Having no other option at my disposal, I hereby release Mr. Henry Born of the charge of horse theft due to a lack of sufficient evidence."

The judge hammered down the outraged growls and gasps of shock that rippled through the half-filled courtroom. Dutch Henry cleared his throat as the guard unlocked his manacles.

"Yes, Mr. Born? You wish to say something?"

"Just that as I am now even with the army and I am even with the Indians, it is time for Henry Born to bury the hatchet and smoke the pipe of peace and go straight."

And, after decades of rustling, Dutch Henry Born kept his word. When he got out of prison, he took to mining in Colorado, then purchased 160 acres along the West Fork of the San Juan River, a day's ride from Pagosa Springs, Colorado. He established a fish farm there, and the spot would become known as Born's Lake. He even married, fathered four children, and refused to keep a gun on the premises, claiming he'd had his fill of killing.

Dutch Henry Born lived a long life, blessed with good fortune and more lucky breaks than any slippery swindler has a right to expect. It was not a lynch mob's noose, nor a posseman's bullet that laid Dutch Henry Born low. In the end it was pneumonia on a cold January 10, 1921, that did the final task, at age seventy-two. Born is buried at Pagosa Springs, Colorado. No word on whether any of his kids ever carried on the (first) family business and took to the owlhoot trail.

BLACK JACK NELSON

A. C. Simmonds had grown up in the Great Basin region of Utah hearing stories of his family's neighbor, Black Jack Nelson, and the man's reputation as a notorious outlaw. But Simmonds never would have guessed that one day he would buy Nelson's ranch from the old rustler himself. Years later, in 1906, when Black Jack was in his sixties, he sat down with Simmonds and told him the whole truth of his exploits—tales of a murder and a stagecoach robbery and numerous rustlings and crop thefts—tales he'd never told another person.

"Jack," said the younger man, who himself had a touch of gray in his beard. He swigged again from the bottle they were sharing as if he'd been about to ask something but had lost his nerve.

Nelson smiled a little. "Go ahead and ask. I'd say you're eager to know something."

Simmonds nodded. "Okay then, Jack. Did you ever shoot a man?"

Nelson sipped from the bottle, then said, "I did once, yes. It was an Injun. Felt badly about it ever since. But it was what had to happen. Elsewise he woulda kilt me."

Then he leaned forward and lowered his voce. "That's the truth of it. But that ain't no way close to the most exciting thing that ever happened to me. Now," he took another sip of the whiskey. "I always was different, I guess. When Pap and the family decided to move to Utah, I had me two brothers, Will and Joe. But they was older and we wasn't never close. I had a tendency early on that kept me from taking a liking of work. Oh, I don't mind spending my energy, but I didn't want some other man telling me what to do and how to do it. So I took to the owlhoot trail, as I've heard it's called. It's a romantic name for something that just means you're doing things most folks wouldn't never try. Took me a while to get the hang of it, you see."

He smiled at the memory, closed his eyes, and for a moment his younger companion thought the older gent might have dozed off. Then Nelson spoke, and as he did so his face seemed to lose its gruff look, his ruddy cheeks appeared less wrinkled, his moustache twitched, bushier, more gray than reddish now. Then his eyes popped open. He was smiling.

"I expect I can tell you a few things that not another soul alive or dead ever knew . . . no one but me, that is." He leaned in. "Oh, there were plenty of law dogs who thought they knew the truth, but them not quite knowing ain't the same thing as knowing, now, is it?"

"I guess not, Mr. Nelson."

"Call me Jack. Or Black Jack. Heh, that's what they used to call me."

"How'd you get that name anyway . . . Jack?"

"I gave it to myself! I figured if I was to rustle cattle and horses, by gum, I ought to have a name to strike fear into the hearts of them that would give chase. Really all I hoped was that it would make them think twice before taking off after me. All that double-thinking might give me a few more minutes to get on up the trail."

"So you did . . . steal cattle?"

"Yes, yes, I did. And I should say that I repent and I regret it and all that palaver. But the truth is, I liked it. Oh, not every minute of it, but who likes everything they do in life?"

"Not many. I can't say I like everything I do in a day's time, that's for certain."

"There, you see?" Black Jack slapped his knee and gave the bottle another tug. The warming liquid loosened his tongue and cleared his mind. He felt fine, felt like he hadn't felt in a number of years. "I have stolen just about anything there is worth to steal up in these here parts of the country. I made off at one time or another with cattle, horses, gold, wheat. And then there's a certain payroll from a certain stagecoach."

"You mean to tell me that story was true?" Simmonds poked the sweat-stained hat back off his forehead. In the dim lantern light, it seemed to him that Nelson was smiling broader than ever.

The outlaw nodded. "You see, back in 1873 I was doing business over along the border of Idaho and Oregon. I'd already rustled cattle and horses and been tossed in jail for them too. I was looking around for greener pastures. So while I was over that-a-way, I discovered something I had not been aware of—a whole lot of money, and I mean a whole lot of money, was running through there. I'm talking about gold from Boise Basin and silver from all them mines in Owyhee. And payroll and money all them greedy merchants made off the miners.

"And you know where it was headed? South on the Central Pacific line on down to Nevada, to Winnemucca, and over to Kelton, Utah. So I says to myself, 'Jack?' I never call myself Black Jack. 'Jack,' I says. 'You need to decide if you like being caught rustling cattle for pennies on the pound or would you rather risk more time in jail for something that will keep you in high style.' And I decided that someone was bound to liberate all that money before it reached those railroad goons anyway, so it might as well be Black Jack Nelson.

"It was a bright, fine morning with nary a cloud in the sky. I recall it was July 25, 1873. Don't ask me why I recall that, I just do. Come to think on it, maybe it's because it ain't every day that a man makes a fortune in one fell swoop." Jack cackled again, slapped that knee, and continued. "It was me and Sam, that'd be my old pal, Sam Colyer, a nicer fella you'd be hard pressed to find, but numb as a hammer-struck thumb.

"He was willing to take direction from me and be glad with whatever scraps I tossed his way. Like a big dog he was. Anyways, me and Sam were holed up along the road, about three miles south of that ford in the Snake River. We were hunkered there with our shotguns and kerchiefs pulled high up on our faces, cinched tight just below our eyes, our hats pulled down too. While we still had time, long before I heard the stage a-comin', I told Sam, no matter what, not to use my name. . . . 'Why not?' said Sam. 'What am I supposed to call you?'

"I sighed. 'Sam, you call me by my name, and I use yours, they're going to find out who we are. Might as well not wear these here face coverings if we're going to go around shouting each others names.'

"'Oh, I see what you mean. Okay.' After a few minutes, Sam spoke again. 'What'll I call you, then?'

"I only had time to sigh before I heard the screech and rattle of the stage, the shouts and whistles of the driver. Then the pounding of the horses' hooves. It was a four-horse team and I give some thought to taking the horses, too, but I wasn't so sure about leaving anyone afoot out there. It was a whole lot wilder in those days than it is today, I can tell you.

"Then there was no more time for thinking, let alone palavering with Sam. For that stage come on quick. We braced it, standing right in the road, no way they could get past without a blast from each of us, but positioned such that we wouldn't deal each other with a face full of buckshot, neither.

"'Ho, there! Ho there, I tell you!' I shouted it as if I was king of the world. In truth, it's like when you're a child and your papa is coming back from a trip to town and he had hinted that there just might be some toothsome treat, like a licorice pipe, somewhere in his coat pocket if you were good and all and help your mama. And you'd wait and wait and then you finally see him riding back home, tall in the saddle and with a big black hat and you're thinking if only that hat was made of licorice.

"And he looks down at you with them sad eyes, sort of surprise, and you just know he forgot to buy any little licorice or any sweetie for you. Well waiting on that stage was just like that feeling. And once I got them to toss down them two sacks of mail, and the Wells Fargo strongbox, it was all I could do to find out if there was something a whole lot prettier and more useful than licorice in that box. I told them all to skedaddle. I didn't want them stopped any longer than they needed to be. Elsewise they might get comfortable with the situation and try something that would force me to use a gun on a man, and that's something I've always tried to avoid."

"And was there?"

"Was there what?" Nelson asked. "Money in the strongbox? 'Course there was! Do I look like the sort of man who'd waste his time on a situation like that otherwise?" He nodded solemnly. "That box was filled with a whole passel of goodness, in fact." He smiled broadly and sipped the whiskey once more. "I give ol' Sam two small bars of pure gold and told him to skedaddle and to keep his mouth shut. Should have known better, but then again, I was dumber in those days."

"How much was in there, Jack? That is, if you don't mind me asking." Simmonds leaned forward, gazing intently at the storytelling old man.

"Don't mind at all. I've gone down this trail far enough I might as well not shortchange you on the details, now, eh? Wouldn't be right. Let's see. . . ." he ran plump, stubby fingers across his whiskered chin. "Near as I recall there was $20,000 in that box."

The man to whom he'd been telling the story, A. C. Simmonds, gasped, sat back in his chair. "Twenty thousand . . . my stars."

Nelson's eyes widened. "That's about what my reaction was!" he slapped his leg once more. "After I sent Sam on his way—which was not without purpose, either, you know. I figured he might work to draw the danger off of me and toward him. It could have worked better, but then again I got away with it, for the most part, didn't I?"

"You did?"

"Sure I did. After that I made my way back to the City of Rocks, you know that place? I found me a cave. Some clever gent called it Big Cave, matter of fact. Up in Western Canyon, up yonder headed to Cache Valley. You get to it from the west, though, elsewise it's a fool's errand. My plan was to hole up there until the snows closed the passes, making it too difficult for me to be followed. What I didn't know at the time was that Wells Fargo was madder than a rattler poked with a sharp stick. They posted rewards for us, imagine that! $2,500 each. I was mighty flattered when I eventually found out about that, I tell you. Makes a man feel proud to be that highly thought of." He winked, laid a finger alongside his nose knowingly.

"But it was that reward that started things a-tumbling. An old rock hound got the drop on Sam, dragged him to Boise, where that rascal, US Marshal Joe Pinkham, rousted him. They made Sam tell them everything. And I know Sam wasn't the sort to squawk without feeling something, maybe pain, you know? So ol' Sam up and admits to it all, spills the whole bean pot, tells them where he hid his two gold bars. They give him five years up to the Territorial Penitentiary in Boise.

"But all this I wasn't to know for some time to come. I was having my own troubles, but mine weren't with lawmen, they were with Indians. It was a hunting party of Shoshoni, all braves. I think they'd come down from Fort Hall. I could just see their fire on down the canyon, hear them laughing, whooping it up now and again. And I know they could see me. Smelled me, I dare say. My fire, my food—who knows?

"After a while they commenced to riding on up to visit me, sometimes one of them, other times two or three together. Not that it was a friendly sort of visiting, you understand. I reckon they thought since I was a white man that I'd have all manner of whiskey. I didn't really care what their thoughts were, I kept my revolver and my shotgun right handy and tethered my two animals, a pack horse and my mount, closer in to camp.

"There was one of those rascals, after a while he just wouldn't leave. Kept lurking. I give him some food, which if you do that with a cur dog, they'll likely stick around. But I felt like I couldn't eat in front of him and not offer the man a plate. But he was a curious sort and wouldn't keep his beady eyes off my gear and horses.

"That kept up for a few hours more, then as the daylight started to hide itself away for the night, the entire band rode on down through the canyon, headed to the mouth that led to the valley below. I saw them all ride on out, all but that one who wouldn't leave me be. I recall by the way he'd been eyeing my pack horse that he was planning on making a play for it. And long after the other braves had filed out of the canyon, I watched that rascal worm his way on over toward the animal. Then all of a sudden he jumped up on its back and began to drum his heels on that poor beast's sides. Well, my pack animal began to move, all right. And if I hadn't had my Colt close to hand, I reckon I might have lost that horse."

Simmonds leaned in. "What did you do?"

"I shucked that Colt Navy and thumbed back on the hammer right quick. I aimed straight at the back of that thief's head and let 'er go. My word, but that noise echoed and rolled and thundered on down that long, narrow, rocky valley, and I knew the other braves would have heard all that crashing sound. I only delivered one lead pill to the brave's head, but it sounded like a full-bore cannon battle.

"I didn't have any time to waste, so I grabbed onto that Injun and flopped him over my shoulder. When I got to the top, I chucked him in a ditch not far from the cave. He flopped and tumbled on down there, and I covered him over with whatever I could find that looked natural, mostly scrub branches, that sort of thing. Good thing I did, too, for not long after, who comes riding on up but them others in his party.

"They seemed to know something had happened because they commenced to annoy me and give me the hard looks, but they couldn't find their chum. Kept on walking around in circles, looking for him. But they never did find him. And I never did get any sleep. They finally left in the morning. They knew I killed him, though. And I figured that if they found him, why they'd kill me right back!

"From there I headed to the Big Range. Figured I'd wait out the winter with my kin. But before I got there I found a likely spot at the base of a mountain out there close by Newton, Utah, called Molly's Nipple. Don't ask me how it got that name," he smiled, winked. "Because I am liable to get a little embarrassed." He laughed, before continuing his story. "So I buried that money and didn't draw off it right then. Plenty of time for spending all that money down the road.

"That winter I visited with neighbors, family. One neighbor had a boy, couldn't have been more than a year or so old. You remember that?" Nelson smiled at Simmonds, who nodded, knowing that boy had been him, though too long ago to recall it.

"Wasn't long after that, along about the next year, I think, 1875 it was, that I made my way through Elko, Nevada, then south a ways toward the White Mountains near Ely. As I passed on through Elko I couldn't help it—I found myself leaving town with a team of horses. Imagine my surprise when the sheriff showed up at my camp. Not only did he catch me with those horses, but he had a wanted dodger on me for the stage coach job! Of all the nerve, rode right into my camp and that was that. I ended up spending the next nine years—nine years!—at Carson City prison. Wasn't until 1884 that I got out and bee-lined it back to Molly's Nipple and my loot. It was all still there too. I will admit—and no shame in it, either, that I lived like a king for a winter.

"By May, 1884, I found myself in Frisco, Utah, and found something I knew a little about—two horses that looked like they needed me to show them the way to a better trail. So the next day when I headed on out of town, why those two horses came with me. Problem was, they belonged to a local rancher who was all worked up over them being missing and all. I managed to hide them, but it didn't matter. They still rousted me at the line cabin on my papa's range.

"They tore everything apart, didn't find hide nor hair of those horses. But they yarned me outta there anyways. Kept me a few days, then had to let me go. I sold those horses for a nice little profit. Oh I spent the next ten or so years moving other people's dogies and ponies from Utah on up to Montana and back again, wherever there was men and money, and mining money, in particular. They always seemed to need good cattle and horseflesh. There was demand, see, and I was filling it. Plain good business savvy.

"After a fashion I grew tired of all that rousting up and down, even though parts of it were still exciting to me. I guess I was just getting older, I don't know. But soon enough I bought me a saloon. I tried to keep on the level and narrow road that so many other men don't seem to have a problem traveling, but so help me, it was all I could do to not shoot myself.

"I ended up making nighttime runs, found me a new product to peddle too." Black Jack leaned forward. "It was wheat," he sat back. "Yes sir. Wheat. I'd scuttle on in under cover of darkness and load up a wagon, drive it north ten miles or so, sell it to a mill, strike off in a different direction, find more, sell it, make my way home. No questions were asked, no answers were given. Now who's the crook, eh?" he laughed again, slapping at that knee.

"I tell you, though, those were tedious years. Still are. That blasted county sheriff, Rob Crookston, has been riding out to my place regular as clockwork, with warrants for my arrest. Ever since 1881 or so on up through today. Any time anything goes wrong, any time someone's kitten goes missing, anything at all goes amiss, and he comes trotting on out to my place, drags me back with him. I tell you it gets downright embarrassing.

"So after a few of those episodes, I hired me a lawyer, one George Q. Rich. He was a good attorney, but I tell you what, there was no competing with a warrant every month, sometimes more than one! I believe it was in 1904 that he got so fed up because I kept him so blamed busy that he sent me a letter. Mind you he sent it to me," Nelson leaned forward, smiling, eyes twinkling, and he said, "The note had just two words on it: 'You're fired.' Ha! Imagine that! My own attorney fired me! Oh but that was a hoot.

"Then those rascals in Newton, they outlawed booze two years ago, and me owning the only saloon in town. Imagine that. How can a man be a man without a bar to lean on and a fine friend to share a few swallows with?" He raised the bottle and saluted Simmonds, passed it to the younger man.

Nelson dragged his coat cuff across his mustachioed mouth and belched softly. "I'm selling up and heading on out of here. It's no fun anymore." He stood and stretched his husky, five-foot-six frame, squared his hat on his head, and shook the younger man's hand. "Be seeing you, Simmonds. Good knowing you."

He walked to the door and Simmonds watched Black Jack Nelson leave, a man not yet old, but no longer young, a man who had lived more adventurous years than any ten men Simmonds knew he was likely to ever meet.

Nelson paused in the doorway of the ranch blacksmith shop and half turned. "And if you ever tell anyone about all these things I just said," he smiled, "I'll deny it all. Ha!" He slapped his leg and walked off, offering a slow wave over his shoulder as he made his way into the night.

Simmonds wasn't sure what to think of this man he'd just heard share secrets to which no one else had ever been privy. Outlaw? Thief? A man who'd swindled and stolen and pillaged up one side of the Big Range and down the other. A man who had stolen from friends, foe, and family alike. And yet, there was something about Black Jack Nelson that was likeable. Legend or outlaw. Or both.

Simmonds swigged the last of the bottle and headed for his house.

CHAPTER 21

OLD SAN FRANCISCO
SINK PIT OF SWINDLERS

Sometimes thievery and swindling take on different forms, become an oozing sickness that runs long and deep, a vein of illness coursing beneath a place, leaching evil upward into the inhabitants, causing good and bad to clash time and again. Sometimes swindling is a deep-rooted hoax rather than the surface-dwelling misdeeds of a fly-by-night thimblerigger. Such was the case with San Francisco when the nineteenth century collapsed, plundered and spent, at the feet of the shiny new twentieth century. But it didn't end there.

The Barbary Coast, a nine-block canker clinging to the wharves of San Francisco, was a premier red-light district, where brothels, saloons, and gambling halls numbered in the hundreds. Seekers of the dangerous district's ills numbered in the tens of thousands, following the overnight bloom of the California Gold Rush in 1849.

Though that hotbed of debauchery certainly existed for more than a decade, it was not until the early 1860s that the Barbary Coast earned its romantic moniker. Sailors pinched the name from the original Barbary Coast, along North Africa's coastline, a notorious region where pirates and slavers looted, raided, and instigated every possible pursuit of vice and corruption. It was a matter of time before someone named California's coastal version the same thing.

From the raw, wide-open hedonism, crime, and deviltry of the Barbary Coast to gang rule and warfare to decades of graft and corruption within the ranks of its elected officials, San Francisco has a fascinating history of lawlessness that exceeds better-known wide-open Old West towns such as Dodge City, Deadwood, and Tombstone. But what can we expect from a city whose population bloomed fifty-fold in a little more than two years following the gold rush? In 1847 San Francisco was a sleepy little coastal enclave of 492 people living in tents and crude shacks. By the time 1849 drew to a close, more than 25,000 people called the spot home.

In 1901, Eugene "Handsome Gene" Schmitz (top, left) was hand-picked by burgeoning political boss, Abe Ruef (top, right), to be mayor of San Francisco. Under the Schmitz-Ruef regime, graft and corruption nearly bled dry the city's coffers, then the Great Earthquake and Fire of 1906 exposed the extent of the chicanery. Indictments were handed down and Ruef went to prison, emerging in 1915, penniless and humbled. (Bottom): In 1856, James Casey, lapdog for corrupt Senator Broderick, gunned down forthright newspaperman James King in the street. A crowd of 10,000 protested, and within days the citizen-led Vigilance Committee tried and hanged Casey for the crime.   *Top left: Complete Story of the San Francisco Horror by Herbert D. Russell, 1906. Top right: Courtesy Library of Congress, Photo by Bain News Service. Bottom: Courtesy Library of Congress, Frank Leslie's Illustrated Newspaper, July 19, 1856.*

So what qualifies nineteenth-century San Francisco as a swindler? In truth, the Bay City was not so much a swindler as it was a haven for them. Indeed, as a locale, it proved itself to be an ideal incubator for individuals and groups actively engaged in bilking others out of their money, their time, their votes, and ultimately, their most valuable possession—their lives.

Had San Francisco, and in particular Barbary Coast within it, not formed as it had—rapidly and with little oversight—there would have been far fewer incidences of swindlers and swindling farther afield throughout the West. But because San Francisco was such a hotbed of chicanery and deceit, like-minded individuals congregated and conjured more of the same until it was impossible for a man to leave a brothel without getting waylaid and robbed as he stepped out the door on his way to a saloon two doors down.

It wouldn't be long before the city became fractured into various neighborhoods filled with gangs, frequently allied or divided by nationality or political or social agendas. One of the earliest such gangs was a clot some sixty strong, tightly organized like a modern-day biker gang. These men, calling themselves the Hounds, set up shop in 1848 and made a business of the prevailing disorganized and unruly individualistic pursuits of swindling, thieving, corruption, and murder, and upped the ante to almighty heights.

The Hounds were discharged Mexican-American War volunteers, many of them former gang members from New York City with axes to grind. They tormented anyone of Spanish descent and shook down local merchants for protection money, promising woe to those who refused to pay up. The Hounds set upon the belligerent with a fury, and with a few quick flashes of knives or razor blades, they removed noses, ears, eyes, fingers, toes, or worse. Not surprisingly, the newly scarred merchant usually paid the extortion fee and continued to do so—minus an appendage. . . .

"Hey, Paco. . . ."

The slight, swarthy man tried not to let on that he'd heard the call, but it had hitched his step. So he thought, keeping his hands balled tight in his coat pockets. Tonight is my night, the thing I have been expecting is about to happen, unless I can run faster than them. He didn't quicken his pace until he heard the boot steps draw closer—it sounded like two men somewhere behind him, closing in.

"Hey, I'm talking to you, Mexican!"

Here we go, thought the man, and he slid his hands out of his pockets even as he bolted forward down the mud street, splashes of ooze spraying upward with each footfall. Behind him he heard shouts, "Get him! Stop that man!"

He ran faster, leapt over the remnants of a shattered wooden crate, dodged to his left to avoid piling into two scantily clad women leaning against each other. *Have to get away*—he knew what would happen to him. His only crime was working hard to make money to get out of the city.

He knew that the two men behind him were members of the Hounds, and the Hounds hated him because he was Mexican and because he owned a small business selling rough-weave shirts and trousers to miners. It wasn't his business the Hounds objected to, but the fact that he had refused to pay them the money they demanded. And he knew what would happen because he witnessed the results of their so-called protection. But business had been slow and he had no money to pay them, even if he had wanted to—which he didn't.

And now it would not matter—they were hard on his trail. His shop front, such as it was, would not exist tomorrow, of that he was sure, and he would owe money for the inventory.

As the shouts increased and the sound of the men's voices drew closer, he knew he might not make it away from them. Might not, but he had to try. His breath came in quick gasps now, hot and stinging in his chest. Sweat stippled his face, ran down his cheeks and nose, he felt its salty tang on his moustache. He might just make it—the shouts of the men were not as close as they had been seconds before.

And then a man ahead, a tall, thin-looking fellow with ratty clothes and a broken cane spun in his direction on hearing the shouts of his pursuers. He saw the man's smile widen, saw the black nubs and gaps where teeth had been. Then he was bolting by the man, then . . . his legs hit something and he heard a cackling laugh as he flipped forward. He landed face-first in a half-muddied patch just outside a saloon filled with drunken men and women. As he pushed himself up, he saw the tall man poking at him with his broken cane and knew the man had stuck his long leg out and tripped him.

The chased man tried to rise, but rough hands were already on him. He heard gasping breaths, smelled the rank reek of old food and whiskey and rot, all clouding at his face, and he struggled to clear the mud from his eyes.

But it was too late. A fist, big and bony, drove into his cheekbone, snapping his head sideways. He felt something crack deep in his head, in his neck, and a numbness built in him. There was blood, and there were faces everywhere, the laughing faces of drunks looking out the windows of the saloon. Now he saw them, the two who had been chasing him.

And he recognized them as the same men who had warned him, the same ones who told him he would be given no second chance to give them the money. Money he didn't have and would never have. But on their faces he saw more than their greedy desire for money. He saw anger. No, it was more than that, he saw disgust and he knew this was only because he was Mexican. These were gringos who had fought in the war, and none of them he had ever encountered felt anything but anger toward Mexicans.

They were dragging him toward the alley, the dark angle of space to the side of the saloon. More sound rushed into his ears, loud, as if he were hearing for the first time. At the same time he felt strength returning to his arms, his legs. He willed them to move, thrashed with them as hard as he could, for he knew he had nothing to lose.

He sensed they were not after his ears or nose or fingers. He had angered them too much. Now these men were after his life, if only to feed their hatred of him. *Fight,* he told himself. *Fight or it will all end and you will die shamed. Fight.*

And he did, kicking and thrashing and flailing and shouting, and they pummeled him again and again in the face with their big fists. He fought long past the point where he felt something low on his side pop, then hot pain like lightning flowered inside him. It washed all over, as if he had been tossed into a vat of hot coals. He screamed, still kicking, for there was nothing else to do.

Again and again he felt the popping and knew it was a knife driving deep into him, over and over, his life's blood leaking out into the mud of this filthy street in this filthy city. And all for money. He should have listened to his sister, to his grandfather, the only ones of his family left back in Mexico. But he wanted to make money to help them, and now they did not even have him.

It all came to a head in 1849 when more than two hundred local men, tired of giving over their hard-earned money, formed their own gang, the Regulators, and retaliated. This new militia clashed with the Hounds in their den in the Barbary Coast. The Hounds promptly tucked tail and scattered, running for parts unknown. But the militia's work had barely begun. For a more entrenched and thriving collective had set up shop in 1849, and these newcomers were no mere striplings. They were boatloads of hardened criminals from Australia.

Calling themselves the Sydney Ducks, they moved in, took over established businesses, and proclaimed it Sidney Town. They looted without impunity throughout San Francisco, setting fire to entire blocks of vulnerable wooden structures a half dozen times by 1851. While the fires raged, the Ducks pillaged, raped, and murdered unseen.

Once again the common citizens could take no more and the militia that had run the Hounds out of town re-formed, stronger and more organized this time. They called themselves the Vigilance Committee, and merely running the Ducks out of town was not on their agenda. They had had enough and wanted a more permanent solution to the growing plague of crime in their midst.

The vigilantes made quick work of rounding up two men, Robert McKenzie and Samuel Whittaker, men they knew to be guilty of participating in the recent spates of arson and looting. A quick trial was held and the two men were hanged. This stunned the brazen Ducks, and it wasn't long before the rest of them waddled out of San Francisco. At last, the Vigilance Committee had secured a period of relative calm. It lasted for two years before a newer, more insidious entity rose up, and this time it came from within the ranks of paid city officials.

In 1852 corruption at the highest levels became exposed. The spider at the heart of this web of graft and corruption was state senator David Broderick. Others may have held positions of seeming importance in Frisco, but Broderick called the shots. Whenever anyone assumed public office, he demanded they split their earnings with him, ill-gotten or not, right down the middle. The city's own bank accounts had become threadbare, caused by bloated salaries and kickbacks from projects that never saw fruition.

Public anger ran higher with each day, but it would take the murder of a lone voice of reason before San Franciscans were forced to act. . . .

"King!"

James King stopped in his tracks, one hand resting on the doorknob of his newspaper office. He was in a hurry, late in fact, to get this latest slice of misfortune inside to be typeset for the paper. The last thing he needed was another interruption.

His eyes clapped on the man who'd shouted and King instinctively sneered. He curled a finger around the damp cigar stub jutting from his mouth. "James Casey. I've been wondering when I might again have the displeasure of addressing Senator Broderick's lapdog. What do you want? I'm a busy man."

Casey stepped closer, his hands holding back the sides of his unbuttoned frock coat, his hands resting lightly on his waist. "Oh, I know you're a busy man, King. Busy spreading lies and rumors about the good senator. And it has to stop."

King took a step toward Casey. "Are you threatening me, Mr. Casey?"

By then a number of people had paused in the street, regarding the rising voices of the two known enemies.

"You know what I am doing. I am telling you to stop maligning Senator Broderick, King, or you'll find I'm not so nice."

King felt his face redden, and he poked the air before him with a rigid finger. "Now see here, Casey." He bulled forward, savoring any moment he was able to tell anyone at all just what a filthy, lying thief Broderick really was.

"No sir, your words will not stand!" Casey's face had reddened considerably, and quick as lightning he shucked his sidearm and raised it level with King's chest. The newspaperman spat disgustedly and took another step toward Casey.

Casey thumbed back the hammer and, without waiting, fired a shot at King's chest, then another. King spun to the side, slamming his back against the door of his beloved newspaper office. The cigar stub had dropped from his mouth, and he slumped to his side, one leg bent beneath him. The sheaf of papers he had been carrying splayed across the sidewalk and down the steps.

It took seconds for Casey to be subdued, strong-armed to his knees by a handful of men, while others eased King against the wall. *He is still alive . . .* murmurs rippled through the rapidly growing crowd.

"Let me go! Broderick won't like this! Let me go, I tell you!" Casey writhed, but the men holding him told him to shut up, that he was going to jail. Some said he would swing for killing the only true voice the citizens of San Francisco had on their side.

Minutes later, whistles and shouts parted the crowd and two policemen arrived. They took in the scene, shouted that someone needed to get Mr. King to the hospital. But that had already been addressed. The crowd was waiting on the arrival of the doctor who lived around the corner.

The police manacled Casey, took the revolver with them as evidence, and hustled him to the jail, not far away. A growing crowd surrounded them as they pushed Casey along. By the time they arrived at the jailhouse, the crowd had grown to one of the largest either officer had seen.

"This ain't no good, Dudley. Keeps up we're going to have to join in or get on outta here."

"Nothing doing, Peters. We'll hold them off until he gets a meeting with the judge."

"You can't let them—"

"Shut up, Casey. Nobody told you to speak."

The shooter ignored them. "You send word to the senator, tell Mr. Broderick I have been unfairly arrested. Do you hear me?"

They tossed him in a cell without responding. What a mess, thought the guards. This cannot end well. And it didn't.

Barely two hours later a crowd of ten thousand irate citizens of San Francisco surrounded the jailhouse, pressing close and shouting in a frenzied mass.

"You guards in there!" A big fellow with a tidy suitcoat spoke for the crowd. "If you don't give Casey up, we're coming in, and we won't have any trouble taking him from you. You go along now and it will all be better for you. Trust me, boys!"

They didn't need to be told twice. The handful of jail guards backed off and the crowd's representatives moved forward, snatched the keys from the hand of one guard, and jerked the key in the cell lock until the steel door squawked open. Casey was still manacled inside the cell. But instead of the blustering shooter of an hour before, here was a man whining and cowering as he retreated to a back corner of the cell.

"This isn't right! Senator Broderick will hear about this! It's not right! I know you—and you! I know you all, and I say he had it coming, just like you all will if you don't unhand me!"

A storm of voices shouted him down, told him to shut up, that he'd get what they doled out and like it. Finally they jerked him forward, men to either side of him, and dragged Casey stumbling and unsteady out of the cell, down the long hallway, up the stairwell, and out onto the front steps. The rest of the crowd roared its approval and venom all at once, and Casey shrunk in on himself, did his best to dodge the angry groping hands and slamming fists. He'd never seen so many people, hundreds, perhaps thousands! All of whom bellowed for justice—an eye for an eye, they shouted.

Casey pleaded with his captors to listen to reason.

Finally one man turned on him and snapped, "Reason? The way you gunned down Mr. King? And on the steps of his own newspaper! You will get what you deserve, Casey."

"But . . . this isn't right. . . ."

"Not right? Now then, what did you think was going to happen, Mr. Casey? Did you think that you were going to get away with murdering the one man in this town who had the nerve to call that rascal Broderick on the carpet for all his swindling ways?"

By the time the man finished his brief diatribe, his face shook, high color rose in his cheeks, and spittle flecked his lips. With that he turned away and the crowd roared even louder as they hustled Casey toward the waterfront.

He spent his time manacled and shivering in a makeshift cell in what his captors called the new headquarters of the Vigilance Committee. They gave him bread and water for nearly a week. Then on the sixth day, a grim-faced man stood before the cell. "James King died in the night, Casey. You will be tried for murder." He left before Casey could think of what to say.

That day they began what the man on the stand, a judge of some sort, called James Casey's trial.

"This is a farce!" shouted Casey, straightening in his chair.

"No more so than the murder you committed."

"We have laws in this city! In this country!" Even as he shouted it, Casey knew how absurd that would sound. He had shot a man in front of dozens of people on the street, after all. He slumped back in his chair and waited for what he knew would soon happen.

He was worn down, regretting the entire affair. He still harbored a deep hatred of James King, the so-called journalist, and his foul newspaper. He figured he had a right, no, an obligation to defend the senator from the scurvy-ridden newspaperman and his foul rag. But it had all gone off in a direction Casey could not have foreseen. How could all these thousands of people be so deluded by the journalist?

He ground his teeth tight together, half wished that King had not given up the ghost. Maybe then Casey could live, too, to fight another day. But that was wishful thinking, and he barely heard when they pronounced his sentence, a sentence he knew was coming.

Before the fifteen thousand people who attended the journalist's funeral could file past King's coffin, the Vigilance Committee had tried, convicted, and stretched the neck of Mr. James Casey.

To ensure that law and order continued to rule the teeming streets of San Francisco, the Vigilance Committee, enjoying full public support, moved into a fortress-like facility complete with jail cells, a court room, and an outer wall defensible against any expected attacks by a larger military presence. The vigilantes called their new digs Fort Gunnybags, and they ruled the streets of the city with a steely gaze and an iron fist. It worked, and within two months they reduced criminal activity to a handful of minor robberies and no murders, where before there had been almost daily killings and lootings around the clock.

But that is hardly all there was to San Francisco's history of corruption and vice. In fact, its darkest days lay ahead. Within months following Casey's hanging, the Vigilance Committee once again backed down and turned the reins of power over to the city's hired officials, convinced that a proper government was preferable to the long-term health of their fair city. Unfortunately history repeated itself. It would take a few years, but corruption once again reared its mangy head.

The city's first line of defense against the ever-increasing influx of lowlifes was a paltry police force that was underpaid, overworked, and overwhelmed by the sheer numbers of miscreants. By 1871 the city had a mere one hundred policemen, a ratio of one officer to 1,445 long-term and transitory inhabitants, a shocking figure when compared with New York's ratio of 1 to 464. By the 1890s the city was home to more than three thousand establishments with liquor licenses and another two thousand operating without licenses.

Most of the customers of these dens of debauchery, from saloons to can-can houses to dance halls, were men. And most of the employees were women instructed to chat up the men to get them to buy overpriced, watered-down drinks.

If that didn't work, they would drug the mark's drinks, making it easier for thugs, also employed by the establishment, to subdue them later in the alley. Often the hired hooligans would hit the hapless drunks too hard and kill them—all in a night's work along the Barbary Coast. The most common patrons of these dives were sailors looking for a quick, good time. Frequently they ended up drugged and robbed, and when they came to the next morning, they found themselves shanghaied, coursing out at sea aboard a strange ship. What a hangover.

One of the most corrupt individuals in San Francisco's history (now that's say-ing something), Eugene Schmitz was also the mayor of that city at the turn of the century. In fact, for years following his conviction on a bevy of charges of corruption, he was the poster boy for graft and greed among politicos nation-wide. And yet, as corrupt as Schmitz was, the man who worked his puppet strings was even more corrupt. Abraham Ruef was an attorney and a behind-the-scenes, high-powered manipulator, the man who made Schmitz and many others the corrupt cads they were.

Interestingly, Abraham Rueff (he would later drop one "f") pursued a budding interest in politics while a young student at the University of Cali-fornia at Berkeley. Though he majored in classical studies and graduated with high honors at eighteen, this young man, considered a prodigy—he spoke eight languages—while a student also developed a keen interest in the raging corruption of the local politics of his hometown of San Francisco.

With friends, Ruef established the Municipal Reform League, a think tank whose members corresponded with like-minded individuals through-out the country, including young Theodore Roosevelt. Over time Ruef's ide-als blunted while sparring with corrupt politicians and businessmen such as those of Southern Pacific Railroad, which wielded considerable control over both the Democratic and Republican parties.

Eventually Ruef grew tired of swimming against the current. But instead of resorting to time-tested but wearying strong-arm tactics employed by behind-the-scenes political haymakers, the erudite, sophisticated young Ruef wined and dined, smooth-talked and sweet-talked his way into indispensible positions in city government. Though he aspired to a position of power, the pervasive allure of money was not as big a draw to Ruef. Rather he sought a way to pose serious opposition to the entrenched big-money machine manipulating San Francisco politics. His trump card was his intense study and budding knowledge of the rise of the organized labor movement.

So, in 1901 Ruef set about building his own political machine, the Union Labor Party, a force he expected would be so formidable that it would one day soon take control of the city. He felt he could count on no one but himself to steer that ship, though he would appoint yes-men, answerable only to him, to key positions within city government. An early order of business was to fill the position of mayor. As luck—or more to the point, proper planning—would have it, 1901 was an election year in San Francisco.

Ruef selected a man who he was confident could become his ideal mayoral candidate. So far ahead did Ruef speculate that the position of mayor would be but a stepping stone to the California governor's seat—not for himself but for his groomed appointee.

He chose Eugene "Handsome Gene" Schmitz, a tall, charismatic, young married man with two children and a clean record—no mean feat in San Francisco. Poor Eugene, if he knew what was coming, would have skipped town in the middle of the night.

Before becoming Ruef's stooge, Schmitz was a promising young violinist and composer. He also led the city orchestra and eventually became president of the Musicians' Union in San Francisco—the extent of his political activity prior to being beckoned by Ruef.

Ruef set about building the perfect political candidate, literally schooling Schmitz in everything from the California Constitution and San Francisco city articles (which he insisted Schmitz memorize) to telling Schmitz how to dress. He wrote all of Schmitz's campaign speeches and tightly controlled the man's social and political appearance calendar. And it paid off.

The only man unsurprised by Eugene Schmitz's election to the office of mayor in the fall of 1901 appeared to be Ruef. He smiled and nodded, already busily planning the future. Not only did Schmitz win the election, but in doing so he became the first Union Labor Party candidate to be elected mayor in the United States. The next five years were busy, heady times for the upstart political boss. In addition to the office of mayor, in time Ruef exerted control over the chief of police, a handful of judges, and the city's Board of Supervisors.

His first real misstep—it had to come at some point—was in appointing William L. Langton as district attorney. Shortly after he assumed his role in 1905, he did what the young Ruef had been so passionate about: Langton set into motion plans that would demolish the power broker's carefully constructed enterprise. He revived all-but-buried vice laws, ignored for so long because they were regarded as impediments to the welfare of the city, more to the point, the wallets of the city's power brokers.

Still the premier go-to place for all manner of illicit entertainment and discrete distraction, San Francisco's numerous brothels, gambling dens, and dance halls thrived for decades because their owners and operators paid huge bribes and kickback fees to city officials. This look-the-other-way approach kept much of the city afloat, most notably the Barbary Coast district.

This had gone on for so long it was seen as the easiest and most legitimate way of keeping the clanking machinery of City Hall in operation. Trouble was, it was illegal . . . and thriving more than ever under the Schmitz (read: Ruef) administration. But not only was DA Langton no one's stooge, he was also unimpressed with and embarrassed by his city's dubious national distinction as a sink pit of debauchery.

Bolstering Langton's efforts in his crusade of cleanup from within the belly of the beast was an increasing hue-and-cry from a citizenry long disgusted with the goings-on of the Barbary Coast district. Add to that was the growing national prohibitionist movement inciting equal parts interest and ire in the city.

Ruef had long since left behind his old chums intent on reforming the corrupt political machine and had himself become puppet master of that very machine he long before had reviled. But his old cronies hadn't let go of their dreams of reform. In fact, they'd only grown more powerful, and they did not like what Ruef had done to their fair city.

DA Langton had the backing of the town's most powerful publisher, Fremont Older, and his newspaper, the *Bulletin*. Not only that, but Older attracted the well-connected millionaire Rudolph Spreckels to the cause. Spreckels jumped in with both feet—and a sizable wallet—and funded a federal investigation into the rampant corruption at San Francisco City Hall. Just when it looked as if headway was being made, and heads would soon roll, Mother Nature intervened.

At 5:12 a.m., on April 18, 1906, a tremendous earthquake, magnitude of 7.8, violently fibrillated the heart of San Francisco. Immediate and devastating fires broke out citywide, causing unprecedented damage. The earthquake and fires ultimately destroyed more than 80 percent of the city and caused the deaths of three thousand people.

That first day rioting and looting ran rampant throughout the city. Schmitz responded with a shoot-to-kill edict regarded as heavy handed:

Proclamation by the Mayor: The Federal Troops, the members of the Regular Police Force and all Special Police Officers have been authorized by me to KILL any and all persons found engaged in Looting or in the Commission of Any Other Crime.

I have directed all the Gas and Electric Lighting Co.'s not to turn on Gas or Electricity until I order them to do so. You may therefore expect the city to remain in darkness for an indefinite time.

I request all citizens to remain at home from darkness until daylight every night until order is restored.

I WARN all Citizens of the danger of fire from Damaged or Destroyed Chimneys, Broken or Leaking Gas Pipes or Fixtures, or any like cause.

E.E. Schmitz, Mayor, Dated April 18, 1906

The initial tumult of San Francisco's Great Earthquake and Fire of 1906 eventually subsided to a constant but low-level thrum of activity of rebirth and rebuilding. And the political reformers were more determined than ever to sweep clean the offices lining the cracked corridors of City Hall.

Just what had been going on in those dens of greed? Privileges, favors, and palm greasing of the most blatant order. Despite long and loud citizen opposition, the privately owned street railway company sought the right to transform overhead cables for use with its street trolley system. So it paid someone at city hall a $200,000 bribe and its request was granted. A telephone company forked over a sizable wad of cash to prevent its rival from horning in on its turf, and then the rival upped the ante. The gas company fixed its rate from the expected, lobbied-for 75 cents to 85 cents.

In 1907 Ruef, Schmitz, and a long list of other city officials, as well as on-the-take street railway, gas, electric, and telephone company bigwigs, were all indicted by the grand jury. Their longtime schemes of corporate greed had been outed. Mayor Schmitz was indicted on twenty-seven counts of graft and bribery. He was convicted and received the maximum penalty allowed by law. However, his conviction, as well as most of those earned by the others, was overturned on appeal.

A number of the guilty turned state's evidence, ratting out their fellow felons, in order to evade imprisonment. That left Abe Ruef alone on the dais to take the full brunt of the long-corrupt system. There were rumors of anti-Semitism on the prosecution's behalf, which played against him and in favor of his former cohorts, whose punishments were lessened.

Ruef's trial was a protracted affair peppered with appeals and much media coverage. In the end his wealth, power, and political connections did Ruef little good—he was convicted in 1911 of bribery and was subsequently sent to San Quentin, where he was to serve fourteen years, the maximum allowed for the crime.

Oddly enough, his staunchest enemy, the publisher Fremont Older, felt that Ruef's punishment was unduly harsh. He and Ruef, once enemies, struck up a correspondence while Ruef moldered in prison, and the newspaperman even paid Ruef to pen a detailed account of his long experience in and around city politics, which was then serialized in the *Bulletin*.

Older actively pursued appeals and pardons on Ruef's behalf, but none materialized. However, Ruef was released in 1915 after vowing he would abstain from engaging in politics. Apparently he was true to his word. Sadly, Abraham Ruef has been thus far remembered almost exclusively for his part in the corruption of the city, something that predated his time in San Francisco politics and something that continued to linger like a bad odor long after he left.

As with so many men whose reach exceeded their grasp, Ruef was much more than a corrupt political boss. He left behind a number of contributions to his city that he never crowed about. Though he was worth a million dollars when he entered prison, he passed away a pauper on February 29, 1936, in the city he had three decades before presided over. To his end, Ruef maintained his intelligence, poise, and quick wit, and rarely spoke of those long-gone, heady days when he ruled San Francisco, inside and out.

CHAPTER 22

DR. JOHN R. BRINKLEY
GOAT GLANDS AND RADIO WAVES
(AND ANOTHER CONNING QUACK!)

In Kansas in 1917, "Doctor" (in the loosest sense of the word) John Romulus Brinkley began implanting goat testicles into impotent farmers, sexually frustrated housewives, and libidinously lax folks of all stripes. He parlayed this outlandish procedure into a long-term lavish lifestyle. And because of it, he became the wealthiest surgeon in the United States and went on to run—twice—for governor of Kansas (and nearly won!).

Despite being pursued and exposed as America's "most daring and dangerous" charlatan time and again over many years by his nemesis Dr. Morris Fishbein, who represented the American Medical Association, and despite directly causing many dozens of deaths due to ignorance and carelessness, Brinkley's fortunes rose to tremendous levels throughout the 1920s and 1930s.

Brinkley will also go down in history as being responsible for introducing the United States at large to country and blues music, inadvertently plowing the ground for rock 'n' roll to flourish. And if that weren't enough, he used his massive "border blaster" radio station, operated just over the Rio Grande in Mexico, as a unique marketing tool for his own quack remedies, unwittingly becoming the father of the modern infomercial.

If ever there was a man whose life was one long slide into chicanery and intentional ill-treatment of others, it was that of John Romulus Brinkley. In his fifty-six years he was a bigamist, an evader of the law, a writer of bad checks, a prisoner, a buyer of false diplomas, and a practitioner of medicine without a license. But before all that he was a young man with much promise. . . .

Born in 1885 to John Brinkley and Sarah Burnett, herself the niece of his father's wife, John Romulus Brinkley showed signs early on of mental prowess, sharing a similar keen mind as his father, a medic in the Confederate States Army during the Civil War. His father was also fond of the ladies, marrying and outliving four wives, as well as at least one out-of-wedlock paramour— young John's mother.

When John Romulus was five, his mother died of tuberculosis, and when he was ten, his father died, leaving John to be raised by his father's wife, the woman he came to call "Aunt Sally." Despite the small family's long experience with financial hardship, young John was able to attend a one-room log school and thrived there. By the time he turned sixteen, he had gained all the schooling available to him. Though secretly yearning to study medicine and one day perhaps become a doctor, John accepted his lot and took on work as a letter carrier. In his spare time the industrious young man learned the craft of telegraphy, a skill that would prove useful in the years to come.

In 1906 John was twenty-one and living in New York, then New Jersey, working as a telegraph operator for various railroads. By the end of that year he had returned home to North Carolina to care for his beloved Aunt Sally, the woman who had raised him. Alas, she died on Christmas Day, 1906. His grief was assuaged, however, by the amorous ministrations of an old school chum, Sally Wilke, one year his senior. They soon married, and here's where Brinkley came into his own, at least according to public record, as a classic huckster.

The newlyweds traveled the rural regions of the southeast states, passing themselves off, oddly enough, as Quakers who also happened to be doctors. As with so many others of his bilking ilk, Brinkley's traveling medicine show existed for the sole purpose not of helping the poor and weak, but of selling patent medicinals that could cure all manner of alleged ills. Before long the young quack Quaker joined forces with a "Dr." Burke in selling virility tinctures to rural men in need of a bold boost.

By the fall of 1907, Brinkley and his wife relocated to Chicago, and the tricky twosome soon became a trio when their first child, a girl named Wanda Marion Brinkley, was born. At the same heady time, Brinkley realized a life-long ambition by enrolling in medical school. Unfortunately for the American public and the world at large, Brinkley chose Bennett Medical College, a dicey institution with serious credibility issues. Nonetheless, he was the scholarly sort and by day worked as a student and at night as a telegrapher. A second child, a boy, was soon born, but lived only three days.

Mounting debt soon fractured his marriage. His wife took their daughter and left him, filing for divorce and demanding monetary support. Brinkley complied for a time, but it wasn't long before, in a fit of pique, he tracked them down and absconded with his daughter, taking her over the border into Canada. Rather than have the father of her child risk prison, Brinkley's wife dropped charges against him. They resolved their tiff, and once more settled in as a family in Chicago, where Brinkley continued his schooling.

The Bennett Medical College was known for a curriculum based on the dubiously named "eclectic medicine," a quasi-medical pursuit reliant on unusual forms of therapies and abnormal treatments. In his studies, Brinkley learned of the effects of glandular extracts on humans, and his findings quickly developed into a lifelong fascination.

Once again owing to debt and other marital issues, plus the addition of a second daughter, Brinkley and his wife separated. It was his third year of school, but he left his studies and chased after her, leaving a smoking trail of debt behind. He tried his hand at practicing medicine, billing himself as an "undergraduate physician," but met with little success. He ricocheted, family in tow, to St. Louis, Missouri, to resume his schooling, but because of a small mountain of money owed to his previous school, he was unable to obtain his scholastic records.

Poor Brinkley, at his wit's end, obtained an official-looking certificate from the Kansas City Eclectic Medical University—in truth nothing more than a diploma mill—and soon another daughter joined the odd family. He dragged them all to Chicago, where he intended to set up shop as a bona fide medical man. It didn't work out and his wife left him once more, heading home to her kin in North Carolina.

Brinkley drifted to South Carolina and went into business with a like-minded partner by the surname of Crawford. The duo billed themselves as the "Greenville Electro Medic Doctors," and here is where Brinkley, with past experience as a snake-oil salesman and present know-how as a budding quack, settled into his true calling as shameless self-promoting sham shaman.

The two hucksters, preying on men fearful of losing their virility, injected their patients with a special tincture they called "Salvarsan," a so-called "electric medicine from Germany." In truth it was nothing more than colored water. Charging a hefty $25 per dose, they nonetheless quickly built up a steady stream of patients. The shady pair also lived beyond their means, amassing much debt for rent, utilities, clothing, and medicinal supplies. On the verge of discovery as charlatans, they fled in the night and decamped to Memphis, Tennessee.

While there, Brinkley met a young woman named Minnie Jones, herself the daughter of a physician. He wooed her for all of four days, then married her. There was only one hiccup—he was still very much married to Sally! Oops. . . .

After his (second) honeymoon, life began to work against poor Brinkley: He was tossed in the clink for practicing unlicensed medicine and for skipping town and leaving a trail of bad checks in his wake. He ratted on his partner, Crawford, and settled out of court for monetary damages. Just in time for a visit by his first, and only legitimate, wife, Sally, who was unimpressed with her estranged husband's activities and promptly accused John of bigamy. Nearly broke, Brinkley once again tried his hand at practicing medicine, this time on women and children. Luckily for his patients, he soon learned this would not alleviate his faulty financial situation. So he turned to the army, joining the Reserve Medical Corps.

Brinkley's abiding passion throughout these tumultuous years was to complete his medical degree. He eventually paid off the debt he owed to Bennett Medical University, and by the fall of 1914 he was officially sanctioned as an honest-to-goodness medical practitioner in eight states. He quickly landed a job as company doctor for the Swift meat-packing company in Kansas City. While there he stumbled on what became the foundation for his biggest and most dangerous medical discovery. But it would be another few years before he tested it on live subjects. . . .

In the meantime, he filed for divorce from Sally, lying to the court as to her whereabouts, afraid that she might somehow prevent the proceedings. Freed of his marital obligations to her, he legally married Minnie. However, he failed to sit out the six-month waiting period following the divorce.

World War I was raging and the army called its reservists to action. Soon Brinkley found himself on active service. He gave it a paltry two months, during which time he claimed with increasing angst and much lamentation to be too nervous and addled with anxiety to serve. Rather than listen to his bellyaching a moment more, the army discharged Brinkley.

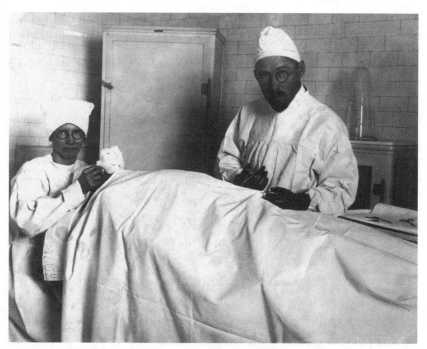

A "doctor" in the loosest sense of the word, John R. Brinkley (above, operating on a patient) nonetheless conned thousands into fraudulent medical procedures involving the implantation of goat testes directly into their bodies. Said to relieve impotency, these and other quack fixes made him rich. But it was Brinkley's pioneering use of radio as a marketing medium for his procedures and products that made him even wealthier and famous nationwide. Then in 1939 the American Medical Association revealed Brinkley for the fraud he was, and the IRS stripped him clean.   *Courtesy Kansas Historical Society, 1920.*

So what does all this have to do with a shady swindler in the Old West? Within months of leaving the Army, Brinkley found a newspaper advertisement placed by the town of Milford, Kansas, stating that it was in need of a medical man. Before long "Doctor" Brinkley found himself in Milford, up to his elbows in the very thing he'd always yearned for—a thriving medical practice. His arrival coincided with the spreading influenza pandemic of 1918, and by accounts of his time there, he was most successful at nursing flu victims back to health. His practice blossomed, and he employed a number of people as assistants.

During his early days in Milford, he was approached by a patient who claimed he was sexually weak—was Brinkley aware of a procedure that might help? He immediately recalled his time at the Swift meat-packing plant, something he had learned there about the powerful glands of billy goats. Brinkley rubbed his palms together as the sound of a ringing cash register filled the dark spaces of his quack mind, for he knew just what to do.

Shortly thereafter he performed a breakthrough operation on the impotent patient, a procedure Brinkley was under no illusion would bring him anything resembling fame and fortune. Still, what could it hurt to try? So he transplanted goat testicles into the man's groin. Yes, you read that correctly—goat testes. And the man paid Brinkley $150 for the pleasure. Though the man did not die, it didn't do him any good either. Not initially, anyway.

Not only was the procedure unproven, but Brinkley surely knew there was no way it could work. Undaunted, Brinkley turned it into a full-blown moneymaking scheme. His clinic business, already brisk, soon thrummed with activity. He upped his rates to $750 per operation, and in no time he was implanting the testicular glands of goats into the bodies of sexually desperate but wealthy men. In the best possible post-operation scenario, the man's body would be able to merely absorb the goat testes. Sometimes it worked; often the patient became sick. None died . . . yet.

"Will it hurt?"

"Just in your wallet," said Brinkley, who kept his straight face for a few moments, before flashing his wide amiable grin and chuckling. The patient caught on and offered his own nervous chuckle.

"Seriously, though," said Brinkley. The doctor canted his head, his face assumed a thoughtful, considered look. Finally he said, "It is true that any surgical procedure is invasive. However, my methods are, and I don't mind saying, far beyond what are considered commonplace at present in this country." A slight smile played across his mouth. "In short, no, Mr. Mulravey. You won't feel a thing."

"And will I . . .? Will I be able to . . .?" the man reddened, looked down at the old hands curled in his lap like two tired birds. "Will I be able to, um . . .?"

Again, a knowing smile, not condescending but kindly, as Brinkley nodded and said in a quiet voice, "Yes, all will work . . . as it once did."

The old man's moist eyes brightened and his mouth stretched into a wide grin. He seemed to sit straighter in the wooden chair, even though he was clad only in his undergarments. "Well, that's fine. That's just fine. I suspected as much. It will be a pleasure to be, ah, back in action, as they say."

A short while later, with the old man safely toddling his way down the sidewalk out front, Brinkley's smile drooped from his face as he turned to his secretary. "I assume the check he just gave you is made out correctly?" He didn't wait for her to answer, but bent over the desk, straining to see the writing on the check's front.

"Yes, doctor."

"Good. I believe that makes six as of today, up from two last week." He smiled. "I do believe I'm onto something. You wait and see if I'm not right." He tapped the counter with his finger.

"Yes, doctor." The secretary nodded.

"Now, you take today's payments on over to the bank. That's why we're here, after all, isn't it?" He winked and turned to the empty waiting room, picturing it filled with wealthy, needy men, a line trailing out the door. "Soon, Doctor Brinkley," he murmured to himself as he headed back to his office. "Soon." And he smiled all the way.

It wasn't long before Brinkley began implanting the same glands into women's abdomens. And though his surgical abilities were feeble, his science unfounded, and his very right to practice medicine a mere house of cards, people flocked to him for the procedure. By this time he had begun to claim the operation was a miracle cure for no fewer than twenty-seven afflictions ranging from excessive flatulence to dementia. In a bit of perfect timing—and incredible coincidence—Brinkley was able to announce that his very first implant patient had recently become a father following the dicey procedure.

Newspapers from all over the country descended on the quack's offices and made him a national sensation. A born huckster, Brinkley knew a good thing when he saw it, and he made the most of all this free publicity. He worked up slogans, posed for the camera, and claimed his operations were able to transform the weak and timid into "the ram that am with every lamb."

All this attention drew not only the wealthy-but-desperate class so keen to make his acquaintance, but also the interest of the American Medical Association. The powerful organization soon sent an undercover investigator to Kansas.

There were other doctors at the time who were experimenting with similar procedures and theories, but none had gained the rising-star status of Brinkley. The press loved him, though as time wore on, his shine began to tarnish as a growing number of patients died from complications arising from the procedures. Brinkley was also accused repeatedly of performing operations while inebriated and of working in less-than-sanitary conditions.

Lawsuits reared their heads, but so well-loved was the charismatic—and wealthy—Brinkley that he swatted his detractors down like flies. He was invited to demonstrate his techniques at a Chicago hospital operating theater. During the proceedings he implanted goat testicles into a number of high-profile folks, men and women, eager for relief from whatever afflictions they claimed troubled them. A whopping thirty-four people in all received his ministrations that day, including a judge and the chancellor of a university law school.

He returned to Milford a bigger celebrity than ever, and his specialty operations increased in both price and frequency. Just when it seemed his star could rise no higher, his most high-profile procedure came about. The owner of the prestigious *Los Angeles Times* offered a challenge: If Brinkley could successfully transplant goat glands into one of the paper's editors, he would be rewarded with the best sort of positive press no amount of money could buy.

If the procedure was deemed a failure, however, the famous publisher, Harry Chandler, claimed he would ruin Brinkley in the press. Brinkley took the challenge, and by all accounts the operation was a thumbs-up success. Enough so that he picked up a roster of high-profile patients, a number of Hollywood stars among them.

That pesky investigator for the AMA, Morris Fishbein, himself a (legitimate) doctor, had seen through Brinkley's charade all along and recognized him for what he was—a charlatan and huckster of the highest order. Fishbein did his best to draw attention to Brinkley's blatant chicanery. Brinkley, he claimed, was not merely duping the gullible out of their money with a simple sleight-of-hand card game, he was playing with their very lives—and with increasing frequency the patients were the ones losing. Worst of all, it was obvious to Fishbein that Brinkley didn't care. Operating under the auspices of the AMA, Fishbein dogged Brinkley relentlessly, using every opportunity to expose chinks in the quack's armor.

Brinkley grew increasingly confident as his fame spread and more patients signed up for procedures with each month that passed. But as his popularity increased, so too did his incidence of casualties. And yet it didn't seem to matter to the public that the man they adored was also maiming and killing the very people he was supposedly helping.

Ever the opportunist, Brinkley was not satisfied with his current level of success. He reasoned that reaching an even wider audience would bring in more patients, and more patients equaled more money. And it was while in Los Angeles that Brinkley figured out how to do so. He became obsessed with the idea of advertising to masses of people using the broad reach of the relatively new technology of radio.

A marketer to his marrow, Brinkley eschewed the accepted notion of radio being merely a vehicle for entertainment and fluff. Rather he viewed all those tempting airwaves as a way to reach untold numbers of new patients. As a venue for hosting and promoting his various remedies, cures, and quackeries, Brinkley knew he had discovered a treasure chest of promise. Never mind that America's fledgling airwaves were at the time rarely used as an advertising medium, Brinkley started the station KFKB ("Kansas First, Kansas Best"), and never had a platform more suited a man, nor come at a better time in his career.

Meanwhile, the American Medical Association continued to cast its net wide, pulling in practitioners of medical chicanery such as snake-oil salesmen and diploma mills. Not surprisingly, one of them happened to be the very place Brinkley had obtained his diploma years before. The grand jury in San Francisco handed down indictments to various individuals, Brinkley among them. But since he was in Kansas and they were in California, the grand jury required legal authority by way of the governor of Kansas before Brinkley could be extradited to the Golden State to stand trial.

But the governor of Kansas nixed the idea of extradition because Brinkley was far too precious an earner, crucial to the state's economic well-being. Having dodged that bullet, most folks in Brinkley's position would exercise humility.

But John Romulus Brinkley was no ordinary fellow. The first thing he did on learning extradition from Kansas wasn't in the offing was fill his radio station's airspace with blustering, bravado-filled speeches about his own importance, about how he had personally defeated the American Medical Association, and how Morris Fishbein was no threat.

Brinkley took to radio like a duck to water, and found it was so much easier than standing before a crowd of skeptical hayseeds not eager to part with their hard-earned coins. Now, day after day he spent pleasurable hours perched before the microphone telling huge numbers of listeners, men and women, why they needed his treatments, appealing to the insecure and desperate. He assured them he was there with a simple cure—goat glands.

As his wealth grew, so grew his needs for a more stable infrastructure to handle the increased demands on his business. Brinkley burrowed deeper into the hearts of Milford, Kansas, by splashing out for upgraded sewage and electrical systems for the town, housing for his employees and patients, a larger post office—in part to accommodate the increased correspondence his business generated—and he sponsored a Milford baseball team named—what else?—the Brinkley Goats. He was also made an honorary admiral in the Kansas Navy—a hollow-sounding title if ever there was one.

He shamelessly trolled Europe seeking more false validation by way of honorary degrees and found one in Italy. But such was the mounting pressure and influence of Morris Fishbein and the AMA that Benito Mussolini, the Italian dictator, had the degree revoked.

Oddly enough, by 1927 Brinkley and Minnie had been married fourteen years and only then were they able to have a child of their own. This drew unwanted questioning of the efficacy of his goat gland treatment. Brinkley deflected the rumors and turned his attentions to his enormously successful radio call-in program, *The Medical Question Box*, during which he fielded questions about health and offered cures such as notions, lotions, nostrums, and tinctures that he himself owned the rights to. Pharmacies that carried these over-the-counter medicines wired money back to Brinkley to the tune of $14,000 per week—at today's rates, the equivalent of more than $10,000,000 a year.

But all the money in the world wouldn't afford Brinkley immunity from the woes that were to come. Merck and Company, one of the pharmaceutical outfits whose products Brinkley was giving a bad name, sicced Fishbein and the AMA on him. At the same time, competitive radio stations began running reports critical of Brinkley. But the frosting on the cake came when the Kansas Medical Board investigated him and began procedures to revoke whatever license he'd been granted years before.

Their decision was based on the fact that Brinkley had been signing death certificates in growing numbers—forty-two by 1930. It was also noted that very few of those people were enfeebled or ill at all before visiting his clinic. In revoking his license, the KMB stated that Brinkley "has performed an organized charlatanism . . . quite beyond the invention of the humble mountebank."

Barely half a year later, the Federal Radio Commission denied his request to renew his broadcaster's license, stating that his output was nearly all advertising and little else. They also said he was in violation of a number of laws and had broadcast obscene information. Brinkley sued the FRC but lost. The case, *Brinkley versus FRC*, has since become regarded as a landmark in broadcast law.

But instead of slowing him down, these setbacks seemed to invigorate the man. Brinkley had enough reserves of self-confidence that he took a run at the office of governor of Kansas. His main motivation? To appoint his own minions to the medical board and, in a roundabout way, get his medical license back.

During his campaign he pulled out all the huckster stops he could think of—he hired a pilot to ferry him in his own plane to all campaign stops. He sent a goat to a reporter who had been critical of him, and he made all manner of outlandish promises. Should he be elected governor, Brinkley vowed that each county in the state would have a lake, and that all citizens would enjoy low taxes, pensions for the aged, free textbooks for schoolchildren, and promises of better opportunities for blacks.

He was a write-in candidate, and a last-minute alteration to the qualifications for including him on the ballot resulted in his loss. It was later found that a huge number of ballots were disqualified on the barest of technicalities that, had they been overlooked, would have afforded him the win. Two years later he once again ran for governor, and once again he lost.

Faced with encroaching failure, Brinkley sold up in Milford, Kansas, and headed for the US-Mexico border. Mounting scandals notwithstanding, the Mexican government was keen to host such a personality as Brinkley. Whereas in Kansas his radio station offered but paltry power, in tiny Villa Acuna, Coahuila (now Ciudad Acuna), Brinkley's newly built "border blaster" station thrummed with fifty thousand watts of brute strength.

He named it the "Sunshine Station Between the Nations" and his broadcasts could be heard all the way to Kansas. By late 1932 he was given permission to broadcast at an unprecedented one million watts. Brinkley's broadcasts were picked up as far north as Canada. There are accounts of car headlights flicking on because of his broadcast strength, of telephone calls being saturated by the station, of steel bedsprings humming with the broadcasts, and of farmers and ranchers hearing it through their steel fences.

And what did Brinkley do with all this raw power? Why, he told his listeners—a vast, broad audience, arguably the biggest audience anyone in the history of the world had ever had—to buy his pills and tinctures and tonics and injections so that they might once again be sexual dynamos. He continued offering his illicit surgical procedures—primarily prostate operations—out of the hotel in which he lived.

Brinkley also sold air time to hucksters who were so shameless Brinkley himself might well have blushed at their claims. One man sold autographed pictures of none other than Jesus Christ, another sold something called "Crazy Water Crystals," and long-distance hypnotists mesmerized the masses. Brinkley also peppered the many hours of broadcast time with young musicians to the relatively new country-music scene, giving broad early exposure to such future stars as Red Foley, Gene Autry, Jimmie Rodgers, the Carter Family, and others.

The head huckster continued in this manner until 1934 when the Mexican government, snapping under pressure from Washington, DC, closed him down. So Brinkley opened a new clinic in San Juan, broadened his surgical offerings to include procedures for the colon, and continued with glandular implants, vasectomies, and "rejuvenations" to prostates. And he made, and spent, more money than ever. He built a mansion with lavish grounds on sixteen acres that included a swimming pool, a greenhouse, a fountain, an eight-thousand-bush garden, exotic animals from all over the world, a dozen Cadillacs, and more.

A cut-rate competitor opened shop nearby in Del Rio, so Brinkley pulled up stakes and headed to Little Rock, Arkansas. Soon enough his competition set up a new facility, specializing in cancer treatments, in Eureka Springs, Arkansas. (The man who did so was, perhaps, sleazier than Brinkley himself. And you'll read more about him—and the horrors he inflicted on desperate people—later in this chapter.)

Then, in 1938, the good times began swerving and screeching to a halt. Morris Fishbein published a brutal, wide-open, two-part article, "Modern Medical Charlatans," detailing and exposing Brinkley's entire professional career. Enraged, Brinkley sued Fishbein for libel, demanding $250,000 in damages. But he should have left well enough alone, for that was just the reaction Fishbein and the AMA had hoped for. The trial, set in Texas, kicked off on March 22, 1939, and Fishbein emerged the victor. The jury said of Brinkley that he "should be considered a charlatan and a quack in the ordinary, well-understood meaning of those words."

And then the lawsuits really began rolling in, seeking damages totaling many millions of dollars. Reeling emotionally and hemorrhaging financially, Brinkley had no time to catch his breath, for the IRS descended and rummaged in every aspect of his life, from his accounts to his closets, claiming massive tax and mail fraud. Brinkley declared bankruptcy in 1941, nearly died from a trio of heart attacks, then had one of his legs amputated due to poor circulation.

"Doctor" John Romulus Brinkley dragged himself through another couple years before expiring, on May 26, 1941, in San Antonio of heart failure. He is buried in Memphis, Tennessee, at Forest Hill Cemetery.

NORMAN G. BAKER: CANCER QUACK

As frightening and bizarre as is the life story of John Romulus Brinkley, the story of Norman G. Baker is, if anything, horrifyingly more fascinating. Born in Iowa in 1882, Baker showed signs of brilliance from an early age, an attribute no doubt gleaned from his accomplished parents. His father was an inventor with 126 patents to his name, and his mother, a writer.

Baker started his own business as a young man, the Tangley Company, maker of the Tangley Air Calliaphone, a modified version of the steam organ. He toured the country with his vaudeville act, showcasing the talents of mentalists, mind readers, and the like. Eventually the potential of radio caught his attention and it seemed an obvious venue for someone such as himself, who not only wanted to make money but rile anyone opposing his often-outlandish schemes.

By this time Baker was no stranger to litigation, bringing lawsuits against larger corporations such as AT&T and Western Electric for suspected conspiracies. He toured the country, railing against everything from fluoridated water and vaccination to the evils of aluminum cookware—which he claimed to be the source of at least 50 percent of cancers.

In April 1930 Baker had opened the Baker Institute in Muscatine, Iowa. Its claim to fame was a cancer cure unaffordable to all but the very wealthy. The ingredients of his wonder drug? Watermelon seeds, corn silk, carbolic acid, clover, alcohol, and water.

Not only was he injecting people with his terrible and ineffective tincture, but they were dying from it. Indeed, at the outset of his venture, all five of his initial test subjects died. Undaunted, Baker plowed ahead and began amassing a fortune. He also attracted press to his ventures by publicly denouncing the American Medical Association, calling it the "American Meat-Cutters Association."

Baker often held mass healings on the grounds of his sprawling complex, attracting thousands of people desperate for cancer cures. Once there, his persuasive and fiery oratory style convinced them to purchase his products. At one of his healings, he performed what he said was an operation on the brain to cure a patient of brain cancer. The gathered crowd watched as Baker cut into the man's head, without anesthetic. (It was later revealed that the man had not had cancer—he had a condition that caused part of his skull to swell.)

The Baker Institute, which he ran with his partner, the perennially imprisoned quack Harry Hoxsey, was raking in $100,000 a month. Baker continued his rants extolling the tenets of populism, claiming that the good, hardworking prairie folk of Iowa were being exploited by monopolies. He ran failed campaigns for various public offices, including governor and senator, but remained a crowd favorite.

Despite his popularity among the people of Iowa, Baker was soon forced to relocate south of the US-Mexico border—Iowa had run him out on fraud charges and for practicing medicine without a license. As had Dr. John R. Brinkley before him, Baker fired up a massive "border blaster" radio station that promoted his cancer cure, as well as offering various on-air entertainments, usually including him ranting about Jews and Catholics, and sometimes even ranting while having sex with a mistress.

In 1937 a very wealthy Baker cast about for a new location where he might reestablish his cancer treatments. He happened on the once-grand town of Eureka Springs, Arkansas, and the dilapidated but still grand Crescent Hotel, a popular destination for the well-heeled prior to the onset of the Great Depression. Baker bought the place with cash, renamed it the Baker Hospital, and transformed it into a high-end resort for cancer patients.

Soon he was treating thousands with his poisonous tinctures and injections, pulling in half a million dollars a year from desperate cancer sufferers looking for a cure. What no one knew was that deep in the bowels of the massive old hotel, Dr. Baker kept a dank operating theater where he performed autopsies and cruel experiments.

But it all caught up with him in 1939 when the federal government nailed Baker and his partner, R.A. Bellows, on seven counts of mail fraud. Baker was given four years in jail and fined $4,000, a pittance considering the barbarous treatment he'd been subjecting his patients to for years. By January of 1940 he was ensconced, as inmate number 58197, at Leavenworth Federal Penitentiary in Kansas.

During the trial various experts and investigators provided testimony, including the following: "Our investigation indicates that Baker and his associates defrauded cancer sufferers out of approximately $4,000,000. Our investigation further shows that a great majority of the people who were actually suffering with cancer who took the treatment lived but a short while after returning to their homes from the hospital. We believe that the treatment hastened the death of the sufferers in most cases."

A BRIEF GLOSSARY OF
SWINDLING LINGO

Apple: Also known as the victim, the mark, the sucker.

Big con/big store: A fake storefront or gambling den easily dismantled once the sucker splits.

Bilk: To sucker someone out of something.

Buck the tiger: To play the card game faro (odds are against staying in the saddle!).

Bumpkin: A rube, naïve and inexperienced in the ways of the world.

Bunco: A confidence game.

Bunco artist: One who orchestrates a confidence game.

Claim jumper: One who steals another's claim, usually a mine.

Con: The swindle, the game, the grift.

Con man: Short for confidence man, one who swindles for a living.

Dove: A prostitute. Also soiled dove.

Dry gulcher: One who ambushes another for nefarious purposes.

Faro (sometimes pharo): Derived from the French game pharao; the most popular nineteenth-century game, in which players bet on which order cards appear.

Filch: To steal or thieve from another.

Fourflusher: One who bluffs and cheats, especially at cards.

Greenhorn: A naïve person inexperienced at a task.

Grift: A con, a game, a swindle in which the grifter uses wit rather than violence.

Grifter: A confidence man who uses wit instead of violence to make a living.

Gold brick: Brick of fake gold, often junk metal with a plug of real gold for "testing."

Hawk: To lure someone into a game; to sell one's shoddy wares.

Hornswoggler: One who gets the better of someone through cheating or deception.

Huckleberry: The ideal person for a job, usually a dim-bulb underling.

Hustler: A cheating gambler on the make to bilk a sucker.

Mark: The sucker, the intended victim, the apple.

Monte: Common abbreviation for the card game three-card monte.

Poke: A wallet, coin purse, gold-dust bag, usually belonging to a miner or cowboy.

Roper: One who ushers the mark into the con; a steerer.

Rube: A bumpkin, naïve and inexperienced in the ways of the world.

Rustler: One who steals another's horses or cattle.

Shell game: A game of chance involving the manipulation of three walnut shells and a dried pea.

Shill: A participant in a con game (not the mark).

Short con: A con game requiring little time.

Snake-oil salesman: One who sells a substance of no worth or medicinal value.

Snitch: To rat on a con man; one who rats or informs.

Soap game: Short con in which the grifter appears to wrap bars of soap in valuable cash to sell, with his shills getting the goods.

Soiled dove: A prostitute. Also dove.

Steerer: One who ushers the mark in to the con; a roper.

Sting: The moment when the sucker's money is taken.

Sucker: Also known as the victim, the mark, the apple.

Thimblerig: A game of chance involving the manipulation of three thimbles and a ball of paper.

Thimblerigger: One who operates a thimblerig.

Three-card monte: Easily rigged card game, using just three cards, in which the dealer's dexterity overrides chance.

Tiger: Another name for the card game faro.

ART AND PHOTO CREDITS

Page 3: Portrait of Ned Buntline. Napoleon Sarony.

Page 15: Soapy Smith in his saloon. Peiser, 1898. Skagway, Alaska. Alaska State Library, Historical Collections, ASL-P277-001-009.

Page 29: Asbury Harpending. Photograph in *The Great Diamond Hoax and Other Stirring Incidents in the Life of Asbury Harpending*, edited by James H. Wilkins. A. Harpending, 1913. The James H. Barry Co.

Page 41: $1,250,000 gold bullion, Miners and Merchants Bank in Nome Alaska. Lomen Bros., 1906. Library of Congress, LC-DIG-ppmsc-01961.

Page 53: Clark Stanley's Snake Oil Liniment label. Illustration in *The life and adventures of the American cow-boy: Life in the Far West* by Clark Stanley, better known as the Rattle-Snake King. Clark Stanley, 1897.

Page 63: George H. Devol, 1829–1903. Illustration in: *George Devol, Forty Years a Gambler on the Mississippi*, 1887 (1st edition). Library of Congress, LC-USZ62-66016.

Page 73: James Addison Reavis imprisoned at Santa Fe, New Mexico Territory. *The Land of Sunshine*, Vol. 8, No. 3, February 1898. Land of Sunshine Publishing Co.

Page 87: Bird's-eye view of men panning gold in Nome, Alaska. Lomen Bros. Library of Congress, LC-DIG-ppmsc-01699.

Page 97: Title page. *The Emigrants' Guide to Oregon and California* by Lansford W. Hastings, 1845.

Page 110: Top: Albert and Bessie Johnson (left) had a surprising decades-long friendship with Death Valley Scotty (right). National Park Service. Bottom: Scotty's Castle, Death Valley National Park, California. Jennifer Smith-Mayo, 2014.

Page 121: Prisoners, from Black Kettle's camp, captured by General Custer, traveling through snow. Sketched by Theodore R. Davis. *Harper's Weekly*, December 26, 1868. Library of Congress, LC-USZ62-117248.

Page 136: The Gem Variety Theater and Dance Hall, Pioneer Days in Deadwood. Deadwood History, Adams Museum Collection, Deadwood, South Dakota.

Page 144: Pegleg Smith Monument, Borrego Springs, California. Jennifer Smith-Mayo, 2014.

Page 157: Plummer's Men Holding Up the Bannack Stage. John W. Norton, 1907. *The Story of the Outlaw* by Emerson Hough. The Outing Publishing Company.

Page 170: Nate Champion, who was killed in the KC Ranch fight by the Invaders. Hoofprints of the Past Museum, Kaycee, Wyoming.

Page 186: "It's my hand against your eye. Watch me close!" *Marion Daily Mirror*, October 13, 1911.

Page 197: Mugshot from Colorado State Penitentiary Record of Lou Blonger #12258. Colorado State Penitentiary, 1923.

Page 209: Puter at work in his cell, revealing the author in his customary attitude while engaged in preparing the manuscript. *Looters of the Public Domain* by S. A. D. Puter, 1908. Portland Printing House Publishers.

Page 221: A Winning Miss. Buxom woman rolling dice, 1911. Library of Congress, LC-USZ62-58977.

Page 232: "Ride Low—They're Coming!" Illustration by Frank E. Schoonover, 1917. *The Rustler of Wind River* by G. W. Ogden. A. L. Burt Company.

Page 248: Top left: Eugene Schmitz. *Complete Story of the San Francisco Horror* by Herbert D. Russell, 1906. Top right: Abe Ruef. Bain News Service. Library of Congress, LC-B2-1148-15. Bottom: Assassination of James King, corner of Montgomery and Washington Streets, San Francisco, California.

Frank Leslie's Illustrated newspaper, July 19, 1856. Library of Congress, LC-USZ62-103212.

Page 267: Dr. John R. Brinkley performing surgery. Kansas Historical Society, 1920.

BIBLIOGRAPHY

Adams, Brewster. *The Prospector: Values in the Rough*. Reno, NV: Reno Printing Co., 1940.

Adams, Ramon F. *Cowboy Lingo*. Cambridge, MA: The Riverside Press, 1936.

———. *Western Words: A Dictionary of the Range, Cow Camp and Trail.* Norman: University of Oklahoma Press, 1945.

———. *From the Pecos to the Powder; a Cowboy's Autobiography, as Told to Ramon F. Adams by Bob Kennon*. Norman: University of Oklahoma Press, 1965.

———. *The Language of the Railroader*. Norman: University of Oklahoma Press, 1977.

Allen, Robert Joseph. *The Story of Superstition Mountain and The Lost Dutchman Gold Mine*. New York: Simon & Schuster, 1971.

Anderson, Elliott and Robert Onopa. *TriQuarterly 48, Spring 1980*. Evanston, IL: Northwestern University, 1980.

Batman, Richard. *The Outer Coast*. New York: Harcourt Brace Jovanovich, 1985.

Belden, L. Burr and Mary DeDecker. *Death Valley to Yosemite: Frontier Mining Camps & Ghost Towns: The Men, The Women, Their Mines & Stories*. Bishop, CA: Spotted Dog Press, 2000.

Bennett, Estelline. *Old Deadwood Days: The Real Wild West of My Childhood*. Santa Barbara, CA: Narrative Press, 2001.

Berton, Pierre. *The Klondike Fever: The Life and Death of the Last Great Gold Rush*. New York: Carroll & Graf, 1989.

———. *Stampede for Gold: The Story of the Klondike Rush*. New York: Sterling Point Books, 2007.

Birmingham, Stephen. *California Rich*. New York: Simon & Schuster, 1980.

Block, Lawrence, ed. *Gangsters, Swindlers, Killers, and Thieves: The Lives and Crimes of Fifty American Villains*. Oxford, NY: Oxford University Press, 2004.

Blumberg, Rhoda. *The Great American Gold Rush*. New York: Bradbury Press, 1989.

Bonner, Robert. *William F. Cody's Wyoming Empire*. Norman: University of Oklahoma Press, 2007.

Bristow, Gwen. *Golden Dreams*. New York: Lippincott & Crowell, 1980.

Brown, Dee. *The Gentle Tamers: Women of the Old Wild West*. Lincoln: University of Nebraska Press, 1968.

———. *Hear That Lonesome Whistle Blow: Railroads in the West*. New York: Holt, Rinehart and Winston, 1977.

———. *Wondrous Times on the Frontier*. Little Rock, AR: August House Publishers, 1991.

Brown, Robert L. *An Empire of Silver*. Denver: Sundance Publications, 1984.

Bruns, Roger A. *The Bandit Kings*. New York: Crown, 1995.

Bryan, Howard. *Robbers, Rogues and Ruffians: True Tales of the Wild West*. Santa Fe, NM: Clear Light Publishers, 1992.

———. *Wildest of the Wild West: True Tales of a Frontier Town on the Santa Fe Trail*. Santa Fe, NM: Clear Light Publishers, 1988.

Carter, Robert A. *Buffalo Bill Cody: The Man Behind the Legend*. Hoboken, NJ: J. Wiley & Sons Inc., 2000.

Cleere, Jan. *Outlaw Tales of Arizona*. Helena, MT: TwoDot, 2006.

Crampton, Frank A. *Deep Enough: A Working Stiff in the Western Mine Camps*. Norman: University of Oklahoma Press, 1993.

Davis, William C. *The American Frontier: Pioneers, Settlers & Cowboys (1800–1899)*. Norman: University of Oklahoma Press, 1999.

DeArment, Robert K. *Knights of the Green Cloth: The Saga of the Frontier Gamblers*. Norman. University of Oklahoma Press, 1982.

Death Valley Tales. Death Valley, CA: Death Valley '49ers Inc., 1970.

Demlinger, Sandor. *Mining in the Old West*. Atglen, PA: Schiffer Publishing, 2006.

Devol, George H. *Forty Years a Gambler on the Mississippi*. Bedford, MA: Applewood Books, 1996.

Dixon, Kelly J. *Boomtown Saloons*. Reno, NV: University of Nevada Press, 2006.

Dobie, J. Frank. *Apache Gold and Yaqui Silver*. Austin: University of Texas Press, 1996.

———. *Coronado's Children: Tales of Lost Mines and Buried Treasures of the Southwest*. Austin: University of Texas Press, 1984.

Dow, James R., ed. *Wyoming Folklore*. Lincoln: University of Nebraska Press, 2010.

Drabelle, Dennis. *Mile-High Fever: Silver Mines, Boom Towns, and High Living on the Comstock Lode*. New York: St. Martin's Press, 2009.

Drago, Harry Sinclair. *The Great Range War: Violence on the Grasslands*. New York: Dodd, Mead & Co., 1985.

Eberhart, Perry. *1536-1968: Treasure Tales of the Rockies: Lost Mines and Buried Bonanza*. New York: Ballantine Books, 1969.

Enss, Chris. *Hearts West*. Helena, MT: TwoDot, 2005.

———. *The Lady Was a Gambler*. Helena, MT: TwoDot, 2008.

Felton, Bruce, and Mark Fowler. *Felton & Fowler's Famous Americans You Never Knew Existed*. New York: Stein and Day, 1979.

Finch, L. Boyd. *A Southwest Land Scam: The 1859 Report of the Mowry City Association*. Tucson: University of Arizona, 1990.

Fisher, Vardis and Opal Laurel Holmes. *Gold Rushes and Mining Camps of the Early American West*. Caldwell, ID: Caxton Printers, Ltd., 1968.

Gibbens, Byrd, Elizabeth Hampstein, and Lillian Schlissel. *Far From Home: Families of the Westward Journey*. New York: Schocken Books, 1989.

Glass, Andrew. *Bad Guys: True Stories of Legendary Gunslingers, Sidewinders, Fourflushers*. New York: Doubleday, 1998.

Golay, Michael. *The Tide of Empire*. Hoboken, NJ: John Wiley & Sons Inc., 2003.

Grant, Marilyn. *Montana Mainstreets, Volume 1: A Guide to Historic Virginia City*. Helena: Montana Historical Society Press, 1998.

Griffith, T. D. *Deadwood: The Best Writings on the Most Notorious Town in the West*. Helena, MT: TwoDot, 2010.

Hardesty, Donald L. *Mining Archeology in the American West*. Lincoln: University of Nebraska Press, 2010.

Harpending, Asbury. *The Great Diamond Hoax and Other Stirring Incidents in the Life of Asbury Harpending*. Norman: University of Oklahoma Press, 1958.

Higginson, Thomas Wentworth. *Travelers and Outlaws: Episodes in American History*. New York: Lee and Shepard, 1889.

Holland, Barbara. *Brief Histories & Heroes*. Pleasantville, NY: The Akadine Press Inc., 1998.

Holliday, J. S. *The World Rushed In: The California Gold Rush Experience: An Eye-Witness Account of a Nation Heading West*. New York: Simon & Schuster, 1981.

Hollihan, Tony. *Gold Rushes*. Edmonton, AB: Lone Pine Publishing, 2002.

Horwitz, Tony, ed. *The Devil May Care: Fifty Intrepid Americans and Their Quest for the Unknown.* New York: Oxford University Press, 2003.

Hunt, William R. *North of 53: The Wild Days of the Alaska-Yukon Mining Frontier 1870–1914.* New York: MacMillan Publishing, 1974.

Jackson, Donald Dale. *Gold Dust.* Edison, NJ: Castle Books, 1980.

Jackson, Joseph Henry. *Anybody's Gold: The Story of California's Mining Towns.* San Francisco: Chronicle Books, 1982.

Jahoda, Gloria. *The Trail of Tears.* New York: Random House, 1975.

Johnson, Dorothy M. *The Bloody Bozeman: The Perilous Trail to Montana's Gold.* Missoula, MT: Mountain Press, 1983.

Johnson, Dorothy M. and R. T. Turner. *The Bedside Book of Bastards: A Rich Collection of Counterirritants to the Exasperations of Contemporary Life.* New York: Barnes & Noble Books, 1994.

Katz, Jane. *Messengers of the Wind.* New York: Ballantine Books, 1995.

Kelly, Bill. *Gamblers of the Old West: Gambling Men and Women of the 1800s – How They Lived, How They Died.* Las Vegas, NV: B&F Enterprises, 1995.

Kelly, C. Brian. *Best Little Stories from the Wild West.* Nashville, TN: Cumberland House Publishing, 2002.

Kluger, Richard. *The Bitter Waters of Medicine Creek.* New York: Vintage, 2012.

Knowles, Thomas W. and Joe R. Lansdale, eds. *The West That Was.* Avenel, NJ: Wings Books, 1993.

Lavender, David. *Let Me Be Free: The Nez Perce Tragedy.* New York: HarperCollins. 1992.

Levy, Joann. *They Saw the Elephant: Women in the California Gold Rush.* Hamden, CT: Shoe String Press, 1990.

Lewis, Oscar. *The Big Four.* Sausalito, CO: Comstock Editions Inc., 1971.

Lockley, Fred. *Conversation with Bullwhackers, Muleskinners, Pioneers, Prospectors, '49ers, Indian Fighters, Trappers, Ex-Barkeepers, Authors, Preachers, Poets, & Near Poets & All Sorts & Conditions of Men.* Eugene, OR: Rainy Day Press, 1981.

Mackay, Charles. *Extraordinary Popular Delusions and the Madness of Crowds.* Hampshire, UK: Harriman House, 2003.

MacKell, Jan. *Red Light Women of the Rocky Mountains.* Albuquerque: University of New Mexico Press, 2009.

Marks, Paula Mitchell. *Precious Dust: The Saga of the Western Gold Rushes.* Lincoln: University of Nebraska Press, 1994.

Mayer, Melanie J. *Klondike Women: True Tales of the 1897–1898 Gold Rush.* Athens, OH: Swallow Press, 1989.

Mayo, Matthew P. *Cowboys, Mountain Men & Grizzly Bears: Fifty of the Grittiest Moments in the History of the Wild West.* Helena, MT: TwoDot, 2009.

———. *Sourdoughs, Claim Jumpers & Dry Gulchers: Fifty of the Grittiest Moments in the History of Frontier Prospecting.* Helena, MT: TwoDot, 2012.

McMurtry, Larry. *Oh What a Slaughter: Massacres in the American West: 1846–1890.* New York: Simon & Schuster, 2005.

Meeker, Ezra. *Ox-Team Days on the Oregon Trail.* Yonkers-on-Hudson, NY: World Book Company, 1932.

Morgan, Lael. *Good Time Girls of the Alaska-Yukon Gold Rush.* Vancouver, BC: Whitecap Books, 1998.

Murphy, Clair Rudolph. *Gold Rush Women.* Portland, OR: Alaska Northwest Books, 2003.

Nash, Jay Robert. *Encyclopedia of Western Lawmen and Outlaws.* New York: Da Capo Press, 1994.

O'Brien, Mary Barmeyer. *Across Death Valley: The Pioneer Journey of Juliet Wells Brier*. Helena, MT: TwoDot, 2009.

Oppel, Frank, ed. *Tales of Alaska and the Yukon*. Edison, NJ: Castle Books, 1986.

Pace, Dick. *Golden Gulch: The Story of Montana's Fabulous Alder Gulch*. Virginia City, MT: Dick Pace, 1962.

Pasternak, Jody. *Yellow Dirt: An American Story of a Poisoned Land and a People Betrayed*. New York: Simon & Schuster, 2010.

Place, Marian T. *The Yukon*. New York: Ives Washburn Inc., 1967.

Prassel, Frank Richard. *The Great American Outlaw: A Legacy of Fact and Fiction*. Norman: University of Oklahoma Press, 1996.

Raymond, C. Elizabeth and Ronald M. James. *Comstock Women: The Making of a Mining Community*. Reno: University of Nevada Press, 1997.

Reading, Amy. *The Mark Inside*. New York: Vintage, 2012.

Reid, Robert Leonard. *A Treasury of the Sierra Nevada*. Berkeley, CA: Wilderness Press, 1983.

Reynolds, Clay. *The Hero of a Hundred Fights: Ned Buntline*. New York: Union Square, 2011.

Ripley, Thomas. *They Died with Their Boots On*. New York: Pocket Books, 1964.

Roop, Connie and Peter, eds. *The Diary of David R. Leeper: Rushing for Gold*. Tarrytown, NY: Benchmark Books, 2001.

Sagstetter, Beth and Bill. *The Mining Camps Speak*. Tarrytown, NY: Benchmark Books, 1998.

Schofield, Brian. *Selling Your Father's Bones*. New York: Simon & Schuster, 2009.

Secrest, William D. *Dangerous Trails: Five Desperadoes of the Old West Coast*. Stillwater, OK: Barbed Wire Press, 1995.

Seelye, John D., ed. *Stories of the Old West: Tales of the Mining Camp, Cavalry Troop & Cattle Ranch*. Norman: University of Oklahoma Press, 2000.

Shally, Dorothy and William Bolton. *Scotty's Castle: Death Valley's Fabulous Showplace*. Yosemite, CA: Flying Sur Press, 1973.

Shermeister, Phil and Noel Grove. *National Geographic Destination: The Sierra Nevada*. Washington, DC: National Geographic Society, 1999.

Sherr, Lynn and Jurate Kazickas. *Susan B. Anthony Slept Here: A Guide to American Women's Landmarks*. New York: Times Books/Random House, 1994.

Shirley, Glenn. *Law West of Fort Smith*. Lincoln: University of Nebraska Press, 1969.

Sifakis, Carl. *Hoaxes and Scams: A Compendium of Deceptions, Ruses, and Swindles*. Facts on File, 1993.

Siringo, Charles A. *A Cowboy Detective: A True Story of Twenty-Two Years with a World-Famous Detective Agency*. Lincoln: University of Nebraska Press, 1988.

Snow, Edward Rowe. *Ghosts, Gales and Gold*. New York: Dodd, Mead & Co., 1972.

Steele, Phillip W. *Outlaws and Gunfighters of the Old West*. Pelican Publishing, 1991.

Steele, Volney, M.D. *Bleed Blister & Purge: A History of Medicine on the American Frontier*. Missoula, MT: Mountain Press, 2005.

Stein, Gordon. *Scams, Shams, and Flimflams: From King Tut to Elvis Lives*. Detroit, MI: UXL, 1994.

Thornton, Brian. *The Book of Bastards: 101 Worst Scoundrels and Scandals from the World of Politics and Power*. Avon, MA: Adams Media, 2010.

Time-Life, eds. *The Old West Series*. 26 vols. Alexandria, VA: Time-Life Books, 1973–80.

Titler, Dale M. *Unnatural Resources: True Stories of American Treasure.* Englewood Cliffs, NJ: Prentice-Hall, 1973.

Townshend, R. B. *A Tenderfoot in Colorado.* Boulder: University Press of Colorado, 2008.

Utley, Robert M. *The Indian Frontier of the American West, 1846–1890.* Albuquerque. University of New Mexico Press, 1984.

Vestal, Stanley. *The Old Santa Fe Trail.* Lincoln: University of Nebraska Press, 1996.

"Vigilante Justice, 1851" Eyewitness to History. www.eyewitnesstohistory.com, 2006.

Walker, Dale L. *Legends & Lies: Great Mysteries of the American West.* New York: Forge Books, 1998.

Walter, Dave. *Speaking Ill of the Dead: Jerks in Montana History.* Guilford, CT: Globe Pequot Press, 2011.

Weir, William. *Written With Lead: America's Most Famous and Notorious Gunfights from the Revolutionary War to Today.* New York: Cooper Square Press, 2003.

Wellman Jr., Paul I. *A Dynasty of Western Outlaws.* Lincoln: University of Nebraska Press, 1986.

West, Elliott. *The Saloon on the Rocky Mountain Mining Frontier.* Lincoln: University of Nebraska Press, 1996.

Willard, John. *Adventure Trails in Montana.* Billings, MT: John Willard, Publisher, 1986.

Wilson, Robert. *The Explorer King: Adventure, Science, and the Great Diamond Hoax: Clarence King in the Old West.* New York: Scribner, 2006.

Zinn, Howard. *A People's History of the United States.* New York: HarperCollins Publishers Inc., 2003.

INDEX

ranch of, 117–19
visits Scott, 116–17
Johnson, Royal, 82
Johnson County War, 168, 175,
176, 182–83
See also Wyoming Stock
Growers Association
Jones, Chubby, 234
Jones, Minnie, 266
Jones, Orley, 175
Jones, Samuel J., 216
Jones, William, 70–71, 196
Judson, Bethany, 5
Judson, Edward Zane Carroll,
1–12
and Cody, 10–11
death of, 12
and Hickok, 8–10
literary success of, 10
"Ned Buntline" byline, 1–8
photo of, 3
politics of, 6
relationships of, 11–12
Judson, Levi Carroll, 5

K
Kanavuts, George, 201
Kelley, Robert P., 214–17, 218
Keys, Bill, 112, 114
King, Clarence, 38
King, James, 248, 253–54,
255, 256
King of the Riverboat Gamblers.
See Devol, George H.
Klondike Gold Rush, 21

Knickerbocker magazine, 5
Know Nothing Party, 7
Knox, Henry, 121

L
Lakota Sioux, 130
Lane, George, 166
Langton, William L., 259
Larkin, Thomas, 95
LeBlanc, Dudley, J., 60–61
Le Grand, Alexander, 143, 150
Lent, William M., 38
LeRoy, Kitty, *221*, 224–26
Logan, John, 129
Longfellow, Henry Wadsworth,
130–31
Looters of the Public Domain (Puter),
209, 213
Lyons, Haze, 166

M
MacArthur, Alfred, 115, 116
Mackay, John W., 81
Mahpina Luta. *See* Red Cloud
(Indian chief)
Mason, Richard, 95
Masterson, Bat, 7, *197*, 233
and Born, 234–36
McClellan, General, 38
McDonald, Thomas, 206
McKenzie, Alexander, 85–94
arrest of, 92–94
mine legislation by, 85,
90–91
McKenzie, Robert, 252

Smith, Bascomb, 20, 198

Smith, Jefferson Randolph "Soapy," 13–26, 196

  in Alaska, 21–24

  bar of, 20

  and Blonger, 198

  and Burns, 205

  in Colorado, 14–19, 20–21

  early life of, 13–14

  photo of, 15

  and Reid, 24–26

Smith, Thomas L. "Pegleg," 143–55

  horse thief story, 153

  Indian attack on, 145–46

  memorial to, 144

  quartz/gold discovery of, 143–45, 154–55

Smith, Tom, 172

Smoky Hill Trail, 103, 104–6

"snake oil," 52–53

  See also Stanley, Clark

Song of Hiawatha, The (Longfellow), 130

Southern Pacific Railroad, 78, 79, 211, 212

Spangler, Michael, 46–47

Spreckels, Rudolph, 260

Staininger Ranch, 118

Stanley, Clark, 52–59

  early life of, 55

  government lawsuit against, 59

  liniment of, 56

  at world exposition, 56–59

Stewart, John Douglas, 24

Sting, The (movie), 60

Stinson, Buck, 161, 163

Sublette, Martin, 151, 152

Sutter's Mill, 95

Swearengen, Al, 132–39

Sydney Ducks (gang). *See* San Francisco (CA)

T

Taft, William H., 212

Tangley Company. *See* Baker, Norman G.

Taylor, Alonzo, 178, 182

Tbalt, Nicholas, 159–60

Teller, Henry M., 128

Territory of Kansas, gold in, 103

thimblerigging. *See* Bennett, Samuel

Thompkins, Carlotta J. *See* Deno, Lottie

Thompson, William, 205–7

Thornton, William B., 186, 194–95

Thurmond, Frank, 228, 230

Tiffany, Charles, 29, 36, 38

Tilghman, Bill 7

Time magazine, 60

Tisdale, John A., 175

Trail of Tears. *See* Cherokee Indians

Treaty of Guadalupe Hidalgo, 74–75

Treaty of Laramie, 124, 125

U

Union Labor Party. *See* Ruef, Abraham

United States

  and Cheyenne and Arapaho, 123–24

ABOUT THE AUTHOR

Award-winning author **Matthew P. Mayo** has written more than twenty-five books and dozens of short stories. His novel *Tucker's Reckoning* won the Western Writers of America's 2013 Spur Award for Best Western Novel. He has also been a Spur Finalist in the Short Fiction category and a Western Fictioneers Peacemaker Award Finalist. His numerous novels include *Winters' War*; *Wrong Town*; *Hot Lead, Cold Heart*; *Dead Man's Ranch*; *Tucker's Reckoning*; *The Hunted*; and *Shotgun Charlie*. He also contributes to other popular series of Western and adventure novels.

Matthew's nonfiction books include *Cowboys, Mountain Men & Grizzly Bears*; *Bootleggers, Lobstermen & Lumberjacks*; *Sourdoughs, Claim Jumpers & Dry Gulchers*; *Haunted Old West*; and *Jerks in New England History* (all TwoDot), among many others. He collaborated with his wife, photographer Jennifer Smith-Mayo, on a series of popular hardcover books including *Maine Icons*, *New Hampshire Icons*, and *Vermont Icons* (all Globe Pequot).

The Mayos also run Gritty Press (GrittyPress.com) and rove the world in search of hot coffee, tasty whiskey, and high adventure. Stop by Matthew's website for a chin-wag and a cup of java at MatthewMayo.com.

8/20